The End of Glory

The End of Glory

An Interpretation
of the Origins of
World War II

Laurence Lafore

WAVELAND

PRESS, INC.

Prospect Heights, Illinois

For information about this book, contact:
    Waveland Press, Inc.
    P.O. Box 400
    Prospect Heights, Illinois 60070
    (847) 634-0081
    www.waveland.com

To my Colleagues
    of the History Department
  of the University of Iowa
with admiration and affection

CONTENTS

The End of GLORY

I

An Epitaph for the European Age

O N March 14, 1918, a special British representative
in Washington wrote to the Prime Minister's private secretary in London, "It is not easy work for
a British Ambassador, as you can well imagine. At
every turn he is met by the obvious but unpleasant
truth that we are very largely in the hands of the
American Administration—that they are in a position almost to dictate the war policy of the Allies."*

The man he was writing about was His Britannic
Majesty's Ambassador to the United States, His
Excellency the Right Honorable the Earl of Reading, Viscount Erleigh, Privy Councillor and Lord
Chief Justice of England. The state of the world
was strikingly described by the juxtaposition of his
titles, smelling strongly of medieval chivalry and
glory, with the surprising fact that a former history
teacher from a Virginia parsonage could dictate
policy to him.

The war of 1914–18 had suddenly conferred upon
the United States of America the dizzying responsibility of leader of world affairs. It was an ex-

*H. Montgomery Hyde, *Lord Reading* (New York: Farrar, Straus & Giroux, 1968),
p. 247.

change of roles equally difficult to grasp, and in different ways equally embarrassing, for people on both sides of the Atlantic.

The situation summarized in Lord Reading's difficulties was more complex than that; the noble lord was in himself the sign of changing times in Europe. His origins belied the odor of medieval chivalry, for he was born Rufus Isaacs, the son of a Jewish fruit merchant, and had risen to position and eminence thanks to what was often described as the best legal mind of his generation. His antique titles were scarcely less significant than the fact that he gloried in them. The old forms of European society and politics were in some places being swept away; in Great Britain they could still gratify, as they absorbed, the gifted plebes, but in the process they were losing substance and meaning, turning into brittle travesties, just as European dominion over the world was becoming a travesty.

What happened after 1918 was the product of the forces so symbolized. The world had for several hundred years been governed from Europe, and the European countries had worked out forms, inadequate but uniquely ingenious, for governing themselves. At the core of this system was a delicate equilibrium between unity and diversity among the European powers. Their relations were, at times anyway, ultimately controlled by common moral principles and the institutions they shared. Among these was the principle of patriotism, the dedication of all citizens—and in particular public servants—to the notion that service to the state was their first duty.

Such allegiance, which had enabled states to survive, to grow, and to perform with stupendous efficiency the tasks society required, was a compound of many elements. From the French Revolution, patriotism had inherited strident enthusiasm with deep roots among the commonalty who had come to see the destiny of their country as peculiarly affecting themselves. As popular government spread, patriotic emotions were most potently and ominously voiced in the cheap press which catered to, and aggravated, the chauvinism and xenophobia of the masses in each country. From earlier times patriotism had inherited the aristocratic abstractions that still counted as civic and personal morality: honesty, honor, courage, loyalty, devotion to duty, chivalry, deference to superiors, and graciousness to inferiors. Such moral principles were conspicuous, in a beneficent form, in the career of Lord Reading, a loyal and useful servant of his king and country. They showed their least constructive aspect among soldiers and sailors dedicated to winning glory for their state in ways sometimes suggesting unconscionable ignorance that warfare with shells and machine guns meant anything different from what warfare had meant at Agincourt.

It was illuminating that in France, the first democracy in Europe and still, in 1914, the only important republic, where the patriotism of the people had begun, the surviving aristocrats still brooded in their moldering châteaux and their Paris parlors, eschewing service in their nation's politics which would have obliged them to take an oath to the "slut," as they called the French Republic. But they did not eschew service in the French armed forces, and so they put themselves in the service of the chauvinism of the populace. The two greatest French generals of the twentieth century were both aristocratic monarchists; of one of them, Marshal Lyautey, who conquered colonies for France, it was observed that he was a royalist who gave a republic an empire. His role in history, and that of Ferdinand Foch, supreme commander of the Allied armies that finally defeated Germany in 1918, neatly symbolized the compatibility, almost the fusion, of the old abstractions with the twentieth-century state.

Glory, balanced by prudence, was in more muted forms the business of statesmen as well as soldiers. In an international system whose essential nature was a fecund but intense competition, the welfare of one's country demanded more than survival; it demanded grandeur. The requirements of grandeur varied a good deal, from the flag-waving of the popular press to protests about who sat next to whom at banquets to the annexation of large and uninviting deserts in Africa, but it always involved the very basic, one may say the atavistic, notion of sacrifice. Fighting in wars had been, from the first clearing of the anthropological mists, associated with personal justification; in the tensely civilized atmosphere of late-nineteenth-century Europe it was, except for a few cranks, still associated with the noble ideals of chivalry and opposed to the creeping materialism of the scientific age. To the persistence of this atavism every war memorial is a graven monument. Europe and its world had been built on the assumption of glory, and its sublimated version, successful diplomacy, still embodied such ideals.

The war of 1914–18 was an earthquake that cracked this fundament. Three important facts became gradually and disastrously clear in the interwar years. The first was that the hereditary practitioners of glory, conscientious politicians in the nineteenth-century tradition, genteel diplomats (and diplomacy was still very much the preserve of gentility), and soldiers whose ancestors had sometimes fought as knights in armor, were frightened by what happened. They knew that they could not afford to repeat it; common humanity and a due concern for the preservation of the social order that allowed them to exist forbade it. It is the oddest and most basic irony of the Second World War that it was made possible by the extreme timidity of the very kinds of people whose bellicosity had caused the first. Conservatism, obsolescent, turned pacifist. Generals counseled surrender before hostilities started.

The second important fact was that the old ideas were espoused and reinvigorated by new and surprising figures who cloaked them with revolutionary novelty: the most warlike men of the thirties were the several sorts of radicals. It was a working-class man, an anarcho-syndicalist schoolteacher, leader of a mass movement, who in the twenties began to preach the purifying idealism of strife. When he became dictator of Italy he dedicated his nation to the virile virtues of the warrior and told his fellow-citizens that they must regard themselves as in a state of perpetual war. It was a house-painter, an obscure German corporal, who dreamed of more than Carolingian splendors for his fatherland. In the past, the game of glory had been played according to strict rules similar to those governing other genteel pastimes such as cricket. Mussolini and Hitler, revolutionary plebeians, were wholly contemptuous of such rules. Memories of Arthurian jousts, discernible in the mentality of the great German generals of the nineteenth century like Moltke or Schlieffen, were alien to the fascist dictators. They played the game for keeps. Still, in their mouths, the idiom of glory was similar—if heightened to the point of madness—to that of the traditionalists. The traditionalists were fooled by it. They responded to the eruption of volcanos with the minutiae of diplomatic finesse. It is interesting that the Prime Minister of Great Britain believed *both* that Hitler was insane and also that he could be lured to sanity by an Englishman's gentlemanly converse and reason. The most extraordinary feature of the whole dismal story of Hitler's success in the years from 1933 to 1942 was the attitude of the German Army leaders to him; it was petulant, panicky, and most of all disdainful.

These were the sources of the terrible inability of constitutional governments to defend themselves, either at home or abroad, in the interwar years. Beneath them lay the fact that Europe as a whole had lost control of the world. The unreality of well-bred Englishmen hopefully reporting that Hitler was an amiable and sincere patriot was matched by the unreality of their efforts to make a wounded society with a staggering economy play the role it had played before 1914.

The third important fact was the revolution in Russia. Like the later revolutions in Italy and Germany it produced a regime controlled by proletarian revolutionaries, determined and imaginative men with vast aspirations whose fulfillment would have destroyed totally the existing social and international order. Their aims were not nationalistic, or at least they were not so in the early years of the Soviet regime, but being internationalist they were more unsettling to other societies since they combined appeals for social justice with no less powerful appeals to the deep fear and hatred of international war that was the heritage of 1914–18. But the Russian Revolution had even more important effects than this; it subtracted Russia from Europe. The vast empire of the Romanovs had been, perhaps, only partly and superficially European, but in international affairs it had behaved like a European state. It had participated in the balance of power and the European system. The withdrawal into hostile isolation, prefaced and symbolized by Russia's withdrawal from the imperialist war in March 1918, meant that there was one less great power in Europe. Geography was drastically changed.

Europe was diminished by the loss of Russia. For a time it

looked as if it might be augmented by the addition of the United States, which would easily offset the loss. In 1918 the United States had been enthroned as the strongest power in the world, but immediately afterward the United States, too, withdrew into isolation.

The superpowers were in the making, but neither of them participated largely in the decisions that were to bring the final destruction of the old Europe. The new war was made by the old great powers in a vacuum left by the absence of the superpowers, and the story of its coming is the story of old practices persisting in a diminished setting. Mussolini and Hitler, for all their precocity, realized their limitations even less clearly than the leaders of France and Britain.

The chief characters in the new *Iliad*, then, are all European; as the climax approaches, they are principally German and British. Germany and Great Britain were by 1939 the only two surviving nations of the old Concert of Europe that still had any freedom of action. The decisive powers, however, lay elsewhere.

Power means different things in different situations. During the last stages of World War I and thereafter, it meant the appealing political ideals of the United States and the Soviet Union, their military potential, and in the case of the United States its overwhelming economic and financial means. But the translation of power into effective world policy requires leadership, the deliberate use of power for the achievement of conscious purposes, and this the Soviet Union was unable, and the United States unwilling, to achieve. It was a phenomenon alien to the old system of world management, for the great nations of Europe had always, for better or worse, used their power to affect the course of history. In the absence of a new system, the old, thus altered, broke down.

The second war saw the situation reversed. After 1941 leadership was exercised with the utmost vigor by both of the superpowers. The change was so sudden and so complete that it is difficult to realize, looking back, how total were the isolation of the United States and the exclusion of the Soviet Union from world affairs in the twenties and thirties. The American press and American diplomatic correspondence of those decades,

when reread today, seem almost incredible in the totality of their
acceptance of American aloofness. The issue is always how to
safeguard that aloofness, very rarely how to alter it. By the
midthirties, when the possibility of another European war began
to appear, Americans of all political opinions were united in their
belief that the one important objective was to avoid any possible
action that could lead to involvement, should it break out. The
affairs of Europe, as the Americans heard about them, seem to
have been transacting themselves on a different planet.

"War," like "power," is a word with a vague and changing
meaning, and what happened after 1939 was entirely different
from anything that had happened before. War acquired a new set
of definitions as the superpowers at last moved into Europe. But
there are certain generalities about the European wars up until
1941 that are defensible and pertinent.

Europe's battlefields had always been the graveyards for its
outworn institutions. They were also the breeding place for new
ones. Not, in general, notable as either a destroyer or a progenitor of *ideas*, the genius of war had been in administration, adaptation, dissemination, and development. The airplane, before
1914, was an ingenious demonstration of abstract theory and a
sportsman's plaything. After 1918, it was a social and economic
fact of the highest importance. Propaganda in 1914 meant a kind
of campaign (developed in the sixteenth century) to win souls for
the Roman Catholic Church through sermons and brochures. By
1918 it was a highly technical exploitation of the mass media, of
espionage, political rhetoric, for the shaping of minds into prede-
termined molds. Mobilization of an industrial economy for
deliberately chosen purposes through the regulation of investment, labor, production, commerce, and consumption was
scarcely practiced in 1914; by 1918 it was commonplace. In the
same way, the "splitting of the atom" was in 1939 discussed in
comic strips as one of those proverbial, slightly farcical, feats for
a brave new world whose deriding has always been a way for
humans to qualify their atavistic fears of future time; in 1945 the
jungle panic was justified, and two provincial cities in Japan
testified to the end of the long autocracy of gunpowder which
had made Europe and its greatness.

All the things that died in the two wars were European things. All the new inventions and adaptations that came out of them were of a sort that diminished Europe and increased the potential of the United States and the Soviet Union. War in the twentieth century was the graveyard of the old Europe, the Europe that had bought and paid for the world with the cash of modern science, modern administrative methods, modern finance. By 1945 that proprietorship had gone the way of gunpowder, the way of the lingering memories of chivalry. Nations that had invented the modern age and implanted its institutions in Japan and Zanzibar and Guatemala were occupied by Russian and American troops. Britannia would not again rule the waves; ruling waves was, indeed, little more than a picturesque pastime. What mattered now was to rule the depths beneath them and the air above.

In 1919, when the peace was made, no one realized what was happening. The presence of the rest of the world was, of course, evident. The President of the United States in its brief moment of leadership was the most conspicuous figure at the peace conference, but the very novelty of his presence had the embarrassing effect of making him seem an otherworldly being whose subsequent, very human, failures were the more shocking as a consequence. The British Dominions and India for the first time added separate signatures to a treaty. Japan and China were also present, and there was some talk of the equality of races. Parts of western Asia, and even of Africa, were dealt with in ways that mumblingly avowed the principle that self-government, even for backward regions, was an ultimate possibility. Democracy was much mentioned.

But the peace was a European peace, and it was perhaps partly from an instinctive recognition of this that the Senate and the people of the United States rejected it. It was not that it favored the interests of European powers against the rest of the world; it was that the rest of the world was considered largely irrelevant to the settling of its own destiny. In making the decisions that mattered, non-Europeans might take part, but what mattered about the decisions was that they were about Europe. Woodrow Wilson affected a certain universalism: the League of Nations was politely ecumenical in conception. He distrusted the sly effeteness of Europe, but he admired and imitated it. The League was designed to perfect and expand, not to replace, the European system.

The process of disintegration of Europe's capacity for leadership had begun much earlier—begun, if one takes a metaphysical view, at the moment when it passed beyond the limits, in time and riches, of all previous civilizations and set sail on the western seas. But whatever the deeper sources of decay, the glittering apogee had been reached only in the twentieth century. In 1910 Europe had never been so rich, so fecund, so imperial. Almost the entire world had been brought under control, direct or indirect, of Europeans or their descendants.

Then in 1914, Europe set about the work of destroying its own supremacy in the world. By 1945 the process was complete. Two wars, two decades of violence, hysteria, futility, and hedonism, and the worst depression in history had carried the decline of world suzerainty to the point of extinction. The generation from 1914 to 1945 lived in one long, uneven nightmare of destruction, the sorry climax of a thousand years of European history. Europe's pomp was at last, as Kipling had foreseen it, at one with Nineveh and Tyre.

Or so it seemed in 1945, and so it still looks almost a quarter of a century later. The emancipation of Africa, logically presided over, at periodic congresses, by the durable *éminence noire* of independence, the Conquering Lion of Judah, is epochal. The independence of Indonesia and Trinidad, Parisian boys dressed in blue jeans, and Congolese politicians solemnly haranguing an assembly, overwhelmingly nonwhite in membership, that is trying to manage world affairs from a glass skyscraper on the East River in Manhattan, most of the world ruled or strongly influenced by communism—these are signs of change that would have been wholly incredible if predicted in 1910; and the change is the collapse of European power and a world governed by its peculiar traditions.

The causes of World War II have never, even at the moment of its outbreak, attracted the same polemical interest as did the causes of World War I. For this there were several obvious reasons. There seemed no need to discuss the question of war guilt, for one thing. Adolf Hitler not only stood convicted of having started the war; he had convicted himself. The archives merely confirmed his enemies' propaganda. In the years after the first war, when the documents were becoming gradually and partly available to historians, the reconstruction of the 1914 crisis and the events leading to it were re-examined and re-evaluated. In general, the effect of historical appraisals in the 1920s was to soften, sometimes obliterate, the charges of "guilt" with which the Allies had labeled Germany during and immediately after the war. An entire school of "revisionists" arose, and the morality of everybody's conduct in 1914 continued to be feverishly argued. It is revealing that the rather simple-minded moral conceptions that had been so shaken by World War I continued to be applied to its causes. It was a fascinating, if not a very rewarding, approach to historical analysis. By the time people came to consider the origins of World War II, analytical history was based on more up-to-date notions. The notions of state power, of ideology, of impersonal forces, had replaced the earlier judgment that events were determined by the moral principles of statesmen. By 1945, moral principles in statecraft were rather cynically seen mainly as a form of public relations.

A more important fact that affected, perhaps distorting and certainly obscuring, the study of causes of Hitler's war, and perspectives on the whole reach of European history in the first half of the century, was that its sorry end was accompanied by the outbreak of another war, cold but costly. It would not be misleading to give the name of World War III to the rivalry that ensued, in the twenty years after 1945, between the United States and its clients and the Soviet Union and the Communist world, and it was this war, not the second, that understandably attracted the interest of both the public and the historians. In a certain sense, 1945–65 was more truly a time of *world* struggle than 1939–45, certainly more than 1914–18. Hitler and Mussolini were dead and fascism gone, while the United States and the Soviet Union were armed in panoply. The events that led to World War II were examined, very often, from the standpoint of developing relations between the superpowers of the fifties.

The public did not really care to reconsider the causes of Hitler's war. The publication of collections of documents from the state archives dealing with diplomacy before 1914 had been breathlessly awaited and passionately discussed in the 1920s. The much more complete collections that appeared in the 1950s were largely overlooked except by experts.

It was not, for the most part, until the late fifties that this relative indifference began to change, as a new generation grew up, infatuated—as all new generations are—by the notion that their parents had behaved like idiots. Naturally enough, the new school of thought appeared earliest and most emphatically in Germany, but in Britain young men wrote analyses of the follies of appeasement not with passion but with disdain. Much of the discussion in English-speaking countries about the causes of World War II centered on the curious passivity of Great Britain, its relations with France, the Soviet Union, Italy, the United States, and the ideological and economic fracases of the dreadful decade of the thirties. The arguments, when there were any, were still of a familiar sort.

The first serious writer to question either the deliberate responsibility of Hitler for the war or the insufficiency of British policy toward him as its basic causes was Professor A. J. P. Taylor, in a book called *The Origins of the Second World War*, published in 1961. His great brilliance and eminence made his interpretation something of a sensation: he held, with what looked to some almost like a perverse determination to revise history simply for the sake of revising it, that Hitler was neither destined nor determined to undertake limitless expansion, and that the British statesmen were not wholly unwise in dealing with him as they did. He held, at least by implication, that the Europe of 1914 still existed and that its institutions were not unworkable.

It is striking that this first notable example of revisionism should have been—in the strictly literal sense—reactionary, but it was logical. Within the limits of European history as conventionally understood and written in the past, no other form of revision was possible: either Hitler was or was not bent on limitless expansion, either Chamberlain was or was not wise in trying to handle him by negotiated concessions. It rapidly became clear, however, that Taylor's revisionism found little favor with other scholars. An increasing volume of material began to appear that challenged, forthrightly or by implication, many of Taylor's conclusions, but counterrevisionism was still largely within a European context.

The most prominent question raised about the origins of the war, then, concerned the nature and consistency of Hitler's motives. Was he, as Professor Taylor has suggested, an improviser maneuvering for advantage? Or was he, rather, a man, perhaps a madman, with a vision consistently pursued, a man tactically improvising but moving strategically toward a fixed goal? On this question hang all the others that interested contemporaries and have interested historians since, including all appraisals of British and French policy. For if Hitler had fixed and visionary goals, they involved changes in the world order so vast that a world war was certain to follow and attempts to control him by negotiation, such as French and British statesmen desperately engaged in, were futile. Were the events of the nineteen thirties, in short, a volcanic eruption of gigantic forces in Europe, or were they a traditional exercise in diplomatic manipulation?

The evidence of a fixed purpose in Hitler's policies is very strong. It appeared first in his autobiography, *Mein Kampf,* written in the early twenties, and while he prudently omitted discussion of ultimate goals from most of his later speeches and writings, there is abundant proof that he constantly and almost obsessively dwelt on them in conversations with his associates.*
Most writers today, therefore, find it difficult to accept Taylor's thesis or to doubt that Hitler always intended to conquer the Soviet Union as an empire for Germany and knew that this would entail dominance over continental Europe and even, perhaps, the world. As the most distinguished English historian of Nazi Germany recently observed, "Not only did he consistently hold and express these views over twenty years, but in 1941 he set to work to put them into practice in the most literal way, by

---

*See, among other examples, Hermann Rauschning, *The Revolution of Nihilism* (New York: Longmans Green and Co., 1939); *The Voice of Destruction* (New York: Putnam, 1940); Edouard Calic, editor, *Ohne Maske* (Frankfurt: Societaetsverlag, 1968); *Hitler's Secret Conversations* (New York: Farrar, Straus and Young, 1953).

attacking Russia and by giving full reign to his plans, which the S.S. had already begun to carry out in Poland, for the resettlement of huge areas of Eastern Europe."*

There have been many revelations, as distinct from revisions, to emerge from the copious flow of scholarly studies in recent years. Most of the work has been specialized, detailed, and technical, and the findings are correspondingly specific. They deal for the most part with useful refinements, making clear the immense complexity of motives and events. Statesmen are never as clear in their minds and policies as their public proclamations indicate, and we know a great deal now about the uncertainties and hesitations, the disagreements, the failures of information, that affected the policymakers everywhere. In general, the new material indicates four important clarifications of the history of the events of the thirties as it was understood twenty-five years ago. The first is the quite drastic reinterpretation of Hitler's Germany, which to many people appeared at the time both monolithic and revolutionary but is now seen as makeshift, divided, and in many ways stagnant, although informed by spasms of extremely intelligent economic and military planning. The second is the role of Italy and its relations both with the western democracies and with Germany; the Rome-Berlin Axis, terrifyingly impressive at the time, is now likewise known to have been a precarious makeshift, a changing pattern of trivial impulses and uncertainties on the part of both dictators. The third is the quite startling picture that has emerged of the inefficiency of intelligence services, particularly in Great Britain but in a remarkable degree in all countries, which distorted the judgments of statesmen and, most strikingly, of their military advisers. The fourth is the mounting and now almost conclusive evidence to support a view, long familiar but once controversial, that the British and French policies were shaped by a defensive mentality, a determination to avoid responsibility beyond their boundaries and to try to maintain the peace of Europe by invoking the aid of others, by paper fortifications and diplomacy, or simply by agonized inaction.

*Alan Bullock, "Hitler and the Origins of the Second World War," *Proceedings of the British Academy,* Vol. LIII (London, Oxford University Press, 1967), p. 261.

The very careful studies that provide these new interpretations have given us, for example, detailed pictures—not perfectly complete or fully agreed upon—of German economic planning for war and of the intention to fight it with brief, carefully prepared, decisive attacks that would avoid the intolerable strains of a long war of attrition like World War I. They have demonstrated the ineffable frivolity of Benito Mussolini. They have revealed that it was the generals, in all countries, who were most timid and most averse to incurring the danger of a general war. They have further illumined the curious ineptitude and languor of many British statesmen. They have shown French leaders in a somewhat more favorable light than they once appeared. But they have not changed much of the larger picture of events as they were understood by perceptive people at the time. The truths now established were always suspected by some. There has been no such drastic alteration of attitudes in the fifties and sixties as there was in the twenties about the origins of World War I and, consequently, about the nature of diplomacy and of war itself.

What has not often been attempted is an appraisal of World War II as a product of the changed position of Europe in the world, of the importance of the contrast between unchanged responsibilities and diminished capacities, of the absence of the nascent superpowers, of World War II as a product of the failure of their leadership. It is important to decide whether Hitler was an improviser or a man driven by the vision of conquering Russia, but it is surely even more important to understand how such a man could have come to power in the first place and could have successfully outmaneuvered the rest of the world.

The weakness, the absence of responsible leadership, of European governments was in part, anyway, the product of the draining of resources and self-assurance in World War I. The fact was not fully understood at the time, and the magnitude of the losses was not understood at all. But it can scarcely be overlooked now, in the light of the almost total disintegration of Europe's colonial empires and the age of the superpowers, of the permanent dependence of all European countries on either the Soviet Union or the United States. Still, much of the writing about the origins of World War II has been in the old context of a Europe that was mistress of most of the world and certainly of its own destinies. The myths and preconceptions and parochialisms born in the centuries when Europe was extending its imperial sway are still very much alive, and still often shape the views of historians and, through them, popular attitudes and the policies of statesmen.

2

A World Safe for Democracy

In the year 1917 began the first act in the long
drama of Europe's fall from world rule. Twenty-
eight years later the play ended. The destruction
of Europe's dominion was complete, neatly symbolized by the handshake of common soldiers of
the invading Soviet and American armies when
they met at Torgau in the center of the languishing
continent they had occupied, among the ruins of
nations whose affairs had been conducted since
their beginnings by the heirs of chivalric and patrician rulers who saluted or bowed but did not shake
hands. The long reign that had begun under the
Lion Gates of Mycenae a millennium or more
before the birth of Christ had now closed, and the
dismantling of a world empire commenced.

The drama, a tragedy in the classic sense,
opened with the Russian Revolution that broke up
the political principles, changing and contentious,
that had nonetheless given Europe a measure of
unity in the past thousand years, and with the
appearance of American troops on the western
front, the first overseas army to play a decisive role
on European soil since the fall of Byzantium.

Before the curtain had gone up on these events

there had been a long overture to the pageant of collapse; still, it was the war itself that in 1917 had palpably led to the American incursion and the Russian Revolution. And this was true not merely in the sense of revealing publicly the underlying weaknesses of "Fortress Europa," as it was to be called later by Adolf Hitler, who laid the final charge that leveled it. The war of 1914–18 was both cause and symptom of Europe's weakness and of the widening confusion that weakness bequeathed to later generations. Europe was bound to share its monopoly of world control with non-Europeans. The European "system" was certainly doomed, so far as Europe was interpreted in a purely geographical sense. But the system might conceivably have survived as a world system, with overseas elements gradually integrated into it, had World War I not happened to destroy, in four years, the shape and sense of its cosmos. For the importance of the war lay not so much in what it did as in the speed with which it did it; the system was destroyed before it could be adapted.

Aside from Japan and Ethiopia, no part of the 1914 world was free from the control, direct or indirect, of Europeans and their descendants. The exceptions were mostly nominal, like Liberia, China, Siam, and the Ottoman Empire, all of them manipulated by competing Europeans. Outside of Japan, no considerable enterprise of manufacturing, transportation, or finance was run by anybody except Europeans and their descendants. With sporadic or unimportant exceptions, few works of art, music, literature, philosophy, mathematics, or science achieving world recognition had, for at least a century, been produced by anybody except Europeans and their descendants. The governments and societies in Europe seemed on the surface either stable and enlightened or moving fairly rapidly toward stability and enlightenment, and their heirs abroad, in the Americas and the antipodes, looked as if they were becoming part of an expanded but still homogeneous European world. Certainly Europe seemed to be moving rapidly in the direction of organizing its growing prosperity in ways to provide reasonable levels of welfare and security for all its citizens.

The stability was illusory. It is possible to argue that the very fact of stability—or imagined stability—made trouble: the kind of trouble associated in history with the boredom of a generation bred in serenity which fails to appreciate the value that its fathers attach to it; the kind of trouble associated with rising expectations; the trouble associated with bland assumptions about progress and the perpetuity of things that have lasted fifty years; the trouble born of new views of the universe which reject the assumptions that produced them; the trouble arising from gradual but fundamental and revolutionary changes in the economy and society when they are dammed up, as it were, behind stability and slow adjustment.

In the years before 1914, really major changes had been taking place in Europe and the world, produced by the very conditions of progress and serenity which they destroyed. Developments in technology presaged—indeed were already making—huge shifts in power and in ways of living and thinking; in the twenty years before 1914 there had been invented or were coming into wide use a staggering list of such developments: the airplane, the automobile, the telephone, the radio, the submarine, the machine gun, the electric light. Increases in population of themselves portended drastic change, and large revolutions were in course: *half of the world's population*, composed of women, was beginning to move, for the first time, toward equal rights with men, and in some places and spheres had already made substantial progress; and the working classes of society were for the first time beginning to achieve not only a measure of economic security that would provide them with independence, but, what was more remarkable, education and political power. These were much larger changes than had ever taken place before.

The world of 1914 that now looks so stable was in fact a whirlpool of enormous forces that its masters could not conceivably have controlled. The palpable changes were complemented by immaterial ones. Theory after theory was being presented, and sometimes demonstrated, to break down the verities upon which men had based assumptions, as drastically as had the ideas of Galileo or Newton. Einstein discovered relativity, and changed the nature of the universe by increasing knowledge of it. Freud had begun the work of revising men's notions of their own natures, and of the nature of good and evil and rationality, which was gradually to sweep away previous views of human character and of morality in much of the world. The sanctity of property was under systematic attack.

As always in history, however, theories of society were either cast in terms of the past or based on false visions of the future. Sociology, anthropology, and political and economic theory had opened fewer frontiers than mathematics or psychology. The popular prescriptions of reformers were almost all—it is now possible to see—unsoundly based, and all without exception suffered from the factionalism that proposals for reform invariably produce. And—as is also always true in history—institutions and the people who ran them lagged even further behind the real changes and misjudged their effects even more seriously than the revolutionaries and reformers. It is in the nature of governments to preserve at least the skeleton of an *existing* order; it is in the nature of radicals to try to correct *existing* evils. Neither offers much useful guidance for right policies for the future, and the gap that thus opened accounted, perhaps more than anything else, for the desperation and the consequent inclination to force and illegality that began, bafflingly to many contemporaries, to trouble the western world before 1914. The first world war was a culmination of this inclination.

The stability of Europe was therefore a crust, and volcanic disturbances were cracking it. We often consider the years before 1914 as a period of profound and unprecedented peace, but there had been ten international wars in the two decades before 1914, and most of these had involved—significantly—major powers fighting against lesser ones. Already, military defeats had been inflicted on European powers by non-European peoples, the Ethiopians against the Italians in 1896, the Japanese against the Russians in 1904, the first such defeats in many centuries. The gulf in power—technological, administrative and psychological—between Europe and the rest of the world had been widening since the discovery of America; it had now begun to close. There was a crescendo of disturbances inside Europe, most ominously the determination to "solve," immediately and by force, certain questions of domestic affairs and of national boundaries and national aspirations, even if the solution clearly involved the likelihood of a civil or a world war; they presaged the disintegration of Europe's seeming serenity. Violence indicated the existence of purposes and emotions that could not be satisfied by playing the game of constitutional government and peaceful diplomacy by the rules; indeed it indicated a passionate loathing of the rules themselves.

By 1918 the old order—which is to say the habits, routines, attitudes, and inhibitions by which the pre-1914 world had lived —had been battered or ruined. No new routines or habits sufficiently widely accepted to furnish a new stability had appeared. Most of the new attitudes were of a sort to provoke deeper division. Inhibitions were positively reduced in number and strength.

The destruction of intangibles included and was aggravated by material destruction. Since men in 1914 were quite unprepared for, and certainly unaccustomed to, physical losses on so large a scale, they tended in 1918 to exaggerate them; physical losses were great but turned out to be mostly relatively minor and curable compared to the loss of impalpables. Still, they were— mainly in unforeseeable ways—of great and lasting importance, and they were given an importance that exceeded their intrinsic significance by the shock they produced, the exaggeration with which they were computed, the sense that material losses were what mattered most and that nothing must ever be allowed to lead men to repeat them.

Both in reality and in men's minds, it was the loss of life that mattered most.

The war deprived about thirteen and a half million people, overwhelmingly young men of the years of greatest vigor, imagination, and productive and reproductive capacity, of their lives, and gravely and sometimes permanently incapacitated another twenty million. Of the dead fighting men more than 95 per cent were Europeans, and over a million European civilians are estimated to have lost their lives besides.

The fact is, both symbolically and in material terms, indicative of what had happened to Europe. A generation was, in the terms of the time, "wiped out" in Europe, and this meant an irreversible loss of leadership.

The incidence of mortality was even more important than the total (from a standpoint other than personal tragedy, which is generally not of concern to the historian). A most important variable in this connection was the trend of national birth rates, and the most depressing effect of World War I mortality was in France. There the birth rate and the population had been nearly stable for a long time, and France, much the largest of European nations in the eighteenth century, had fallen to sixth place by 1914. The effect of the bloodletting on a declining birth rate was indeed to wipe out a generation, not so much the generation of young men slain as of babies unborn. The effects, materially and psychologically, upon the nation that regarded itself as, pre-eminently, *the* great power of the world, the military, political, and cultural leader of a Europe that ran the universe, were terrifying and therefore paralyzing. At the other end of the gamut was Russia. By 1918 the old Russian Empire had suffered some nine million military casualties (dead, injured, and missing), three quarters of its armed forces, about fifty per cent more than total French casualties. German casualties were over seven million, also greater than France's. But, historically speaking, the Russian and German losses were less significant. The effect of the bloodletting on Russia, staggering though it was, was mitigated in the long run by a rising birth rate. The vitality of the population absorbed it, and the rising birth rate replaced it. France, the most mature and the richest of the great continental societies, suffered most from human losses in relative, although not in absolute, terms, since the population did not replace itself.

The qualitative incidence of mortality was likewise varied, and of peculiar importance. The case of Britain is an instructive illustration. Britain's dead numbered only about sixty per cent of France's, but it is often observed—the matter is clearly difficult of proof—that war casualties had a particularly depressing effect in Britain because of their *social* incidence. In the early years especially, the conditions of warfare in northern France were such that the highest losses were sustained by junior officers, who actually led their men in charges across no man's land. NCOs and enlisted men were a trifle less exposed; high brass was generally not exposed at all. But subalterns, lieutenants, and captains were slaughtered. The British Army in 1914 was a small, professional, volunteer body, with its officers drawn almost exclusively from the elegant classes of society, the families that still provided political leadership in Britain, in contrast to the conscript armies of the continent. The slaughter was that of the British ruling order. The patricians who should have governed England between the wars were dead before Ypres or on the Somme—so runs the plausible argument, given force by the appalling memorial plaques in Oxford and Cambridge colleges that suggest that 1914–18 destroyed the élite of modern Britain with the same thoroughness and effect as the Wars of the Roses are said to have unmanned the feudal aristocracy of the fifteenth century. In any case, it is true that few politicians of the first order did emerge from the halls of the ancient universities in the generation that was reaching manhood in 1910. Only Lord Avon and Lord Atlee, among later leading statesmen, were young officers in the First World War.

It has been argued with force (by the late Professor David McKay) that the loss of leadership in France was even more serious, and it is true that there were few young men of authentic stature there, as in Britain, in the interwar years—Léon Blum and Aristide Briand and Edouard Herriot were all mature men by 1900. But the theory about Britain is particularly instructive because it indicates the ironic ways in which the peculiar institutions of late nineteenth-century Britain, a free democracy governed by an old, but adaptable, privileged class, were made unworkable by a war designed to make democracy safe. On the continent, the loss of life was *socially* more evenly distributed.

In every country of Europe, and in the United States as well, the bloodletting had a profound impact on public opinion. This was partly because of the terms of the fighting in the west; the combination of geography, military technology, and the extreme conservatism of many professional soldiers determined that the western front should be remarkably stable for four years, and warfare there was a harrowing and intensely boring alternation of life in trenches with huge artillery duels and sanguinary, yard-by-yard advances and retreats. The new weapons—tanks, poison gas, barbed wire, and air power—all seemed horrifying, perhaps especially because they were unsuccessful in changing the awful war of position into one of movement. Moreover, aerial bombardment of London by Zeppelins, long-range shelling of Paris, and economic blockade reintroduced the world to warfare against civilians.

All this happened at a point in history when mankind had been generally supposed to be progressing in enlightenment, civilization, good sense, humanitarianism, and, above all, ability to control his environment. The contrast between "progress" and what was happening 1914–18 made it seem even more devastating and disillusioning than the facts would, in a different circumstance, have justified. Moreover—and this was more than anything influential in determining the curious impotence of the human mind in the years that followed—there was an even more shocking contrast between what was actually happening and the purposes for which it was supposed to be happening. Europe had gone to war in 1914—it was thought—in the pursuit of traditional, finite, coherent political purposes which were, as the custom of the time demanded, cloaked in appropriate sentiments. By 1916 at the latest, these values were seen to be insufficiently real, or insufficiently important, to justify what was happening. Patriotism, honor, and the sanctity of treaties had already been supplemented by diabolism: by the end of the first month of the war, each side was depicting the other as monstrous and subhuman in its cruelty and irresponsibility and (this was especially important) *guilty* in initiating the war. Positive incitements were also provided: all sorts of good things were promised on the condition of victory—"homes fit for heroes," "a world safe for democracy," "national self-determination," "observance of international law," and many others. The very intensity of the conflict which produced them made the promises absurdly unattainable, and thus generated a bitterness and disillusionment that in some cases preached that all wars were unnecessary as well as immoral and evil, and in other cases that the evils of the particular war just past could only be overcome by fighting another to reverse the decision.

This group of effects of World War I and its losses is matched by, and closely connected with, another, similar and equally important: the nations of western Europe ceased to be creditors and became debtors, and their balance of payments, their fiscal conditions, their commercial policies and relations underwent losses that affected opinion and power as drastically as the loss of men affected minds and morals. In 1914 Great Britain, France, Germany, Italy, and Austria-Hungary, along with most of the small states that bordered them, were creditors: their citizens had lent money abroad and were owed, by foreigners, more in interest and capital than they themselves owed to foreigners. In the case of Great Britain, whose economy was involved with suppliers, buyers, sellers, borrowers, and lenders beyond its borders in virtually every aspect, the overseas investment was enormous, and had been rapidly growing for a long time. British citizens and institutions had invested abroad, by 1914, over 3½ billion pounds, and this yielded an annual income to British people, paid by foreigners, of 185 million pounds.* A comparable situation, on a smaller scale, existed for other western European nations.

This was the product of western Europe's fast economic expansion in the years before 1914. Its citizens had accumulated profits beyond their needs, and they found it advantageous to invest their savings in foreign countries, often less "developed" ones, including those in eastern Europe, where interest rates were high because risks were high. It was a situation in many ways extremely useful both to Europeans and to the rest of the world. The creditor nations found themselves in the enviable position of heirs living on an inherited fortune; they were making money, in the form of interest on investment, which they didn't have to work for. The rest of the world had capital to develop its economy. This was the foundation, and the characteristic institution, of the world economy and the world system as it existed in 1914. It was the token and the imagined guarantor of "progress"—and of European pre-eminence.

But like so many of the institutions of prewar Europe—like, perhaps, any institution—the situation contained weaknesses

---

*This was a substantial portion of total taxable income in Britain, which in 1911–12 was just over a billion pounds.

and drawbacks which contributed to its own destruction. The income from abroad meant, of course, an import surplus: the standard of living, and in some ways the survival, of Europe's economy was dependent on goods that were being paid for by foreign investments. This meant that the European system, and the world order, depended upon the rather fragile fact of foreigners' good manners, upon the hesitation of a foreign country like, say, Mexico, to confiscate European capital investment. And this, in turn, depended upon the political and military pre-eminence of Europe, its authority in enforcing its own notion of good manners. Such enforcement had been relatively easy in the past: gunboats were sent to awe recalcitrant natives; squadrons were landed to collect customs; islands were occupied to intimidate uppity regimes; whole regions were annexed to assure respect for "civilized" powers. But—and this was characteristic of the whole world order—this pre-eminence depended on a condition contrary to fact, the willingness of Europeans to stop their rivalries with one another short of mutual destruction. And the European countries were—it was one of the conditions of expansion and power—highly competitive.

The most clear and present danger arising from the problems of dependence on foreign investment and import surpluses presented itself in Great Britain; and Great Britain, more than half a century after 1914, has failed to solve the critical problem that its dependence produced. To state it in its simplest terms, Great Britain, pursuing the persuasive precepts of capitalist economics, had concentrated in the nineteenth century on producing the things that the British produced most efficiently: that is, the things the free market demanded. They had done it so well that their nation had become highly specialized in certain lines of manufacturing, and had also accumulated large profits to invest abroad. British farming, in some lines uncompetitive with Canadian or American farming, could no longer produce enough food to feed more than half a largely urban population. The necessary imports were paid for by foreign investments and brought to Britain by ship. If the foreign investments were lost, *or* if the surrounding seas fell under the control, even partial, of hostile powers, then the British would be threatened with starvation. Both contingencies developed by 1917. In the spring of that year it was estimated that the British Isles, girdled with German submarines, were within three weeks of starvation.

But this very real and tangible threat was only the beginning of the weakness of Britain's position as revealed and worsened in the war. The overseas investment had gone to build up competing industrial economies; Britain's own industry, less attractive to investors and handicapped by obsolescent equipment, was less and less able to compete with foreign manufacturers created by British capital. Britain's security and power and prosperity all rested, then, on two things in 1914: the continuation of income from abroad provided by foreign investment; and the new diversion of capital into Britain's economy in order to assure new and rapid growth as soon as possible. Precisely the opposite of both these developments took place during, and partly as a result of, the war.

By 1918, Britain had sold more than a third of its foreign investment in order to pay for imports of war materials, including food. It would have had to liquidate much more, and would in fact have been faced with international bankruptcy, had it not been for massive infusions of money from the United States, in the form of war loans amounting, by the end of the war, to something approaching a billion pounds. Moreover, four years of growth, which should have taken place, was replaced with four years of deterioration, and this at a time when Britain's competitors, notably the United States, Japan, and Canada, were growing fast.

What happened to Britain happened to all of Europe. American wartime loans to Europe came to something like nine billion dollars, which of course represented a European debt. And all the former creditors had lost substantial parts of their assets abroad. The German overseas investment held by enemies was mostly confiscated, amounting to a loss of several billion dollars. Much of Germany's total investment had been in central Europe, and that too was lost in the chaos. The French, heavy creditors in 1914, sold off much of their investment to pay for the war; the largest single chunk of it, which was in Russia, was confiscated by the Soviet Government in 1918. By the end of the war, Europe was in debt to everybody, most especially to the United States.*

The shift from creditor to debtor status has an absolute importance which illustrates the complex ways in which the war operated and the decisive effect of timing. It was probably true that the rapid growth of the United States, and the slowing down in Europe that inhered in an import surplus, would have eventuated (in a generation or two) in a similar financial relationship. Almost certainly, the process would have produced in the end the same industrial superiority that in 1918 complemented the new American creditor position; and American military and naval supremacy was also, perhaps, a near certainty.

These were the logical climaxes of tendencies perceptible in 1914. But the shift of power—financial, industrial, and military—took place not in the course of generations but of months. The *rapidity* of the shift was the most notable fact of the twentieth century: neither the Americans nor the Europeans were prepared psychologically or institutionally for what happened. The Americans, with a small-power, debtor mentality, continued to act in ways that suggested that they could, whenever they pleased, withdraw from world responsibilities and let the Concert of Europe reassume leadership. They also supposed, like small-town traders, that they could force the recalcitrant Europeans to repay the money they had borrowed while at the same time continuing to pursue the traditional policies of a debtor: high protective tariffs. They distrusted Europeans because they considered Europeans to be experienced and powerful and wily; and the Europeans, while urgently aware of the need for help from America, were equally unable to adjust to the tidal change in power relations: the British and French handled the Americans as escaped and ungrateful colonists.

The rapidity of the shift of the world center of gravity from the eastern to the western hemisphere is reflected in almost every statistical index. France and Germany did not reach their 1913 national income again until the midtwenties, and (the fact

---

*It was true that Britain was on balance still a creditor, but the credit balance was formed by loans owed by foreign allies, arising from war credits, and did not help Britain in its balance of payments crisis with advanced industrial economies, notably the United States, its biggest creditor.

is of the utmost significance in explaining what happened in the 1930s) most of the countries of central and southeastern Europe *never*, between the wars, approached the 1913 level of production. From 1913 to 1925 the share in world trade of Britain, Germany, and Italy declined, and that of France failed to rise. But in the same period American production and trade were expanding enormously.

Much more had happened to the world order than the making of a colossal economic power in America. One of the reasons why the old order could not be restored, and why efforts at what were called "reconstruction" (which meant trying to restore it) were so unsuccessful, was that many of the essential conditions of continued growth in Europe were destroyed. The most important of these was the stability of currencies.

The stability of money is, like abstention from certain forms of vice, mainly a question of habit. In 1914, it was generally assumed that pounds, francs, dollars, lire, and marks were absolute quantities, like quarts and liters and tons. This looked like the sanctified consequence of something called the gold standard; it was in reality the consequence of a sort of taboo.

It is not at all necessary to explore here the way in which the gold standard worked. But one feature of it should be pointed out: it provided an appropriate fiscal complement to the political system of pre-1914 Europe. There was an international currency whose existence imposed limits upon the freedom of action of national governments, but the limits were not imposed by another government. Sovereignty—unlimited authority—was not impaired.

This system required, for its operation, many inhibitions to supplement the discipline of gold value, among other things a reasonably conservative fiscal policy of avoiding deficits. It was in many ways a financial system that imposed painful and sometimes almost unendurable penalties upon society, particularly the poor, since it required nations to bear deflation and depression without resorting to the alleviations of public spending. But with a fairly stable or expanding world economy, these penalties were generally tolerable. For an understanding of what happened in the twenties and thirties, developments which made the

Second World War, it is necessary to see that the abandonment of the inhibitions of gold as a universal means of payment meant that all fiscal and currency affairs were determined henceforth by government action. This meant that any international agreement to restore an international means of payment or to determine a common fiscal or commercial policy would constitute an invasion of sovereignty and independence, and this governments could scarcely agree to.

Upon the monetary inhibition the prosperity and "progress" of the world before the war had been founded. Like so many other inhibitions, including those of conventional morality, it turned out that a foundation that had seemed as solid and unalterable as the earth itself simply dissolved without much notice upon the outbreak of war. It had been generally expected that the war would be short: like the closing of stock exchanges, the suspension of gold payments—which marked the ending of the' definition of the value of European currency by an objective standard—it was an emergency measure. But the war continued, growing ever more costly, and the value of currencies, determined now by prices, supply and demand, government policy, and public confidence, declined as inflationary prices grew. By 1920 the mark had lost half its gold value, and the pound, which had been most solidly backed and most skillfully managed, over a fifth.

Greater damage had been done to the idea, as well as the facts, of an international economy than the disruption of its standards for exchanging different kinds of money. International trade between enemies had, of course, stopped; between allies and neutrals it had been deformed and distorted by military requirements. In some places shut off from former European suppliers, particularly South American countries like Brazil or antipodal ones like Australia, industrial revolutions began. Almost every country, belligerent or not, had had to embark upon an extensive program of government management of the economy in order to lessen strains, to assure the efficient use of available resources, to control soaring prices and wages. This extension of government controls of economics was one of the most startling effects of the war. Before 1914, government interference with the international economy had been limited mainly to low and on the whole rather stable taxes (tariffs) imposed on goods crossing frontiers. These had not very much hindered the growth of a free international market, although along with some other developments, like the growth of businessmen's agreements (cartels) to allocate markets and materials, they presaged the form that interference with the free market would take. After 1918, the international economy existed entirely at the pleasure of national governments: the prosperity of foreigners would be tolerated only when it did not injure the stability of the domestic economy. To give a single example: the defeated Germans, under the terms of the peace treaty, were required to pay enormous reparations to the French. They could not (or insisted they could not) pay in currency, because they had no gold or francs and could not get any; but they were willing to pay in kind, that is, in goods. Specifically, rolling stock, which French railways urgently needed. The French government was obliged to decline this offer because of the hostility of French labor unions which feared workers in French railway manufacturies would be thrown out of work if German equipment were brought in to the country. The logical, although unexpected, effect of the First World War was to substitute governmental controls—and in particular national governmental controls—for automatic, international economic mechanisms.

One of the most striking symbols of the change that had taken place was in what is technically called the "mobility of persons." This is partly economic—can labor cross frontiers? It is, more largely, a question of human rights. Before 1914, mobility of persons was limited only by inclination or the cost of train tickets: anybody could go anywhere he wanted in Europe (outside of Russia, where travel was strictly regulated both across borders and within the country). Passports were not necessary, and were not much used. No officials asked for "papers" at frontiers. War, and the exigencies of security, made travel difficult, often impossible. After the war, every traveler across every frontier had to be provided with a passport demonstrating that his own government guaranteed that he was who he said he was, and in most cases also a "visa," issued by the consul of a foreign country assuring the frontier officials that the entering alien was not dangerous. It was a symbol indicating that the cosmopolitan world order had dissolved.

Passports and visas were tangible symbols of the intangible losses. Others were paradoxical. The rising egalitarianism, the demand by peoples for participation not merely in the electoral politics but in, for example, the negotiation of treaties or the settlement of international disputes, the demand for full knowledge and publicity of the affairs of state—these seemed to many people good things, tending toward democracy and personal freedom and restraint of the tyranny associated with the fading institutions of militarism, monarchy, and aristocracy. On the other hand, these tendencies produced newspapers and politicians who appealed to the most elementary of popular prejudices. In Great Britain, where among democracies the tradition of patrician leadership survived most strongly in 1914, public opinion displayed its most destructive side. The voters were manipulated by a proletarian demagogue wildly avaricious of power, backed by the frightened and ambitious grandees of a vulgarized Toryism. In 1918, the Lloyd George coalition fought an election with slogans like "Hang the Kaiser."

Not only by pandering to elementary passions did governments seek to harness and exploit democratic opinion; they also manufactured it. The nascent mass media were exploited with advertising techniques, with semiscientific "market research," with planted rumors, with sure-fire appeals to emotions. The purpose was to encourage ever-increasing fear and hatred of the enemy, willingness to make sacrifices, and certainty that sacrifices, however great, would in the end yield victory. This sort of thing went on in every country, increasingly as the war advanced.

Control of opinion, like control of the economy, involved an absolute increase in power, the power of the age of industry and mass communication, to which the state fell heir. This new kind of power of governments was, along with the closely related decay of restraints, among the most notable and universal of wartime developments. Since most people who believed in freedom had thought that state control of society was precisely the thing the Allies were fighting against in 1914, the fact appears as an irony. The irony was not unnoticed by contemporaries: one of the most deeply engaged of French believers in liberty, Elie Halévy, wrote an essay about the war called *The Era of Tyrannies.*

The power of states was encouraged by the very weakening of economies and social stabilities. A regime ill founded and ill poised, faced with depression and subversion, was bound in the postwar years to use all its authority to defend itself and appease or suppress the discontents of a troubled people. The Italian government broke strikes, shot down workers, tried vainly to control a crisis of production, employment, and morality, and then collapsed before a movement which promised, and attained, a much more efficient exercise of state power. The history of Italy from 1918 to 1922, the years of chaos and conflict leading to a dictatorship which deified the very name of the State, illustrated not merely the ineffectiveness of parliamentary government in an age of social strife but also the knowledge that strong government during the war *had* worked, in moments of supreme crisis.

The experience and promise of strong governments and the reality of weak ones helped to produce fascism in postwar Italy. Five years earlier, before the war ended, a rather similar conjunction had produced in Russia the larger and more important phenomenon of the Soviet Union. The Bolshevik revolution succeeded in Russia because the Bolsheviks knew how to use power in a situation when it was not being exercised by the existing state. And there were two other important elements in the Bolshevik success. One was purely Russian: the nature of the Russian state had given ample experience in the techniques of autocracy, and the few inhibitory elements that existed there had always been weak and were destroyed by the wartime experience.

The other notable factor has to do with Marxism itself. Orthodox Marxists, in particular Lenin, among them, benefited from an almost accidental element in Marxism which enabled them to exploit—to ride, one might say—the most important tendency of their day. Marxism included in its predicted process the growth of state power, in the form of the dictatorship of the proletariat. Most nineteenth-century socialists, including Marx, had seen states as inherently bourgeois and oppressive—the state is theft, as one early socialist wrote—and anticipated that the righting of tyrannous wrongs would allow the disappearance of the state as an institution by liberating the natural compatibility of human wills—a typical nineteenth-century view of man that was inherited from the sunny days of the Enlightenment and shared by some liberals. But where anarchists and syndicalists sought to destroy the state by a frontal assault on it, Marxists sought to capture it and use it to destroy capitalism. They thus availed themselves of, instead of opposing, the most efficient, ubiquitous, deeply rooted, and *popular* institution in history. This fact, more than any other, explains why the Communists succeeded in capturing and holding power, and why their success came first in Russia, where the habit and technique of autocracy was real and present, and why, by contrast, anarchism and syndicalism withered away except in industrial centers located in primitive societies, or were transformed into a new form of statism called, in its Italian phase, fascism.

In Russia, then, by the end of the war, the tradition of unleashed state power had triumphed, and the meager traditions of state restraint were dramatically destroyed. The Soviets not only refused to play games by rules; they denounced both the game and the rules while sometimes pretending to accept both. Thus they exchanged ambassadors, in a traditional way, with such western powers as would recognize them, and conventional messages were conveyed between foreign offices in Moscow and abroad. But while this simulacrum of the old procedures of international relations was in course, revolutionary plots and parties were seeking to overthrow western governments. The most important inhibition of the old order had been a respect for the "sovereignty" of foreign states—meaning, in this connection, the legal right of foreign governments to exist without being interfered with. This inhibition was utterly, systematically, and consistently assaulted by the Soviets, on principle.

Similarly, although less important, an essential inhibition forming a foundation of the old order had been the recognition of state obligations as unalterable—certainly unalterable by arbitrary action. Contracts, in effect, were sacred in international law, and this meant both treaties and debts. In the preceding century or so the great powers in Europe had devoted a considerable amount of time and power to enforcing these principles against unstable and recalcitrant peripheral countries. Now the Soviet Union resoundingly announced that all previous "bourgeois" or "imperialist" commitments were by their nature invalid. From the fall of 1917 on, it was made abundantly clear that the restraints which for five hundred years had formed the basis for world order were not ordinances ineluctably imposed by the nature of the universe but a fragile form of social etiquette.

What happened in Russia, perhaps the most important single element in making any real postwar "reconstruction" unthinkable in 1918, was complemented by what happened in central and eastern Europe.

Between the Rhine and the borders of the Soviet Union the changes were less great than in Russia, as regards the way of life in social facts like the family, religion, property, class structure. There were, however, several kinds of changes, all of which made it difficult for the old institutions to function, let alone to improve. By about 1923, when some kind of stability re-emerged in the region between the Rhine and Russia and the Baltic and the Mediterranean seas, the following observations might have been made: *(a)* no state (without exception) retained the same boundaries it had had in 1910; *(b)* every single state in the region had undergone a revolution, and sometimes several; *(c)* every state had seen military action on its territory; *(d)* only one government (that of the kingdom of Hungary) bore any constitutional resemblance to the government that had existed in 1910, and even there the national territory, reduced by two thirds, was so drastically different that the constitutional continuity meant little except the survival of demands to restore the lost lands; *(e)* there were five new states that had not existed at all in 1910, or for centuries previously; *(f)* one vast empire had ceased to exist altogether; *(g)* the richest and most populous nation in the region, which in 1910 had been the best-governed, best-educated, most stable, most powerful, and most rapidly growing nation in

EUROPE AFTER WORLD WAR I
.... Pre-1914 boundaries

0   MILES   500

EUROPE BEFORE WORLD WAR I

the world, had been torn by defeat, revolution, the amputation of much of its territory, almost all of its military and financial power, and all of its colonial empire, and reduced to division, disgust, dissension, and depression.

It was obvious that in this vast area, more than half of Europe outside of Russia, "reconstruction" and "recovery" would involve very drastic therapies indeed. None were forthcoming. And some of the conflicts could not have been appeased at all. The Germans endured losses of territory to recreated Poland, which they tended to regard as a country that had no right to exist; in any case, they were unlikely ever to reconcile themselves to abandoning certain provinces without which Poland *could* not exist. In all the states, as boundaries were redrawn, similar problems existed; there were very large "minorities"— that is people who ethnically and by will belonged in some other jurisdiction than where they were, and the minorities had, in many cases, ample grounds for complaint about their treatment at the hands of alien governments. "Minorities," which is another way of saying the location of frontiers that do not correspond with lines of nationality, had been a chief, perhaps the chief, cause of the First World War. It has been estimated—the matter is one that cannot be appraised exactly, since opinions differ as to just who did and did not constitute a minority—that there were *more* minorities after the First World War than before. In an area where the affiliations of many groups were hard to determine, where national groups were inextricably confused geographically, and where economic and strategic requirements clashed irreconcilably with national boundaries, this was a natural result of trying to redraw boundaries. It was the inevitable result of trying to redraw them to accord with the ambitions and interests of various influential governments and groups within the region.

It is worth observing that the French thought that Czechoslovakia should have a seaport and a corridor to it. Czechoslovakia was expected to become a bastion of French—and anti-Communist and anti-German—influence in Europe, and at the peace conference France sought to favor and strengthen Czechoslovakia. Seaports made nations commercially independent. No Czech or Slovak lived nearer than two hundred miles to any point on the sea, and the intervening territories were all densely inhabited by Germans, Italians, and Slovenes. It was only under American pressure that the French and Czechs reluctantly forewent a seaport. The fact is emblematic.

By 1920, the consortium of states that had run the world was battered and more than decimated. The European Great Powers, a status more or less legally and officially defined, had been six in number in 1914: France, Great Britain, Russia, Austria-Hungary, Italy, and Germany. Together with the colonial empires and associated states they controlled much of the world's population and land surface. With their navies they controlled most of the water surface. Much of the wealth of the world was in the hands of their citizens, and most of the military power.

Russia, defeated and divided, near starvation, and mostly under the control of a government systematically hostile to all other governments and somewhat erratically determined to disrupt them, had been subtracted. Austria-Hungary had ceased to exist; its territory was divided among the "successor states," six in number, none of them Great Powers; Germany was defeated, humiliated, and deliberately deprived of practically all military power and much economic, financial and political influence; the change was unique: *never before had even one Great Power been eliminated by a European war.* Italy, badly battered and also humiliated, much riven by political and social conflict, impoverished by wartime and postwar inflation, deeply resentful of its treatment at the peace conference by its allies, was hostile, momentarily helpless, and isolated; the British and the French, victorious, were much weakened. They were also inclined, like many allies on the morrow of victory, to recrimination and competition. They were both deeply affected by a desire to rest, to bind up wounds, to turn in on themselves. The Concert of Europe that had ruled the world had now ceased to exist.

The United States had replaced Britain and Germany as the most powerful country in the world, militarily, navally, financially, and above all industrially. The Americans had nominally fought to achieve precisely just such moderate, conservatively progressive improvements in the world order as would strengthen the values and institutions that existed in 1914 while diminishing anomalies and eliminating evils. No matter what interpretation one puts on the causes for America's entry into the First World War—the interests of bankers who had an enormous investment in Allied victory, the influence of munition-makers, the naive chauvinism of bullies like Theodore Roosevelt and his anglophile circle of imperialists, the even more naive bourgeois reformism of Wilson and his friends, the outrage at Germany's violations of international laws and duties, or the triumphant kinship, ideological and cultural, with Great Britain —the statement is still justified. The Americans fought in order to strengthen a world order that had until then permitted them the luxury of isolation from world responsibility punctuated by exhilarating adventures in far-away places; they fought, in short, to be allowed to do what they pleased. They saw no reason to pay any price. The job, in November 1918, was done. Whether it had been worth doing, or necessary to do, was open to question. But hands could now be wiped, and business could go on as usual. The Americans refused to take part in the peace settlement, or to join the League of Nations their President had designed.

To rebuild the old system required American support, continuing American sacrifices, and military, political, and especially economic contributions. The consortium needed the full participation of the most powerful country, not only because it *was* the most powerful but also because the decline in power of the old leaders was so immense. The old order was the order of rule by Great Powers, the Concert of Europe; the very enormity and speed that had reduced the old leaders to impotence made it impossible for the new one to replace them. The Americans could never, perhaps, have accepted the role of a new Great Power on the European model. Their traditions were too different, their sense of a separate hemisphere too strong. But they certainly could not accept the change that had taken place so rapidly. Psychologically and diplomatically, they were frontiersmen, privateers singeing the beards of the kings who ruled the world order, a nation of Tom Sawyers turning a shrewd nickel, thumbing noses at the effete lords of the universe, protected by their oceans and their canny know-how from the consequences of their sassiness. Two years—or even seventeen years, the period since Theodore Roosevelt had first begun to convert them to a consciousness of Great Powerhood—were nowhere near enough to extinguish the personality of three centuries.

What was left, then, was a world whose structure, defined in the peace treaties, was supposed to be an improved version of the 1914 world. But the two largest European powers were subtracted from its management and, indeed, determined to destroy it. The strongest power of all would have nothing to do with it. It was left to the weary, shaken, bloodied, French and British to try to run, with ancient methods, a machine whose parts were broken and rusty and whose design was no longer even remotely sufficient to the vast needs of the new era.

This was the situation of the world in the desperate years of the early twenties, when paralysis, inflation, strife, depression, confusion, and vengefulness contorted the Europe that ten years earlier had proudly run the planet.

3

The Years of False Hope

THE world between the wars was still, on maps, a
European world, despite the fatal weakening of
Europe's powers to control it. The disasters of the
First World War had taken place so fast that overseas peoples did not fully realize, anymore than
the Europeans themselves, how vast the damage
had been. And this fact supplemented a subtlety:
the Italians, Belgians, British, and French had *won*
the war, obscuring the more important fact that
Europe as a whole had lost it. This suggested that
the victors would enjoy the traditional fruits of
victory in European wars—greater power, prestige, and stamina. The colonies of the ex-enemies,
Turkey and Germany, passed under the control of
the victors (including Japan and the United States
in the Pacific), and this suggested that their position of overlordship was stronger than ever.
Among the controversies that loomed largest in
the events leading up to the Second World War
was the question of restoring the colonies that
Germany had lost in World War I, and the attempt
of Italy to build an altogether new colonial empire
on traditional lines. It was still thought that who
dominated Europe controlled the spoil of the

world. Unless this is understood, the behavior of Europeans from 1918 to 1939 is inexplicable.

It is interesting to note a striking emblem: Winston Churchill resigned from the British government and shut himself off from influence in the Conservative Party because of his resolute opposition to an extension of self-government for Britain's Indian Empire. It is an irony, one that illuminates the complexities of world politics, that the man who might have prevented World War II was excluded from doing so because of his determination to preserve European dominion in the world.

There were many ways in which the conflict between weakening dominion and the illusion of its permanence showed itself, in all connections and all regions. For example, certain British colonies (Canada, Australia, New Zealand, South Africa, mostly run by European populations) had achieved "self-rule," which meant that their domestic affairs were ordered by an executive authority which had to do pretty much what a locally elected assembly wanted. They were called "dominions." By 1914, several of these had developed into coherent states with some degree of national awareness and a very high degree of resistance to interference from London in their internal affairs or—what was interesting—their freedom to determine their own commercial policies, that is, their right to impose taxes on goods coming from Great Britain. But the notion of the "diplomatic unity of the Empire," which meant that foreign policy was made in London, was still insisted on.

By the 1920s, however, the British Dominions were emancipating their foreign policies from London's control. As a gesture, more than in response to real demands, the British Dominions and (although it was not "self-governing," since decisions made by British representatives were still binding on the local authorities) India, all signed the Treaty of Versailles separately, and were given representation in the Assembly of the League of Nations, which was supposed to embody the element of "equality" among sovereign nations. By the midtwenties, when they had been joined by the Irish Free State, whose government had no sentimental inclination to support the diplomatic unity of Empire, the dominions were beginning to send out their own diplomatic representatives and were signing treaties with foreign nations (the first was Canada with the United States, in 1922) and they were establishing their own foreign offices. The political bond between Britain and the self-governing dominions of its Commonwealth, as it was now being called, were tenuous indeed; the loss of the diplomatic predominance of Europe was here clearly evidenced. Canada, like the United States, disliked the kind of general commitment represented by the League of Nations, and not only discouraged Britain from strengthening the League but persistently tried to weaken it. Canada proposed at the first meeting of the League Assembly in 1920 the excision of the article of the League Covenant which provided (in effect) that no country could be deprived of its territory by force—the outlawing, in effect, of aggression.

The development of authorities and interests liberated from European control was much more striking and disruptive in East Asia than in the British Commonwealth. They affected much more positively the development of world affairs.

A number of unassimilable conditions characterized East Asia, and none of the rules of the traditional international order of European nations affected the participants in the gigantic, unending upheaval in China.

The intromission of Japan into Chinese affairs was in a number of ways illuminating. First, and from the standpoint of later history most important, because of the nature and source of Japanese authority, Japan was able to affect so profoundly the course of European history because it had become, in all the ways that mattered to power politics, a European nation; but it was also hostile to all Europeans, and this fact, not unnoticed, was to provide the paradigm for most future efforts at emancipation in non-European regions. In the best European tradition, but at a time when the age of European empires was ending, Japan was creating an empire; and it behaved with a basic disregard for the old inhibitions of law and diplomacy that would have made the hair of such colonialists as Disraeli stand on end. In 1928, Japan had in the Pact of Paris solemnly renounced war as an instrument of national policy. The next time the Japanese engaged in military operations, they discreetly omitted to declare war, thus keeping themselves in the legal clear. Just as the use by the Soviet Union of diplomats as actors to cover the more basic aims of their foreign policy was evidence of the extent to which the old forms of international relations had become unreal, so was the presence, in the office of the U.S. Secretary of State on December 7, 1941, of Japanese diplomats purporting (and perhaps in honesty) to be seeking to conduct negotiations for the settlement of outstanding differences, while Pearl Harbor was being bombed. Diplomacy had become increasingly unreal for regimes not bound by the conventions of the old European order; the failure of the Americans to grasp the fact made possible the attack that brought them into the Second World War. The failure of many Europeans to grasp it made the war possible in the first place.

Japan was, in short, a most material contributor to the downfall of Europe and the emancipation of unwhite peoples, and its activities distracted Europeans' power and attention from their own affairs.

But before 1939, the contribution was oblique and germinal. It was in Europe that the trouble centered, a Europe deprived rather than enlightened by the three outside Great Powers—the United States, Japan, and the Soviet Union. And the trouble in Europe was essentially of this nature: a group of societies that did not understand how weak and vulnerable they were had chosen—almost perversely, it seemed—to hang separately rather than to hang together.

THE SECURITY PROBLEM

But the perversity was also in large part illusory. The reason for the persistence of internecine rivalries and fears was the very thing that made it indispensable that they be ended: the shock and fear engendered by the First World War. The most illuminating and in all major respects the most important example of this is the situation of France. The future safety of the French homeland and nation, which was called "the problem of Security," lay at the foundation of every dilemma, military and metaphysical alike, that confronted European diplomats.

France had been, pre-eminently, *the* European nation. It was the first to cohere in the centuries when nations were forming; it had equipped itself early on with a workable modern government; it had been blessed by nature with an incomparably rich soil; its people were at every point before the nineteenth century incomparably the most numerous, most productive, and most educated; at most times they were the most fecund intellectually and artistically, and the most dazzlingly civilized in every good sense of that word. They were the original humanists, the original democrats, the original believers in the greatness of the individual. Moreover, they had been, with interruptions, the leading military power on the continent, the arbiter of its destinies. On two occasions, in the late seventeenth and early nineteenth centuries, they had nearly won mastery of Europe.

In the later nineteenth century they had been outstripped, economically and in population, by Britain, then by Germany, the United States, and Russia. Their institutions, earlier more stable than most in Europe, had undergone a periodic series of alarming convulsive changes. They considered that they had been attacked and defeated by a militant Prussia in 1870, under conditions that were not only costly and horribly humiliating but that led to the creation, for the first time, of a much more powerful European state, the German Empire. By hard work and ingenuity in finding allies, they had worked to rebuild their diplomatic position and their armed forces. Attacked (as they considered) in 1914, they had been almost defeated again, but by skill and unimaginable heroism, and with some help from rather unsatisfactory and unco-operative allies, who were often unreliable and egocentric, and distracted by selfish national ends from the war's chief front and purpose, the defeat of Germany and the rescue of France, they had managed to withstand the incredible impact of German aggression. They had finally turned it back and stood, breathless and bleeding, victorious on the blackened battlefields of their homeland.

This is how the situation of France presented itself to Frenchmen in 1918, and this was also, in most respects, a perfectly true statement of the situation. There were additional considerations that affected profoundly the future policies and attitudes of almost all Frenchmen who felt any sense of loyalty of the traditional sort to the *idea* of France as a nation. These were agonizing and provocative, and the emotion they lit was the stronger for a certain egocentricity long noticeable in France, connected no doubt with the long centuries of European leadership.

First: the population of continental France at the end of the war was 39,200,000; that of Germany was 59,850,000.

Second: the number of births in 1920 in France was 834,000; that of Germany was 1,500,000.

Third: The pig iron production of France was 4,426,000 tons in 1911; that of Germany was 15,574,000 tons.

Fourth: Germany had attacked France twice within living memory.

All of these except the last were objective facts; the fourth (which gave the others their political meaning) was arguable, but accepted as true by almost everyone in France, and by most people in the United States and Great Britain.

The inference appeared to the French inescapable. France, twice ravished, must be protected against a renewed attack from Germany. They assumed as self-evident that the Germans were bound to attack again if they thought they had any chance of winning, and in a straight fight they would win. Practically all French foreign policy from World War I until 1940, when they were demonstrated to be correct, reflected these two inferences. The French often appeared obstructionist because they felt it would be unsafe to make any concessions until security had been achieved; they appeared egocentric and parochial because they interpreted all world politics in terms of their eastern frontier; they seemed at times aggressive and vindictive; and at times weak and defensive; and they appeared capricious because changing circumstances, dictating different approaches to security, produced radically various policies. There were conflicts and polemics within France, but their underlying rationale was largely consistent.

During the war the French envisioned a *cordon sanitaire* of states that would be perforce anti-German because they had benefited largely at the expense of Germany and its allies; it was in fact built up, consisting mainly of Poland, Czechoslovakia, Rumania, and Yugoslavia. The governments of all these countries (as of all countries in eastern Europe, where the fluidity of borders encouraged prodigious ambitions) had extensive, and often rather absurd, demands for territory, backed sometimes by ethnic arguments, sometimes by "historic" arguments, sometimes by economic arguments, sometimes by strategic arguments. The French backed almost all such demands against ex-enemies, and this policy sometimes involved actual military support long after the war ended.

For example, the French supported the ambitions of the Poles to extend their eastern frontier several hundred miles beyond the line that the peace conference had determined as just. At the same time, they supported Polish claims to Germany's province of Upper Silesia, a region which had once been Polish, centuries before, some of whose inhabitants spoke a Polish dialect, and which contained a substantial percentage of Germany's mines and industrial capacity. It was eventually divided in a way that infuriated all parties. French anxiety therefore assured for Poland the bitter enmity of its two huge neighbors, a fact that determined the outbreak and course of World War II.

It was not only through the patronage of anti-German governments and statesmen that the French sought security at the expense of reason, humanity, or even good sense. Other and more direct safeguards were proposed. The most direct involved the partition of Germany.

There was, to be sure, general agreement on certain truncations of German territory, of a sort deemed indispensable to render justice to the French (who had lost Alsace and Lorraine in 1871), the Danes (who had lost northern Schleswig, largely inhabited by Danes, in 1864), and the Poles. But the French had larger ideas. They wanted to create, in western Germany, a separate republic under more or less definite allied control, which would include much of Germany's mineral and industrial resources and assure a strategic buffer as well as an economic hemorrhage.

At the peace conference in 1919, such a partition of Germany was flatly and persistently opposed by the British and, particularly, the Americans. Wilson was determined to make a "just" peace, and he said of the French ambitions on the Rhine: "We want no more Alsace-Lorraines." To most people in the world this seemed a logical, wise, and pertinent reproach. To the French it seemed unsympathetic to the point of being pro-German, but they grudgingly abandoned their demands in return for certain substitute guarantees and promises which offered, they thought, a minimally adequate substitute for the absolute security that they considered the Rhineland state would have given.

There were three in particular. The first was that the British and Americans should agree to come at once to the aid of France in the case of another German attack. The second was that an important coal-mining area of western Germany, the valley of the river Saar, which complemented Lorraine's rich iron deposits, should be annexed to France. The third was that the western half of the Rhineland, that is, the territory that lay between the river and the western border of Germany, along with "bridgeheads," small areas on the eastern shore, should be occupied by British, Belgian, French, and U.S. troops and should be perpetually forbidden to German troops or fortifications.

In addition to these substitute demands, the French had other projects to secure the peace from the threat of future German aggression. There were made, and granted, demands of an economic sort which were ostensibly intended to assure that the Germans would pay for the damage they had done in France, but which, taken with a number of other stipulations proposed and mostly inserted in the peace treaty, were designed to harass or even to wreck the German economy. They also tried to provide themselves with guaranteed international military and economic support against Germany in the event of renewed aggression, and it was this that they hoped to achieve partly through the League of Nations. But they had very little confidence in worldwide agencies for co-operation; in certain respects they were able to face realities better than anyone else, and they knew that an organization intended to maintain world peace through voluntary co-operation was the dream of idiots. They thought the League should be chiefly European in its focus and that it must have teeth, in the form of an army, at its disposal. The French, much weakened, would thus be in a position, when they were next attacked, to invoke a large international defense force.

From the point of view of the other powers—and particularly the Americans, who were already facing charges from opposition politicians that the idea of the League was an intolerable infringement on American independence—the suggestion was unthinkable. A League with an army would certainly turn into an arm of French policy, and both British and Americans, discomfited by French obstinacy, were already beginning to suspect the French of wishing to establish a sort of neo-Napoleonic empire, or overlordship, throughout most of Europe. The idea of a League army was, like the partition of Germany, vetoed.

Moreover, the agreement in principle to the three substitute security guarantees was gradually qualified to the point of being most unsatisfactory. The annexation of the Saar was to be partial and temporary: it was to be administered by the League of Nations, and at the end of fifteen years a plebiscite was to be held to determine whether the inhabitants wished to return to German rule or not. (They did, almost to a man.) The Allied occupation of the Rhineland was also to be temporary—for twenty-five years. The most important of the substitutes was the Pact of Guarantees, but the British insisted that their acceptance of it be conditional upon the American. When the United States Senate refused to approve the Treaty of Versailles, Wilson realized that they would certainly not accept the Pact of Guarantees, and never even presented it for approval. Thus the British were freed of their obligation.

By 1920, then, the French appeared, at least to themselves, to have been cheated of most of the fruits of their terribly hard-won victory. They were almost as exposed to German power as ever, and the trend of German politics, where nationalist forces were reviving after the revolution of 1918, confirmed the French fears. They turned away from the League for reassurance and support.

In the next few years the French built up, and strengthened, a system of alliances with the powers that had profited from the defeat of Germany and Austria. Alliances were signed with Belgium and Poland, and later, the "Little Entente" was formed by Czechoslovakia, Rumania, and Yugoslavia, and the French entered into close relations and defensive agreements with these three powers. If Germany could not be partitioned or ruined, it could at least be effectively surrounded. For the next decade, this system of eastern European alliances was a principal concern of French foreign policy. It was, if not exactly incompatible with the provisions of the Covenant of the League, certainly inconsistent with its principles, for the League had been intended to provide a universal security system exactly for the purpose of replacing, or making unnecessary, the alliance system that had played so important a role in the coming of World War I.

The French alliance system is a good example of the persistence of old and unsatisfactory features of the pre-1914 European system, ghosts of the great alliances, as it were. And as in 1914, the real hope for support against Germany seemed to lie in Great Britain, and the attitude of the British toward "the security question" was vague and divided.

BRITISH ATTITUDES

In the immediate postwar years an attitude toward continental affairs developed in Great Britain which expressed itself in two characteristic forms, one reflecting, in a general way, the policies of the Conservative Party, the other of the Labour and Liberal parties. The basic source was disillusionment, which often showed itself in the form of a guilty conscience, sometimes in nostalgia for the lost age of the Balance of Power, and frequently in a parochial and isolationist desire to wash British hands of tiresome continental affairs. In some respects, these reactions were very similar to those of the United States, and in a much less spectacular and defined way British policies resembled the withdrawal symptoms manifested by the Harding and Coolidge administrations.

There were all sorts of conditions that favored these developments. There was, for example, the influential work of Mr. John Maynard Keynes, the economist, published late in 1919 (*The Economic Consequences of the Peace*), which shrewdly (although fallaciously) argued that the peace treaty had wrecked the German economy, and the prosperity of Germany was indispensable to the prosperity of everyone else. The consequences of Mr. Keynes's argument were more moral than economic, as indeed was its motive. The British, bewailing the cruel, unusual, *and* injudicious treatment to which Germany had been subjected, were inclined to blame the French for this wickedness. British opinion more and more inclined to be pro-German.

The second great source of Britain's attitudes toward the continent in the twenties was the postwar depression and the persistent unemployment and economic dilemma that followed it. A serious and world-wide "slump," as it was euphemistically called, followed a brief period of prosperity and optimism after the armistice and preoccupied public attention. So did distracting troubles in Ireland and Asia.

The most vulnerable and fragile of prewar economies, although also the richest, Britain had suffered most basically, and the coalition prescribed very old-fashioned and ineffective remedies. The precepts of capitalist, laissez-faire theory prevailed over the dictates of common sense and popular pressure. These precepts required balancing the budget, reducing production costs, raising taxes, severely limiting public expenditures, and scrupulously honoring all debts, foreign and domestic, government and private, through maintaining and if possible increasing the value of money. It was a program designed to restore "stability," to inspire confidence, particularly among financiers and creditors, and to recapture the economic advantages that had once derived from the enormous prestige and stability of Britain's currency and banking. The difficulty was that it involved economic stagnation and unemployment. By keeping money dear and scarce through taxation and by lowering prices, it discouraged the very investment in domestic industry that was most urgently needed. By making the pound expensive abroad, it forced exporters to try to reduce costs by reducing wages and laying off workers. It represented the triumph of economic theory over good sense. By 1925, when France had pulled 25 per cent above its prewar level of industrial production, Britain was still 15 per cent below it.

But British policy represented in the last analysis a moral rather than an economic choice. It was not a party question: for a long time the Labour Party supported, with equal fervor, the notion that inflation—the stimulation of the economy through deficits and cheap money—would take its first penalty from workers whose savings would be wiped out. But it also represented a half-conscious determination to save the class structure and the confidence of British society in its own permanence. In this, as in some other respects, it was successful. Britain's society, and therefore its cohesion and self-assurance, survived and permitted the nations to survive the Second World War.

Whatever the long-run effects of rigorous deflation, of a policy that might be called deliberate depression, its short-run effects were isolationist. The British were turned away from Europe, toward their own problems and toward the empire and the overseas trade which they associated with the lost capacity for growth and greatness. It is important to understand that these two elements—extreme and weary disillusionment with the war and the peace, and intense preoccupation with economic, social, and colonial questions—played much the same role in British policy as did the obsession with security in French.

Mingled with these universals was the conflict between the parties, which was limited but real. Its terms were also important, for although Labour was in office only a few months in the postwar decade, its programs and pressures had a decided effect in shaping public opinion and, in a negative way, in shaping Conservative policies. The Labour Party, representing a very diverse confederation of trade unionists and middle-class reformers, was dominated in most of its attitudes toward foreign affairs by a series of impulses toward pacifism, internationalism, support for the League, and a general belief that Frenchmen were untrustworthy. In some respects the party was intensely insular, and some of its parts were dominated by what one historian called "the pressure-group mentality," manifesting itself in a national policy that was really an attempt to obtain tangible benefits for workers.

There was a strong tendency to feel that wars were conspiracies by rich men and benefited no one except capitalists; this was

a familiar stereotype of pre-1914 socialists, and had strongly influenced the relatively few Labourite pacifists in World War I.
But it was also noticeable that these attitudes were sometimes
more negative than affirmative. The Labour Party emphatically
opposed most defense measures and, when they could, reduced
expenditures for arms, abandoning, during their tenure in 1929–
31, the most grandiose of imperial defense measures, the fortifica-
tion of Singapore. The Conservatives, not eager to spend money
which would unbalance budgets but officially committed to a
strong defense policy, had their cake and ate it too, being able
to blame Labour for their own laxity in rearmament.

The Conservatives, while skeptical of the League and suspicious of continental entanglements, realized the need for positive action to allay French anxieties. And the need was, indeed,
critical. For by the time Stanley Baldwin formed his second
Conservative government in October 1924, a new Franco-German war had already taken place, and the "European situation,"
as it was called, looked desperate.

THE LOCARNO DELUSION

The war, known as the Ruhr Invasion, was historically the
most important event of the 1920s so far as the origins of World
War II go—less because it diverted the course of events than
because it showed how difficult the course of events was to
divert. Almost every aspect of it was significant.

The French and Belgians sent troops into the Ruhr valley, a
heavily industrialized region just east of the occupied Rhineland,
in January 1923, on the grounds that the Germans had failed to
fulfill their obligations, accepted in the peace treaties and subsequent agreements, to send payments in goods, services, and
money to the Allies as "reparation" for the German misdeed in
starting the 1914 war. The Germans (and most enlightened economic experts of all nations) insisted they could not possibly pay
the "astronomical" sums demanded of them. (The total, decided
after lengthy consideration two years previously, was thirty-
three billion dollars, which would correspond to something like
one hundred and fifty billion dollars in 1969 values. This was to

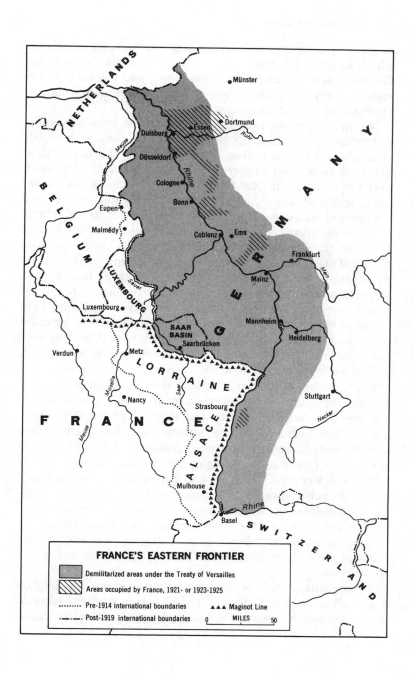

FRANCE'S EASTERN FRONTIER

- (shaded) Demilitarized areas under the Treaty of Versailles
- (hatched) Areas occupied by France, 1921- or 1923-1925
- .... Pre-1914 international boundaries
- ▲▲▲ Maginot Line
- —·—· Post-1919 international boundaries

0   MILES   50

be spread out over an undetermined period.) They said that the efforts to make the initial payments thus far had "ruined" the German currency, and indeed *something* had ruined the German currency, for the mark was rapidly descending in value and German prices were mounting fast.

No one at the time, or since, has understood the economics of reparations, or their connection with the German currency disaster and with other international payments, in a way that was generally agreed to by other experts. But it was clear that whatever the effect of this vast financial problem, its root cause was not financial but emotional: the demand for reparations reflected the sense of injury and of weakness felt by the victorious French.

The Ruhr invasion was a microcosm of this. While the French said that their troops were occupying the Ruhr for the legal reason of German failure to send enough coal, this was obviously a pretext; the invasion represented for some Frenchmen an effort to wreck and perhaps dominate the German economy, for others an attempt to secure French military and perhaps political control in western Germany, and for most Frenchmen an expression of fear and hostility—and of disillusionment with allies who were felt to have let France down if not actually to have betrayed it.

The Germans offered no armed resistance to the invasion, but the government encouraged a policy of non-co-operation which brought the Ruhr to an economic standstill and led to the unemployment of most of its workers. Output fell by two thirds. French and Belgians tried to operate the industry and mines directly and imposed harsh military rule on the region. They also showed their hand by encouraging the establishment of a phony Rhineland Republic which, in October 1923, was "recognized" by the French authorities. The lackey masters of the new republic ejected the German government officials from the area. But British pressure, and the inconvenience and high cost of the occupation as well as the crumbling of German resistance, finally induced the French to withdraw their support and in the end their forces.

What made all this of first-rate importance was, in the first place, what it did to Germany. The Germans, with redoubtable determination, had pushed the vain policy of passive resistance to the point of completing the ruin of their currency. That is, the support of the unemployed in the Ruhr, paid for by government money which was printed for the occasion, finally caused the mark to become valueless. At the end of the inflation, the mark was estimated to be worth about thirty trillion to the dollar. This was a shock of incredible magnitude. In the second place, the same numerous and influential people who had felt that Germany *must* upset by force the onerous and humiliating Treaty of Versailles if it were to survive as a national state were proved right before public opinion, and henceforth the story of German politics was largely influenced by more or less clandestine efforts to conspire against the peace settlement and more or less overt attempts by politicians to curry popular favor by denouncing other politicians as "soft" on international issues.

There were portentous subtleties in these developments even greater than those that appeared on the surface. For one thing —and this was, conceivably, the most important single implication of the Ruhr invasion—the British government and public opinion were driven irrevocably into the position that Germany was a persecuted victim, that France was an irresponsible aggressor, and that European stability depended on righting Germany's wrongs and assuaging its grievances. For another, a considerable portion of the German public was not only alienated from all thought of co-operating with the west but terrified by the prospect of certain internal developments in Germany. For a nation whose people had had an excessive faith in and dependency on the solidity of state and society, the destruction of the currency was psychically quite as disastrous and humiliating as the much less complete defeat of the German army in 1918. Workers very nearly starved to death in some cases, as wages failed to keep up with the farcical rise in prices. Anybody who had a salary, or a pension, or who lived on savings and investments, or insurance payments, found that an income which had permitted him a few years earlier to live in comfort for a month was now quite insufficient to buy a loaf of bread or a postage stamp. The middle classes—not the Marxian bourgeoisie, but the stolid, saving, and rather unenterprising German burghers— were, in the exaggerated and essentially meaningless phrase they used of themselves, "wiped out." Fear of inflation coupled with a sense of indignity in the face of the French incursion were the legacy of the dispossessed.

In November of 1923, during the worst of the inflation and with the French deeply entrenched in the Ruhr, some ambitious, angry, and not very sensible Army veterans and journalists attempted to overthrow the state government of Bavaria in southern Germany. They were inspired by the bull-necked General Ludendorff, who had been quartermaster-general of the wartime army, and in retirement had become a sponsor for all sorts of extreme reactionary and anti-Allied movements. They were representative of a large number of quasi-conspiratorial groups who abounded in these dismal and frightening years in the Bavarian capital, Munich, where a conservative government tolerated them. They expressed what many, many Germans felt: boredom with the dreary years of peace, fury at the loss of the war, a sense that the existing regime and German society in general were corrupt and hypocritical in their grasping capitalism and in the ineffectual reformism represented by the Social Democratic and other moderate parties that ruled in Berlin. They were, in short, typical of their age and, in many ways, of the young people of any age. But what gave them an audience, a certain amount of financial support, and a certain amount of cohesion, was the Ruhr Invasion. The revolutionary attempt was nothing; the police dispersed the rebels in a few hours. But martyrs had been made, and the leader of the rebel group, a man named Adolf Hitler, had emerged as a regional figure of some magnetism.

The significance of the Ruhr was, then, both substantial and ominous. But its immediate effects appeared oddly salutary. Things in Europe began to get better, and in two years they were very much better indeed. The fact that they did so was proof (which no one noticed) of the fact that economics is a matter of myth as much as reality. The terrible shock of the death of the mark was economically much less important than imagined. What mattered was confidence, and confidence was presently restored by the sudden reappearance of the United States in European affairs. As a result of a British appeal to the Americans to assist in providing some way of living with the reparations

problem, a committee including—and indeed dominated by—
the American delegate, Charles Dawes, met in Paris a year after
the French had first marched into the Ruhr. An arrangement, the
Dawes Plan, was worked out for rescheduling reparations and
salvaging the German means to pay them. The German mark
was simply abandoned and a new currency inaugurated, backed
—in effect—simply by faith. It retained its value, the inflation
ended, reparations payments were resumed, the French withdrew from the Ruhr, and, most surprising of all, the German
economy commenced a headlong rush to prosperity.

The faith in the Dawes Plan and in the new mark which made
possible this miracle was correctly founded upon an instinctive
recognition of one of the realities of international politics: the
settlement was backed by an international loan to Germany, and
the loan was in turn largely made possible by the United States.
Thus the most important single element in the world situation,
American money, was brought to bear in salutary ways to miti-
gate the disasters of Europe. In the years that followed, western
Europe dramatically recovered its economic stability and capacity for growth; currencies were stabilized, unemployment fell,
new industries prospered, export revived. By 1928, France, Germany, and some of the lesser industrial societies were back
to, or in some ways well beyond, the 1913 point of development,
and even those countries where more basic disturbances had
existed, like Russia and Britain, were approaching the 1913
level.

Not all of this was due to American capital, of course, but
without American capital it would have been impossible. The
years 1924 to 1929 saw an enormous amount of German borrowing abroad—some five billion gold dollars, half of it from the
United States. This enabled the Germans to pay their reparations fairly painlessly, with plenty left over for expanding their
own industry. The reparations payments thus made enabled the
allies to pay the interest on their war debts to the United States.
A financial circuit, crazy but not vicious, was thus inaugurated,
dispersing dollars and their beneficent influence through the
world. The fact, significant in several ways, was in one way
sinister: just as Europe's dependence on foreign investments

before 1914 had jeopardized its stability, so did the new substitute for foreign investments, American private money; for if American investors decided to stop investing at any time, then the world would collapse into the same chaos from which General Dawes had rescued it at Paris in January 1924. And while it suggested that the first requirement for "reconstruction" and for "security" was money, no one thought to apply the suggestion to the harried countries of central and southeastern Europe. Finally, it showed that in a deeper sense what mattered was not money but power, of which money was an incident, and that power—to solve problems as to save currencies—was seated in the United States of America. There is no more provocative fact in the history of Europe between the wars than this: that despair and catastrophe were in a few months converted into bounding confidence and prosperity by the small, the token, participation of the United States in the affairs of Europe.

The developments that followed the Ruhr in Europe were seriously taken as representing the dawn of a new era. Franco-German relations did appear to be appeased in the years that followed. The milestones of this idyll have some slight importance *because* their importance was so much overrated by contemporaries. There was one principal delusion, and several minor ones.

The first was Locarno. This was the consummation of the unsuccessful efforts that had been made to provide France with security; it was made possible by the exhaustion and despair that followed the Ruhr in both France and Germany, and by the coincident arrival in power of three statesmen who appeared to be prepared to negotiate a European order based on good sense, the forgetting of past illusions and vindictiveness, and a liberal tempering of nationalistic assertions. These men were: in France, Aristide Briand, a renegade socialist but still a strong internationalist; in Britain, Austen Chamberlain, an old-fashioned Conservative seeking to salvage the greatness of the British Empire by damping down the fires of European conflict; in Germany, Gustav Stresemann, who was in fact trying to gain time by an appearance of complaisance in the west before taking action (which was being plotted by the clandestine German Army leadership) to upset the settlement of Versailles in the east.

For the moment, the several duplicities demanded cordiality, and a curious agreement was arranged, designed to buy off German grievances by agreeing not to treat Germany as a criminal outcast. The core of the agreement, executed at Locarno, in the Italian Alps, in negotiations lasting throughout the spring and summer of 1925, was that Germany agreed not to attack France or Belgium or to "militarize" the demilitarized Rhineland area. If something happened that could be construed as a violation of this agreement, then (after careful consideration of a judicial sort) Britain and Italy promised they would come to the assistance of the wronged party. It is now possible to discern some peculiar paradoxes; what was strange about this agreement, hailed as opening a new era of good feeling, was that Germany had *already* agreed to everything that it now agreed to again, and the treaty merely made it more difficult for the French to resist, single-handed, a German attack. According to the cockeyed legalities of Locarno, France would not be able to enforce the Rhineland clauses of Versailles without the approval of Britain, Italy, and the League of Nations. Still, Locarno was hailed, because the German government had voluntarily negotiated it, because it "internationalized" the security question, and because it was negotiated in an atmosphere of amicability. It was taken to mean that France and Germany now *really* accepted a final settlement. In conjunction with the guarantees of the Franco-German frontier, Germany was admitted to the League as a Great Power (with a permanent seat on the League Council, which exemplified Great Powerhood).

Further acts of conciliation followed as the pace of economic recovery and growth quickened and the spirit of Locarno flourished, summarized by Chamberlain's scriptural allusion to the effect that the Locarno Treaties meant "peace for our time."

With security believed, on no grounds except faith, to be guaranteed, the palpable guarantors were deemed dispensable, and beginning in 1925 the Allied occupation forces were progressively withdrawn. By 1930, there were no more foreign troops on German territory; the evacuation anticipated in the Versailles Treaty had thus been advanced by five years. Moreover, other provisions of the treaty which might be interpreted by some as disgraceful and punitive infringements of Germany's dignity and independence (or by others as prudent precautions against German vengefulness) began to be abandoned. Most important was the provision giving the Allies the right to inspect German military establishments to assure that the stringent restrictions of German armament were being obeyed. After 1925 these inspections, never very thorough, were almost entirely stopped, in the interests of good fellowship. Moreover, the Germans' complaint that their own disarmament was supposed to be a preface to general disarmament, in the terms of the treaty, was met by the beginning of laborious negotiations for a world disarmament conference.

In the same years, preparations (eventually ending in 1929, in an elaborate agreement called the Young Plan) were made for rationalizing and further easing Germany's reparations problems, and for establishing an international intergovernmental bank to facilitate public payments in foreign currencies. Briand, the most resolute and in some senses the most perceptive of European statesmen interested in achieving a stable international order, proposed the establishment of a European customs union—which meant, in effect, a common market, in today's terms, designed to stimulate economic growth and economic interdependence as steps toward a European federation, which he favored. And finally, among all the curious and delusory encouragements of these odd years, was the Paris Peace Pact. It bore Briand's authorship, but this was unfair, for he had merely suggested a ceremonial treaty of friendship between France and the United States in an effort to appease the worsening relations between them by invoking the very distant days of their alliance in the War of Independence. The Americans, led by Frank Kellogg, converted his suggestion into an ambitious universal treaty for outlawing war, and in 1928 this project was achieved. All considerable nations in the world (although some with reservations) agreed that they would "renounce war as an instrument of international policy." Nobody, apparently, except the Americans, was much misled by this folly, but the fact that it was signed at all indicated the existence of a belief (still widely held) that international conflict is a bad habit, like smoking, that can be curbed by a show of resolution.

The real difficulty was more like the cancerous consequence of smoking than innocent early experiments with corn silk. No one realized that the symptoms—dependence on American loans, the extreme restiveness of the German Right, the instability of the states of central and southeastern Europe, the gradual stabilization of the Soviet Union, the appearance of an aggressive and unassimilable regime in Italy—meant that the old world smugly administered by the Great Powers of western Europe was deader than ever. The bright years of the late twenties must be properly viewed not as a late twilight or a false dawn but rather as a lightning storm shortly before midnight.

THE CHAOS IN CENTRAL EUROPE

In Britain and America, where guilty feelings about the maltreatment of the Germans, dislike of French irresponsibility, and wishful thinking, were all about equally noticeable in the years between the wars, it was widely believed that Germany after Locarno was a new, promising, constructive society, moving toward acceptance of the peace settlement, deserving of lenient treatment in establishing a stable constitutional structure.

But the situation of Germany in the twenties, like that of Italy and central and eastern Europe, was controlled by elements that made democracy insupportable and belied the easy belief that mechanical adjustments or wise policies could ensure peace.

One dramatic piece of evidence had been made public. Indeed it was flaunted. This was the Rapallo Agreement, signed between Germany and the Soviet Union in 1922. A conference on general economic problems had met at an Italian seaside resort, and the Russians were represented there for the first time in any respectable international meeting since the revolution. The Germans were being subjected to the usual browbeating about reparations. Germany and Russia were then both regarded, and treated, as outlaws; their readmission to the comity of nations was made subject to their accepting obligations (in the case of Russia, the honoring of confiscated international debts, mostly) which they could not meet and which were, in any event, precisely contrary to their principal national and ideological interests. Since the fragile and unreal governance of Europe by France and Britain depended precisely on keeping the outlaws in jail, there was naturally shock (and, less naturally, surprise) when the two powers took the occasion to sign a treaty of friendship that restored diplomatic relations between them.

This treaty, almost as much as Europe's dependence on absent America, demonstrated both the fragility and the unreality of efforts to rebuild the kind of Europe that had existed in 1914. But the profundity of its meaning was not grasped; the treaty was seen as a moral outrage instead of a medical symptom. And the most important feature of the short period of German-Soviet co-operation that now began was not grasped at all.

The outlaws were conniving at German rearmament. In the years that followed, the surviving, underground, General Staff of the Germany Army was enabled to begin, on Russian soil, a large-scale secret training program, which supplemented the various hidden rearmament programs in Germany—in the form of gun clubs, flying clubs, fraternal organizations devoted to midnight drills, and the like. The latter were more or less known to the Allies and disregarded because their military importance was judged to be negligible. But what mattered, in that era anyway, was not military power in being but the will to produce it; and Germany's clandestine rearmament, the affable collaboration of the German leaders with the Soviet regime which, on doctrinal grounds, they detested, showed a will to the recovery of German independence and the revival of German power supported, as a national cause, by most Germans. Two facts were interesting: the Social Democratic paper which printed rumors of the illicit arrangements was harried by the German government *and* by its own liberal and left-wing readers for national betrayal; and Gustav Stresemann, the man who was supposed to represent sweetness and light and the determination to fit a constitutionalized German republic into the western scheme of things, was an author of the government's determination to aid the Army in getting what it wanted. He talked loftily about international co-operation, but his private calculation was the simple and tenable theory that an appearance of "fulfillment" of the Treaty of Versailles and of co-operation with Britain and France and the League was necessary in order to buy time and concessions. Germany's first task, in his judgment, was to rebuild its capacity to defend itself; the second was to regain a position where it could undo, by force or suasion, the humiliating and intolerable peace settlement imposed on Germany's eastern frontier.

Some losses rankled more than others—most notably West Prussia, known as "the Polish Corridor"—because it divided the eastern Prussian province from the rest of Germany. But all of them were regarded as intolerable, and yet without most of them new Poland could not have had much reality or meaning. The destruction of the two great powers that encircled and had partitioned Poland made possible a rather inflated resurrection of the Polish body politic from its century-and-a-quarter-old grave, with some assistance from France. But any cessions to Poland would have been resented; the *existence* of Poland not only converted Germany and Russia into its enemies; it also tended to convert them, from time to time, into friends.

This situation, both as it ramified throughout the world and as it grew confused by more and more local details, is of major importance, not only for the obvious reason that it precipitated the Second World War or because it exemplifies, like the dependence on America, the absolute inability of the French and British to run the world, or even Europe, by themselves, but also because it betokens the immense instability in central and eastern Europe.

Whether that instability could have been remedied is problematical. What was needed was massive infusions of money, intelligently spent to alleviate the costs of war and of redrawing borders, to blackmail the states into some kind of co-operation and some kind of sensible economic planning. The *possibility* of this kind of development existed. But the new states of Europe were supposed to be democracies, they were certainly poorly equipped for sophisticated works of administration, and it was doubtful that battered credit systems in the west could possibly provide the kind of money needed to underwrite the construction of new economies and societies in eastern Europe. The most anybody was prepared to do was to bail out the totally disintegrated Austrian economy with judicious bank loans and advice. Government-to-government transfers of capital that would, in fact, have been outright grants with no prospect of *financial* return were simply not feasible, given the state of public opinion and economic expertise in the west in the 1920s.

The record of the central and eastern states in the twelve years following their creation or remodeling was, unevenly, one of contention, impoverishment, and chaos sliding toward tyranny. Boundaries were made and remade; and nobody was satisfied. The Lithuanians contended with the Poles, the Poles with the Russians, Germans, and Czechs, the Yugoslavs with the Italians, the Greeks with the Bulgarians, Turks, and Albanians, the Rumanians and the Hungarians with *all* their neighbors. A number of quite sharp wars were fought, although military action had largely ended by 1925. Nowhere except in Czechoslovakia and Finland, whose populations and economies were a good deal more mature than most, was anything like economic growth or a reasonable opportunity for individual welfare possible. Currencies varied from the precarious to the calamitous. The new states were, except for Czechoslovakia and Austria, overwhelmingly agricultural: their economic "function" was to serve as a breadbasket and kitchen garden for western Europe, but the production of wheat, livestock, and fruits and vegetables was lamentably backward. Production per acre in Rumania, perhaps the most elemental of all the regions, was less than one sixth that of Denmark. People reflexively thought of eastern Europe as a sort of colonial sphere, where cheap labor produced cheap raw materials to support the sophisticated cultures of the metropolitan west.

The signs of decay were everywhere, and not only in the cluttered combats that passed for international relations from the Baltic to the Balkans. The democratic governments optimistically installed under Allied tutelage—perhaps Allied blackmail —began to founder almost as soon as they were set up. Hungary's was the first to go, in 1919, when a liberal republic was replaced first by a hair-raising experiment with communism and then by a White reaction which installed the rule of the haughty Magyar landowners as a well-run but entirely stagnant oligarchy. Austria was torn, in the late twenties, by armed conflict between monarchists and conservatives and the powerful and vigorous socialists of industrial Vienna: their paramilitary organizations fought in the streets of the city. Yugoslavia, a collection of provinces inhabited by peoples with entirely different backgrounds and nothing in common except a misty racial connection, was riven by regional as well as social disputes, and in the end the king, Alexander III, suppressed the constitution and established a personal dictatorship in 1929. Bulgaria underwent a series of bloody disturbances and Greece a whole series of revolutions. In Poland, where a class of landowners almost as retrograde as those of Hungary had maintained their dominance, the trafficking of politicians made the government unworkable and a military dictatorship was established in 1926.

"Democracy," which was supposed to solve everything, had not worked. Or, more precisely, it was shown that parliaments and bills of rights were absurdities in societies where elemental and unacceptable social and economic conditions prevailed.

FASCISM AND THE EUROPEAN ORDER

The delusions should have been dispelled, or at least the immensely complex reality should have been suggested, by what was happening in three other, older, more sophisticated, and more important countries, countries that belonged, in popular thought, to "the west." These were Spain, Portugal, and Italy, where the forms of constitutional government also collapsed in the twenties.

Both Spain and Italy evidenced, in macrocosm, the kind of cravings and frustrations that beset peoples like the Liths and the Bulgars. They were troubled by citizens who thought that the war had been an embarrassing experience—in Spain's case because it had maintained what seemed to some an inglorious neutrality, in Italy's because it had been defeated and because its victorious allies had failed to provide sufficient booty. They were both troubled by the kind of elemental economic and social

conditions that afflicted places like Rumania but here complicated both by islands of modern industry and finance—mainly
Milan in Italy, mainly Barcelona in Spain—and, perhaps even
more confusing, by an educated elite that contained both proud
aristocrats and superbly educated and productive scholars and
artists. Both were troubled, in short, by extremes of anachronism
and modernity, primitivism and sophistication. And both had
witnessed, in the years since 1900, a rising tide of rebellion,
particularly among young intellectuals, against the corrupt and
inefficient political order that paraded as liberal democracy. Nowhere in Europe before 1914 had bombings, riots, and protest
movements been so lurid as in Spain and Italy. By the midtwenties, both were equipped with dictatorships; what was ominous
was that the Italian version, unlike the stodgy dictatorships in
Yugoslavia or Poland, professed to appeal to rebellious young
people eager for new ideas, and presented itself as pathfinder to
the future. Its anthem was entitled "Youth."

   The Fascist regime in Italy was installed by the leader of a
movement called *fascismo,* which meant roughly "unity." Benito
Mussolini was a psychopathic anarcho-syndicalist of the most
destructive sort, and he had put together an organization, largely
of veterans, which in its early stages presented a program that
matched the most leftist and revolutionary programs of the time:
abolition of monarchy and nobility, anticlericalism, anticapital-
ism. As it moved toward popularity and power, *fascismo* was
tempered by expediency. It sought the support of "respectable"
elements—the peasantry, businessmen, civil servants, the clergy
—by proffering its program as an alternative to Red revolution,
and two elements of its program began to become more prominent. One was a wild chauvinism, a sort of burlesque of the
refined idea of freedom for nationalities from foreign oppression
which had animated nineteenth-century liberals and had inspired Wilson's academic ideal of national self-determination for
the peoples of Europe. The other was an upgrading, almost an
idolatry, of *organization,* of society organized into groups, each
controlled by a superior authority, and culminating in something
that Mussolini called "the state." He later wrote, as a slogan,
"everything within the state, nothing outside the state, nothing

against the state," and this appealed to those who had grown up with the sorry silliness of Italy's maddening parliamentary regime.

In the dismaying confusion of postwar Italy, torn by disillusion and depression, confronted by riotous strikes that threatened national paralysis if not insurrection, *fascismo* gained support. It never gained the support of anything like a majority of voters, and in October 1922, when Mussolini was called to the prime ministership, his success was due much more to the perplexity and fear of the Italian king and governing authorities than to any irresistible tide of national sentiment. Fascism, when its leader reached power, was still mainly a movement of gun-happy action groups.

In power, Mussolini and his followers moved to extend the party's grip over the government, to establish a brutal domination by persecution, frequently accompanied by murder, of political opponents. But they moved slowly and sporadically toward any real innovation in policy. King and nobility remained; so did capitalism; and the Church was actually lured into an agreement, the Lateran Treaty of 1929, which ended the long tug of war between it and the Italian government, dating from Italy's annexation of Rome in 1871, and gave the regime the support of the most powerful institution "outside the state." There was much talk of "the revolution," and of "renewal," but little substance. Elaborate pageants and rhetorical references to a revived Roman empire, together with a fancy program for subjecting the economy to state control and eliminating the social conflict between labor and capital by grouping everybody into "corporations" which would run the economy and regulate the professions, cloaked a policy that was in every sense conservative.

Still, in both Italy and, to a much smaller extent in Spain, the dictatorships of the twenties represented something more significant than conservatism. What they represented was, and is, subject to controversy, even polemics, but whatever it was it was ecumenical in character. It is ironic that a movement whose most conspicuous symptom was violent nationalism could be international; but Mussolini's methods and manners, and to some extent the inward nature of his "movement," exerted a powerful appeal abroad. Almost every country in Europe and the western hemisphere eventually had its fascist movement, with the trappings, more or less superficial, of fascism—its uniforms, its vocabulary, its appeal to those who distrusted or detested the workings of a liberal democracy that had once been an aspiration and had now become a parody. Most important, of course, Mussolini's paraphernalia of pageantry and passion blended with, and fortified, the purposes of Hitler's group in Germany.

Fascism appeared to many, and undoubtedly was, a blend of paradoxes. Mussolini recognized it, and boasted of it: logic, consistency, and rationality were, he said, the false shibboleths of a dogma that denied man's capacity for visceral greatness. It is interesting that, not long after the consolidation of his regime in Italy, three influential books published in America presented three triangularly opposed interpretations. The first, by a Harvard political scientist, William Y. Elliott, was called *The Pragmatic Revolt in Politics* and described fascist and other authoritarian movements as basically a pragmatic reaction against a constitutional liberalism which did not work. The inefficacy of Europe's parliamentary governments when faced with the calamities of the postwar world simply made people accept the need for efficiency, and therefore authority. The second, *The Revolution of Nihilism,* written by a renegade Nazi, Hermann Rauschning, presented German fascism as a form of mass destruction, inspired by hatred of the traditions, the privileges, the very *power* of those who occupied responsible positions in German society. In the third, *The End of Economic Man,* Peter Drucker, a perceptive publicist, argued that liberal democracy had been based upon a purely hedonistic and mainly materialist conception of mankind which denied the force and virtue of emotion; and that it lost its reason for existence when the pragmatic political system based on it failed to satisfy material needs. A fourth interpretation, more important in the end than any of these, was the Marxist, accepted then (as now) in its major outlines by many people who were not at all inclined to espouse communism. This interpreted fascism simply as a tool invented by the property owners in Italy, Germany, and elsewhere, to protect the existing capitalist order through a combination of fraudulent propaganda and brute force.

Any of these four positions is susceptible of defense. The gradual development of historical detachment in recent years, and the accumulation of serious analyses by scholars, adds another and significant element: both the Italian and the later German dictatorship were to a considerable extent the work of cheap political jobbery. They were makeshift, pragmatic in the narrowest sense, and uninventive in the highest degree; and their most conspicuous features were corruption and infighting. The most remarkable of fascism's successes was that this aspect of its character was concealed from so many people. It was not a serious political movement, and the element of jobbery now looms so large as to diminish, although not to eliminate, the elements of pragmatic revolt, of blind destructiveness, of a quest for new ideals, of a conspiracy of rich men to protect themselves.

In short, what fascism was concerned with were power and gain and the satisfaction of individual egos, and its leaders were perfectly prepared to say anything they thought would sound attractive to a given audience. Foreign policy was, in Mussolini's Rome, mostly a matter of impulse and expediency wholly undisciplined by the slightest regard for traditional rules of diplomacy or by principles or long-run objectives. Both Hitler and Mussolini were prepared to use the conventions of traditional diplomacy to *conceal* what they were doing. It was not ideology that determined policy. In this respect, fascism was the opposite of communism, although it had the similar effect of destroying the basic assumptions of European order and converting international relations into a duplicitous farce.

The most illuminating, and the weirdest, Fascist exploit in foreign affairs came before the Fascists assumed power, even before they had developed as a coherent party. It revolved around the port of Fiume, at the head of the Mediterranean, which had been part of the Habsburg Monarchy before its partition. Good sense, good economics, and self-determination all indicated that Fiume should belong to Yugoslavia, once that polyglot kingdom came into existence. In September of 1919, however, a private force organized by the revolutionary nationalist poet of Fascist sympathies, Gabriele d'Annunzio, simply seized the city and held it until 1921, when he was eventually expelled and the place went to Italy anyway, on the eve of Mussolini's call to power, after a treaty was negotiated with the Yugoslavs. D'Annunzio maintained in Fiume, for more than a year, a silly but highly ideological state, equipped with much medieval pageantry and a lot of nonsensical proposals for the complete reconstruction of everything, along "corporate" lines. It was, in fact, a regime of more poetry than truth: no reality matched the oratory. But he *did* occupy the city and maintain his regime, in defiance of law, order, reason, logic, common sense, and the combined hostility of the embarrassed Italian Government and of foreign powers great and small. The age of the political buccaneer had opened in Europe.

The second illuminating episode of Fascist foreign policy took place less than a year after Mussolini's appointment as Prime Minister; it may be regarded as his first major venture in diplomacy. On August 28, 1923, Italian forces bombarded and immediately occupied the Greek Adriatic island of Corfu. This was also the outgrowth of the slow, painful, and often bloody business of settling disputed borders: an international commission was trying to draw the frontiers of Albania. Somebody shot an Italian member of the commission on Greek soil near the disputed border. As retaliation, the Italians seized the Greek island (which was not in any way involved in the border dispute). The Greeks appealed to the League of Nations, which ordered the Italians to withdraw; the Italians, in effect, refused to pay any attention. They later withdrew under pressure from France and Britain, but only after the Greek government had been forced to humiliate itself. The violent aggression by Italy, and the undercutting of the League by the Powers, in search of a "solution" without regard for justice or law, showed that a determined major power would react only to resistance by major powers. The prewar system had been based on this assumption and had sought, sometimes effectively, to constrain such action through the balance of power and the Concert of Europe; but it required resolution by the opposing powers and some sense of restraint and the expediency of obeying the rules on the part of the would-be attacker for the system to work. In the small episode of Corfu, both were shown to be lacking, and the League was no substitute for them.

On other occasions, Mussolini seemed anxious to appear respectable; he showed up at League Council meetings in Geneva dressed in a morning suit and behaving like an elder statesman. There was a strong tendency in British circles especially to suppose that time and responsibility would discipline him, and to find virtues ("Italian trains now run on time," "He stamped out Bolshevism," "He is forcing the lazy Italian people to get down to work at last") in his domestic arrangements. He had done nothing very bad, except to stultify an unsatisfactory parliamentary regime, outlaw some contentious political parties, establish censorship, murder a few dozen political opponents, and occupy a small island. But his intromissions in foreign affairs had at their best an atmosphere that could be interpreted either as low farce or irresponsibility. Although Italy eventually took a decently co-operative role at Locarno, Mussolini had appeared there during the negotiations and ranted, shouting irrelevant demands. Journalists of the world press refused to attend his press conference, and the Belgian delegate to shake his hand, because he had just caused the murder of the distinguished Italian Socialist leader, Mateotti. He publicly contradicted himself by demanding that Italy's new Alpine frontier with Austria be guaranteed as part of the same agreement that guaranteed the Franco-German frontier, while at the same time assuring the Germans that he neither needed nor wanted such a guarantee. And while he talked about permanent peace, he told the Italian Chamber of Deputies, now nothing more than a Fascist Party forum, that Italy must be regarded as in a state of perpetual war, directed toward restoring the imperial grandeur of Rome. This sort of thing might be dismissed as a sign of political naïveté, which indeed it was; but it was also a symptom of the built-in fact that fascism, by its nature, could have no foreign policy except such action as was dictated by impulse and would submit itself to no restraint except that provided by fear. Fascism was nothing more than a compulsive need to swagger translated into government; international conduct could not be separated from domestic.

THE SOVIET UNION

The most bizarre of the obstacles to rebuilding a new world on the foundations of the old, and potentially the largest and most intractable, was not the presence of Fascist Italy but the absence of Soviet Russia. In this respect, as in many others, the role of the U.S.S.R. was analogous to that of the United States in the affairs of a world that was still, by default, directed from western Europe. The two absent powers in a world that was supposed to be run by Great Powers were the two greatest. And—this is what made the world situation so unpliable—the nature of their power was entirely different from that which had formerly been the basis of diplomacy. Neither the Americans nor the Russians had, in the 1920s, an international position based on ingenious states-men or on large armed forces in being. Neither could seriously threaten the world militarily. Their power was potential: financial, intellectual, revolutionary.

The role of the Soviet Union, unlike that of the fascist dictator-ships, was determined by a hard, coherent doctrine tempered, and often distorted, by struggles for power and the pressure of circumstance. One of its most important formative influences was the terror, amounting sometimes to lunacy, that it inspired outside of Russia; an important reason for this terror was the devoted body of its foreign admirers who became, at times, its agents.

Communism, as defined by Lenin and, after his death, prac-ticed by Stalin, inherited the deep distrust and anxiety that nine-teenth-century revolutionary movements, some violent and terrorist and all aiming at the transformation of bourgeois so-ciety, had inspired in the smug but apprehensive Europe of hierarchical classes and sound currencies. But the peculiar qual-ity of horror that the Soviet Union evoked was associated with the revolution itself.

The revolution, and its aftermath, had been singularly blood-curdling for several reasons. First, its actual course had involved an absolutely unprecedented bloodletting of every conceivable kind, civil war (which was not the Communists' fault), Red Terror (which was), the nightmare disorganization of society that proceeded from war, isolation, and a violent reorganization of the economy. Nothing in modern European history had approached it for sheer destructiveness. But it was the nature of the Bolshevik regime, rather than the staggering human and material losses over which it presided, that was in the long run more serious. From the outset it was avowed that Soviet Russia was the beginning and instrument for a Soviet world. Lenin had excluded his country and his followers from any honest participation in the international order that existed elsewhere. He had withdrawn Russia from the war, thereby committing, in the eyes of Russia's allies, a murderous criminal act. He had summarily dispersed the only freely elected representative institution Russia was ever to know. And he had renounced all Russia's foreign debts.

It was this last which was to prove the greatest material obstacle to any negotiation with the west after the unexpected staying power of western Europe dispelled the Bolsheviks' expectations of early world revolution. This was partly for symbolic reasons: the bourgeois countries, true to their nature, took a willingness to honor debts as the basic requirement for releasing Russia from the prison of pariahship. But there were real reasons, too: the French were much the heaviest investors in Russia, and the loans, begun in the 1890s for patriotic and diplomatic reasons to strengthen the alliance against Germany, had been widely distributed among ordinary people in France. In the serious state of shock, and the serious financial problems under which France labored in the early twenties, this real hardship became entwined with the problem of security. In France more than anywhere else, Communist Russia was feared and hated, a response not lessened by the fact that a small but active Communist Party had developed there.

The fear and loathing were somewhat modified as it became clear on the one hand that world revolution was not immediately feasible and, on the other, that counterrevolution in Russia was equally remote. Britain and France, each briefly governed by a liberal, left-wing party, "recognized" the Soviet Union, exchanged ambassadors with it, and tried to negotiate commercial treaties. The debts were finally abandoned as irretrievably lost, except by the United States, where anticommunism (aggravated, curiously enough, by the fact that the Soviets were antireligious) was even more emotional and much more general. The United States followed suit, finally, in 1933, after a more "liberal" administration had come to power.

But this advent of outwardly normal diplomatic relations (short-lived in the case of Britain) was matched by no conformity on the part of the Soviet Union to the rules of the comity of nations; or at least it represented one of two conflicting tendencies within the Soviet Union about how best to exploit that comity. The matter is one of extraordinary complexity and much obscurity, but, to oversimplify it greatly, it is possible to sketch out two quite different authorities and purposes in Moscow pursuing different and sometimes conflicting forms of what, in an earlier day, would have been called "foreign policies."

One was the Third International, in theory a purely party affair whose job it was to assure the international unity of the working-class movement, which in practice meant simply giving orders to all foreign Socialist parties that would obey them. Throughout most of this period, when the balance inside Russia between "socialism in one country" and "world revolution" was still uncertain, the object of the International was to embarrass, disrupt, and if possible to destroy the stability of all bourgeois governments. But the Soviet government itself, with its own commissariat of foreign affairs, followed a different objective in Europe. Like Stresemann in Germany, it often tried to seek to reassure potential enemies, and to behave according to *their* rules, in order to secure such practical objectives as trade, capital, security. The two institutions were to some extent in competition, and they were frequently in ignorance of one another's activities. The most striking illustration of the conflict between them came in 1925, when the Soviet government was trying eagerly to improve relations with Germany, placating and supporting its government in order to strengthen the "spirit of Rapallo" and break its own isolation, and the Comintern thoughtlessly ordered the Communist Party in Germany's state of Saxony to revolt. The revolt was hastily cancelled, but not until serious damage had been done the German government's confidence in the U.S.S.R., and not until the Saxon Communists had come close to seizing the state government.

The situation was exemplary. The rudimentary re-entry of the Soviet Union into world affairs was both slow and, so far as any early prospect for real accommodation went, meaningless.

By the end of the postwar decade, then, the intractable facts of the twentieth-century world were obtruding everywhere. Britain and France, at odds and much weakened, were attempting to revive a world whose structure had rested on the overpowering dominance of a Europe composed of competing but generally polite Great Powers. The nature and location of power had alike changed; the League, an institution which was supposed to revive the principles and strengths of the old system while eliminating its evils, had proved to be little more than a forum for Anglo-French debates. People who had no interest in the world order, and other people who were trying to use its outward forms to wreck it, were coming into control of the seats of power. A modest stability, and in some places a considerable economic progress, had been attained by 1929; but in that year its fragility was spectacularly demonstrated. What happened in one week to the values of stocks traded in Manhattan reduced the entire world to chaos, revolution, and war. Never in human history was a basic fact of life, previously unrecognized, so melodramatically illustrated. The world depended on the United States.

4

The End of the State System

In the 1930s, the procedures and agencies through which authority had been exercised and order maintained in the world for four hundred years stopped working. This was largely because Europe no longer possessed either the power or the internal coherence that would have permitted it to continue its dominance. A vacuum formed. The German government began to perceive and explore—not consistently or even deliberately—the possibilities offered by the ruin of the system of Great Powers and to move toward dominance over the whole continent. In a sense the Germans who engaged in this process were more blinded by the surviving remnants of the past than anyone else; they still believed that Europe was the center of the universe, and that an empire of Europe would be a world empire; but they also, reflexively in most cases, thought that the inadequacies of European power and coherence would permit them to manipulate themselves into supremacy. Hitler and most of the Nazis, parochial and ill-educated, were particularly "eurocentric." They failed because they did not see that the potential of the Soviet Union was enormous or that the

United States would be drawn into, and must eventually master, the conflicts among the suicidal dynasts of what were now micropowers.

The thirties and early forties were the times when this situation was progressively revealed. But ghosts are remarkably tenacious, and few remarked that traditional forms of international relations were lifeless or that governing power lay elsewhere. The French, and particularly the British, and the people of smaller powers, continued to have some faith in traditions. The illusion lit the scene of the thirties in odd and lurid ways. Phantoms and shadows walked. "Incidents" and "crises" of a sort that would have given real grounds for alarm before 1914 caused terror now, and agreements and conferences brought corresponding reassurance. A British Prime Minister thought he had secured peace because he had persuaded the Chancellor of Germany to sign a statement that he would not go to war—but the war Chamberlain so laboriously averted in 1938, and at such cost, was the war of 1914.

The illusions were themselves important; they determined both the making of policy and the appraisal of observers and, for a time, of historians. In political affairs illusions are usually the product of a failure to appreciate change; but such failure— usually a necessary and perhaps salutary part of human affairs— becomes, when the change is very fast, not a stabilizing conservatism but a form of deception resembling lunacy. The inability of men in the twenties to work for a new order based on new forms and new centers of power in the world beyond London, Paris, Berlin, and Rome, was the consequence of the sudden changes produced by the explosions of 1914–18. In the same way, in the thirties, the failure to perceive what happened next was due to the suddenness and the magnitude of changes brought by the Great Depression.

THE DEPRESSION

It is possible that had there been no Great Depression, the makeshift stabilities of the late twenties might have survived, and permitted a gradual reconstruction of world order on more

workable foundations. But the argument is in a measure sophisti-
cal, for it was the very situation that produced those stabilities
that also produced the Great Depression.

It is of both real and symbolic significance that the Depression, set off by the American stock market crash in October of
1929, was precipitated—the word is a precise metaphor—by the
incompatibility of two urgent needs that American leaders faced
in 1928 and 1929: the obvious need to "cool" the rapidly heating
atmosphere of speculation which was driving the New York
stock market, and with it the wild expansion of borrowing in
America, to dizzy and dangerous heights; and the no less obvious need to try to prevent Europe from losing its new-found and
precarious prosperity.

The structure of stability and economic growth in the late
twenties in Europe, upon which the welfare of the world and the
hope of peace was correctly seen to depend, was the result of the
loans which Americans were making to Europe. These were in
considerable part made possible by the fact that the interest rates
in European money markets were higher than in the United
States. But interest rates work both ways, and if Europe attracted
American lenders by its high interest rates, the American money
market, by its low ones, attracted borrowers. Interest rates in the
United States are in general controlled by a public authority, the
Federal Reserve System, whose directors decide on what terms
to finance bank loans and thus determine within limits the loan
policies of the bank. During the three or four years before the
Crash, the extremely low price for borrowing money encouraged
many Americans with resources slim or nonexistent to buy
securities on credit. This demand for stocks, among other things,
caused the prices of securities to rise fairly steadily and very
rapidly. By the beginning of 1928 stocks were being bought and
sold purely as a gamble, without regard for the assets or prospects of the companies whose ownership they represented and
without regard for the assets of the purchasers either. It was
quite clear that this development might—and if not curbed must
—end in a collapse of security prices when any substantial number of people decided simultaneously to stop buying and to try
to sell, to "realize" their profits. The Federal Reserve System

was aware of this; it could have curbed the speculation, but it did not do so because in the beginning of the bull market, when it could have been done without disaster, it was reluctant to enter into competition for loans with Europe. A higher interest rate would have attracted capital away from Europe. The German bankers and government would have had less foreign exchange with which to honor their reparations debts and to finance business expansion; without the reparations payments Britain, France, Italy, and the other allies would have had insufficient foreign exchange to honor the interest payments on their war debts to the United States and to finance *their* business expansion; and the United States government and investors would, at third hand, have suffered. The curious machinery devised to pump blood through the veins of a sick international economy would have come to a halt. The Federal Reserve authorities hesitated, and then it was, or seemed, too late: by 1929 they had an angry bull market by the tail.

The bull died, horribly, in November of 1929, when the stock market had crashed, and the Americans who had borrowed to buy stocks against the security of those same stocks saw the security become almost worthless, faced urgent demands for repayment, and went bankrupt. Nobody had any funds to lend to Europe, or any impulse to lend them. All the credit in America was being used in a frenzied effort to redeem the borrowings of its own citizens. The purely formal nature of finance was strikingly evinced. Money is credit, and credit is loans, and a loan is an act of imagination and of confidence. In 1929 American confidence was struck dead, and wealth shrank like a punctured balloon. By 1930 the world Depression had set in. In two years, industrial production fell by a third, industrial prices by a fifth, and agricultural prices by half. Unemployment spread; it affected almost half the labor force in Germany. Within a few years, every nation in Europe had abandoned the gold standard and raised barriers to trade. Most had extended state controls over all aspects of the economy, and the machinery of international trade and finance was in ruins. The foundations—economic but also psychological and moral—of the old world order had simply disintegrated. All of the intricate problems and negotiations of the prosperous years had become meaningless and absurd.

But no one fully realized it, perhaps because of the very optimism that had previously been generated. Much was happening, in the summer of 1929, that portended a new and better age in international affairs. The Germans—disingenuously, in some measure—were appearing to co-operate, and had been rewarded with the soothing measures of a further reduction and rationalization of reparations, and with the withdrawal of the occupation forces in the Rhineland. Briand was proposing his European customs union. A conference on naval disarmament was in course, and presently achieved a remarkable victory—chiefly remarkable, as it turned out, because it straitened British and American naval power while placing nothing but paper inhibitions in the path of Japanese and Italian naval expansion. A conference—ten years later than anticipated—was being discussed for disarmament of land forces. All of these hopeful forms of therapy for international relations proceeded through the next two years just as if the patient had not died, and the inertia that permitted them to do so persisted long after the whole fragile structure of war debts, reparations, arms control, the League of Nations, and conciliation of democratic Germany had collapsed.

It is not necessary here to consider either the deeper causes of the Depression, or the story of its baleful consequences, as economic phenomena (which remain, indeed, highly controversial matters) in any save chosen aspects of particular importance to the approaching war. But several observations about the background of the world economic crisis, and its course, are indispensable. It should be noted that to some uncertain but decided degree it was linked with the First World War in other ways than through the tortuous mechanisms of international finance. The war produced the debts and the reparations, and it also produced, in some regions of the world, a gross overproduction of raw materials, including food and minerals. High wartime prices had led to greatly expanded production, and, in the years of prosperity after 1925, commodity prices remained low and indeed began to fall. A very considerable portion of the planet's consuming population was in trouble at the moment when feverish optimism was infecting investors and manufacturers. The

price of farm products, and therefore the market for manufactured goods among farmers, did not keep up with the cost of
producing them.

When the financial and industrial communities joined the
commodity producers in penury, there was no cushion of demand or prosperity or security for anybody to fall on. The failure
of markets for farmers had helped to break the boom; it worsened and prolonged depression when it came, and it assured that
the pace and gravity, and the accumulated despair, would appear
in different forms in places which had not shared the profits of
good times.

This was of importance everywhere; in some places it was
critical, and the most illuminating example, as well as the most
important, was in Germany. Much of German agriculture was
not very efficient. Where grain was grown the Depression
brought disaster to groups who had long suffered bad times.
Landlords of great estates, who still had influence, demanded
and got state subsidies. They were able to work through their
connections, and particularly through the President of Germany, Paul von Hindenburg, an old soldier who liked to associate with, and think of himself as a member of, the landed
aristocracy that was closely associated with the past glories of
Prussia and of the German empire. The influence of the landlords
had a good deal to do with the President's disruption of parliamentary democracy in Germany and with the establishment of
incompetent reactionary leaders who tried desperately to make
deals with the would-be dictator, Adolf Hitler. The story of these
developments is dark and confused; but the role of desperate
German farmers in the making of the Nazi dictatorship is in
other connections clear and overt: in the purely agricultural
province of Schleswig-Holstein, a land of threatened small farmers, the Nazis won the highest percentage of votes anywhere in
Germany in 1932.

Comparable disasters were happening elsewhere in the
agrarian east. In Rumania and later in Hungary, Austria, Bulgaria, and Greece, and in the three small Baltic republics, the
simulacra of constitutional government fell, for reasons in each
case directly connected with the problems of the peasants who

composed the majority of the population—in most cases the great majority. The futile trafficking of parliamentary politicians, never very edifying, became intolerable when people were starving. The Greek, Rumanian, and Bulgarian kings established, in their own right or as sponsors of strongmen, dictatorships like that which already existed in Yugoslavia. They were symptoms of what depression did to the disheartening remnants of Wilson's noble dream of free men in free nations.

The largest and most ramified product of the crisis in commodity prices was in a place that was largely untouched by world depression: the experience of the Soviet Union showed that the "farm problem," if ecumenical, was also native, since the fall of world prices did not much affect the Soviet economy. But the unproductive nature of Soviet farming, the existence of innumerable small peasant holdings and a few larger capitalistic ones, the shortage of capital and the inconsonance of rural Russia with the Socialist paradigm, combined painfully with the familiar disparity of price structures. The Soviet regime had to do something, or thought it did, and—having achieved a restoration of the 1913 production level and a degree of domestic political tranquility by 1929—what it did was to start collectivising agriculture. The whole vast society was forcibly reconstructed overnight, in an effort to make a modern, high-yield, socialist rural economy. The effort was accompanied by a famine and by a ruthless repression of protest that cost the regime of Josef Stalin the confidence on one side of the most idealistic of Russian Communists, and on the other of the most practical of them. The result was incipient sedition and the necessity, as it appeared to Stalin, to kill people in very large numbers. So widespread was the mounting opposition to the dictatorship that half the higher officers of the Red Army were executed or exiled. By the end of the thirties, the military efficiency of the Soviet Union was very gravely attenuated, although the massacres had served their purpose well, and the regime was for the time being secure.

But the really remarkable thoroughness of Stalin's extermination policy, which exceeded in magnitude anything that the Nazis accomplished in Germany before the war, was not at all matched by a similar ferocity or fervor in the pursuit of Soviet foreign policy. For one thing, the crisis of the regime required the elimination of the independent power of the International, and with the early thirties the strange schizophrenia of Communist policy almost disappeared; from then on Communist parties served, directly and as obedient agents, the interests of the dictatorship with the same unity of purpose as did its spies, its ambassadors, and its consuls. For another, Stalin naturally had no interest in courting international attack, of which he was seriously frightened. So Soviet foreign policy, in Europe and the western hemisphere, at least, became guileful and, at times, conciliatory, instead of sporadically assertive and revolutionary.

The change in this direction took place in Soviet policy in 1934, leading to the improbable membership of the Soviet Union in the League of Nations and an eager co-operation among Communists and bourgeois liberals. The precipitating cause of this revolution was the menacing rise of Nazi Germany; but the basis of it was Soviet weakness, and Soviet weakness was in large part the product of the agricultural crisis.

In the west, economic crisis tended to have other effects; it turned countries in upon themselves and disposed them to non-co-operation. Isolation—the need and desire to be let alone to solve domestic problems—was fortified in the United States, and in Britain and France it replaced the futile effort to carry the burden of world leadership. In Germany, and to a lesser extent in Italy, highly nationalistic economic policies complemented not a desire to be let alone but a need to develop national "identity" and national power; taken together they required expansion. In the cases of the fascist dictators as well as the democracies, however, the politics of the period reflected the effort to deal unilaterally with the Depression and its aftermath.

The reason for this series of attempts to solve nationally what was (everyone agreed) an international problem was obvious on the face of things. The fact simply was that there was no agency capable of effective action except the national state.

The first and in a way the most striking instance of this development came in Great Britain. It was both paradoxical and logical that it should be so. Paradoxical because in Britain economic liberalism had been born and had taken deepest roots, and because, more than in any other major industrial country, Britain's economy was most intimately connected with, and dependent on, the world economy for its prosperity and survival. But it was logical too, and partly for this very reason, that damage to the world economy was most rapidly and urgently demanding of restorative measures by the British government. And for other reasons as well. The effects of the 1914 war, and particularly of the postwar policies, had been in some respects more severe here than elsewhere. Unemployment remained high in Britain in the days of prosperity, and for a long time governments—Conservative and Labour both—had encouraged a measure of protection, subsidy, and monopoly in various British industries. Government-sponsored monopolies—of broadcasting, of shipping, of electric power, and in varying degrees of other industries—were already well established.

In 1930, when the Depression began to affect Britain with falling prices, larger imports, and rapidly increasing unemployment, a Labour government, dependent upon the votes of the small Liberal Party in the House of Commons and led by the impressive but inadequate and already senile Ramsay MacDonald, was in office. Labour, reflecting in its leadership a combination of doctrinaire, if non-Marxist, socialist intellectuals, ambitious politicians, and tough, narrow-minded trade unionists, was in a poor position to deal with the crisis. Most Labourites, naturally, wished to protect the working class against the pains of a capitalist crisis by maintaining and even increasing unemployment relief, and this imposed upon the treasury a very heavy burden. It was a burden, indeed, that could not be borne without recourse to deficit financing, or to devaluation of the pound, or to the adoption of protective tariffs to force up British prices and prevent the outflow of gold and capital from Britain. None of these three alternatives commended themselves to the Labour Party, which was extremely orthodox in its fiscal traditions and which had long opposed tariffs as a form of tax on the workingman's food.

In the summer of 1931 there took place a critical decline in Britain's situation. It illuminates the nature of the problem, for it took the form of a withdrawal of funds on deposit in British banks (in whose interest the policy of a stable pound had been partly insisted on) by German bankers. The German banks were in serious trouble because of a crisis of confidence in central Europe; this crisis was worsened, if not produced, by the failure of the great Austrian bank, the Kreditanstalt, in June 1931. The failure of the Austrian bank was, in turn, closely connected with actions by the Council of the League of Nations.

In 1925 M. Briand had first proposed a European customs union. It was a beginning for his project to consolidate Europe, to compensate for the obvious fact that a system of competing national governments was no longer fecund or feasible in a world where Europe was no longer dominant, although Briand was more interested in bringing security to France than in stabilizing the planet. Nothing came of the suggestion, but in 1930 he proposed to the League a much larger step toward a consolidated Europe, a sort of federal union. The Austrians had suggested, in the League, that a step in the direction of European union might be taken by developing regional customs unions, and immediately undertook to implement this proposal—in secret, at first— by negotiating a customs union with Germany. The notion was plausible; the economies were compatible, and Austria's, never stable since 1918 when the Austrian Empire had been partitioned, was now facing catastrophe. But customs unions were regarded as rudimentary economic unions, and economic union was seen as a preface to political union. Political union of Austria and Germany had been proposed and expected in 1918 in both countries, when the severance of all non-German-speaking (and some German-speaking) areas from the little republic had left it without much reason, emotionally or politically, for existing as a separate state. But the French, because they did not want to see Germany augmented, and the Italians, because they did not want a major power on the border of a partly German-speaking province (the south Tyrol, which they had just detached from Austria) were bitterly opposed. Prohibition of Austro-German union was explicitly written into the Treaty of Versailles, and the Treaty of Saint-Germain, which made peace between the Allies and Austria.

In 1931, the League Council, urgently invoked by the French, announced that it would consider the question of the proposed union as a possible treaty violation. The Germans objected. The French were deepened in their suspicion that German desires for aggrandizement lay behind the objections. The Austrian government, intimidated, backed down. In a situation of despair about the economic situation in central Europe, prudent investors withdrew deposits from Austrian banks, the Kreditanstalt failed three weeks later, and every bank in central Europe was shaken to its foundations. Several German banks also failed; to cover deposits, German bankers hastily brought home the funds they had in British banks, and Great Britain was dragged, for the first time in its history, to the verge of national bankruptcy.

This remarkable intertwining of events illuminates almost everything that was wrong in Europe, including the extreme difficulty of doing anything about it. M. Briand's proposals, the most sensible policy suggested by anybody in the interwar years, not only foundered upon the rock of the old system of competing states but also cast a lurid light on the failure to build a workable economic order in central Europe. It showed too that Great Britain, the financial titan of 1900, was by 1931 capable of insolvency brought on by the combined effects of depression and an Austrian bank failure.

The British saved themselves, but only after a political crisis that split and emasculated the Labour Party and produced an emergency government largely dominated by Conservatives and intensely concerned with limiting Britain's susceptibility to foreign perturbations. The solvency of Britain in the summer of 1931 depended on the willingness of foreign banks, especially American banks, to loan the government money—a situation which was to recur with dismaying regularity thereafter in British affairs. The banks, pursuing natural, if unsound impulses, refused loans unless something were done to reduce the looming British deficit, which meant cutting unemployment compensation. The Labour government, deeply split, resigned; and Mr. MacDonald, who very much liked being Prime Minister, furtively formed a new Government with the support of the Conservative Party and the angry hostility of most of his own. The new "National Government" shortly undertook emergency measures, including the abandonment of the gold standard, painfully restored five years before, and the devaluation of the pound, despite solemn promises to maintain the gold value. It fought a general election on the peculiar platform of "a doctor's mandate" (which meant in fact that the ministers had not decided, and could not agree, on what to do next). Supporters of the National Government— Conservatives, "National Liberals," and "National Labour"— won overwhelmingly, a popular majority of better than two to one and a parliamentary majority of 556 to 56. This victory reflected a mood of patriotic resolution and unity (which meant that the British public didn't know what to do either but believed, in a wave of fatigued national feeling, that something drastic needed doing and hoped that a government of national unity would do it).

What was done was, from the point of view of "national recovery," sensible, although not very consistent or well planned. The reduced price of the pound eliminated the most dampening fact in the situation; it raised import prices, and lowered export prices, both stimulating to British producers, and it tended to raise the whole price level in the kingdom. Next, rigid budgetary measures were adopted, reducing costs, and tightening up drastically on unemployment relief. Third, Britain's ninety-year-old tradition of free trade (which meant no taxation of foreign goods sold in Britain), much beloved of Liberals and Labour and increasingly loathed by Conservatives, was abandoned in favor of "Imperial preference" (which meant establishing tariffs—10 per cent in this case—and then reducing them in favor of goods coming from places in the British Empire, in exchange for reciprocal benefits to be given to British goods in Canada, Australia, New Zealand, South Africa, India, Ireland, and other Empire territories that had established tariffs on U.K. imports). This had long been a pet of the Conservatives; it was designed to tighten imperial bonds, and therefore the Empire, which Conservatives reflexively liked, while simultaneously bailing out British exporters and industrialists. The United Kingdom purchased commercial advantages in the Empire at the price of explicit abdication of political superiority.

These measures, along with others, increased the buoyancy of

Britain. Prices began to rise, production to increase, unemployment to diminish, markedly although not dramatically. The threat of bankruptcy receded, although suffering and gloom persisted in many places, especially in the coal country. However, although the British recovery program was probably as successful as that of any country, it had far-reaching and distressing effects elsewhere; it was achieved largely by making British goods more attractive and discouraging the sale of foreign goods in Britain, and by reducing the value and liquidity of all foreign funds held in pounds. What was being done was to "export the Depression."

More than the export of the Depression to countries whose economies were as fragile as Britain's made the National Government the most important symptom and symbol of the final ruin of the European system. No less were its flavor and its personnel reflections of insularity. MacDonald was an old line Labourite and pacifist; Stanley Baldwin, the Conservative leader, now Vice-Premier, was a provincial English businessman, as was Neville Chamberlain, who took the chancellorship of the Exchequer. Most striking of all was the Foreign Minister, Sir John Simon, a conservative Liberal and a highly successful lawyer. None of these men, and most particularly not Simon, had any record of cosmopolitan interests or professional experience in conducting foreign relations or of knowledge of the world outside Britain. Simon's policies, conducted with notable ineptitude, were almost entirely directed to keeping Britain out of troublesome international complications, of trying to solve crises by whatever means would quieten them fastest—by arranging things, in short, so Britain could be left alone to pursue its new domestic and imperial policies in peace. The result of this, in specific cases, was to accept and indeed sponsor the victory of the stronger power whenever disputes arose abroad, and to divest London of any responsibility for any positive action in world affairs.

Something rather similar was about to happen in the United States. The Hoover administration, like the Labour government in Britain, had faced the Depression with a vague but decided sense of international responsibilities and an almost total inability to cope with the demands of the nation's collapse.

Two events showed that Herbert Hoover and his advisers were living in a world of warm nineteenth-century memories and cold twentieth-century hopes. One was the action of Congress; confronted by crisis, it resorted to the measure that was traditional, familiar, and generally popular. It raised tariffs. In the second place, faced with overt and gigantic aggression by Japan in China, palpably in violation of the 1928 Peace Pact and other treaties, Hoover's administration tried to galvanize the other powers, and the League, into some show of effective response without committing the United States to anything beyond a display of good will.

The Hawley-Smoot tariff of 1930 raised obstacles to the sale of foreign products within the United States to quite unprecedented and in some cases prohibitory levels. It was intended, as all previous U.S. high tariffs had been, to "protect" American industry against foreign competitors, thus supposedly assuring higher employment and greater economic growth. It showed that the majority in Congress, while thinking American prosperity could be saved by this method, nonetheless expected foreigners to continue paying their debts to the United States. Hoover was trapped by his previous defense of high tariffs; he and his advisers knew that the Hawley-Smoot tariff was a dangerous absurdity, but Hoover, a good Republican, had always accepted the old Republican Party myths, in this case to the effect that low tariffs would cause grass to grow in American streets. He was a sophisticated man; but the persistence of popular ideas dating from the age when America was isolable, and a debtor nation, prevented his acting on his convictions. The Tariff Act went unvetoed.

The Manchurian Incident, as the Japanese called it, was indicative of what was happening. There was a long history of efforts to establish Japanese power and gain advantages on the Asian mainland, beginning with a victorious war against China in 1895. The Japanese were progressively more enraged and impatient as they watched China heave in the horrifying disorder of decay and other powers attempt to extend their own interests and frustrate Japan's. The Japanese had begun to argue that, as a young, vigorous, and highly efficient modern state, they both *required* and *deserved* space and the supposed economic benefits that an empire on the mainland would bring. It will be seen at once that this was another form of economic nationalism peculiar to the era: if free markets, free commerce, and stable currencies had prevailed, and if Japan had really been interested only in national economic aims, there would have been no particular advantage to conquest or colonialism. But the Japanese thought it necessary to create a closed economy and believed that it must include a larger territory than their own. There was some ground for their argument, considering foreign obstacles to their exports and their own overcrowded soil. Moreover, the coming of the Depression had brought to positions of greater influence men— mostly Army officers and rejuvenated reactionaries—who converted a convenience into a cult: room for expansion became an article of passionate faith, as perhaps any controversial aim, strongly felt by many people, must become.

In the fall of 1931, under the influence of the military, the Japanese attacked the huge northeastern Chinese province of Manchuria, conquered most of it, set up a state of Manchukuo under their control in early 1932, and then proceeded to extend their attacks more and more deeply into the rest of China until, a year and a half after the first assault, the disorganized Chinese forces eventually gave up and signed a truce that accepted all that Japan had ever asked for and more, including the "puppet" state of Manchukuo.

The rest of the world did nothing, or at least nothing effective. The result was to demonstrate that in far-away places the peoples of the powers that were supposed to be maintaining peace were not going to endanger themselves or their policies. The League of Nations, urgently invoked by the Chinese, sent an investigatory body called the Lytton Commission to report. It made moderate proposals, not altogether unfavorable to Japanese ambitions and not at all generous to China, for a settlement. The Japanese simply disregarded them and went on with their war. Japan was then censured, and resigned from the League of Nations. The United States invoked a doctrine, invented years before, called Non-Recognition, which meant that as far as the United States was concerned all arrangements brought about by force in violation of international obligations were illegal. The Japanese were not unduly disturbed. The League, and the West, had failed; and they had failed because they were predictably not prepared to use, or threaten, force—which meant war—against Japan. Mr. Hoover spoke loudly and carried a small stick. Nothing happened.

The episode was prophetic. The powers that were themselves prepared to abide by the old rules were neither willing nor able to force others to do so. Mr. Hoover's administration, emblematic of a small but perceptibly increased American willingness to take part in world affairs, retreated. (In Britain, the National Government had been deliberately limp. The Conservatives who dominated it had no stomach for warlike adventures in remote parts against a power whose activities had the merits of containing Soviet influence. The Labour Party, no more adventurous and even less assertive, proposed an arms embargo on both parties. Labour, as usual, was hypnotized by the importance of arms and what may be called the "merchants-of-death" school of international morality.)

Inaction solved no problems. Japan withdrew from the League of Nations and thereafter continued its policies of aggression with even more determination and ferocity. By the time the war began in Europe, it had occupied most of northern China, and both its enormous ambitions in the Pacific and its violent enmity to the other nations installed there—Britain, France, the United States, the Netherlands, Australia—were increasing. It was a long-drawn-out object lesson in the inutility of passiveness that was to reach its climax at Pearl Harbor in 1941. For ten years before that, the bellicosity of the Japanese had a powerful effect on European politics, for the great naval power of Japan represented a ubiquitous threat. Throughout the thirties, one of the reasons—or excuses—for later British inaction was the well-founded fear that if Britain became involved in Europe the Japanese would act against the British territories, interests, and naval strength in the Pacific. Considerable naval forces were tied down by this menace, and fear of Japan remained an acute and growing element in French and British anxieties. It also distracted American statesmen and public opinion, for whom the Pacific seemed in some ways nearer, a sphere of more immediate American concern, because of the Philippines, than Europe or Africa.

Hoover also tried, with results as dubious as those of his efforts to restrain Japan, to negotiate some settlement of the international debts, Allied loans, and reparations, which had now become monstrously unfeasible. The old American refusal to admit any connection between the money its ex-allies owed it, and the money the Germans owed the ex-allies, was tacitly abandoned when, in June 1931, Hoover proposed something called a "moratorium," which meant a suspension, on all governmental debt payments. The powers agreed—not without some efforts at sabotage by the French, who were still in a favorable financial position and wanted to squeeze the Germans as much as possible. A year's suspension was arranged and, as was predictable, payments were never resumed, except by Finland, which continued to pay interest on its infinitesimal debt to the United States and thereby gained a reputation for honor and heroism that contributed to some confusion in American public opinion ten years later when the Finns became allies of Nazi Germany.

The moratorium, like the policy in the Far East, was a sign that the international obligations the Americans looked to as substitutes for active leadership would not work. In March 1933, when Franklin Roosevelt took office, the new administration conducted affairs in a way that applauded Hooverian internationalism abroad while energetically pursuing purposes incompatible with it at home. The Good Neighbor policy, designed rather pathetically to show the Latin Americans that their northern neighbors were Good Guys, was a mere intensification of Hoover's efforts to reverse the earlier policies of a short-tempered and brutal Big Brother who had intervened militarily in Mexico, Nicaragua, Cuba, Haiti, and the Dominican Republic, and diplomatically everywhere else. The Trade Agreements Act of 1934, largely the work of Cordell Hull, the old-fashioned southern

liberal whom Roosevelt appointed Secretary of State, reversed the long protectionist tradition, although with only minor
and conditional reductions in tariffs, and marked the beginning
of the tardy, slow, and painful recognition that being a powerful
creditor nation limits freedom of choice about commercial
policy. But the most important part of the New Deal was its
rather jumbled recovery program, and this was mainly constructed by people who, like those in the National Government
in Britain, cared nothing for foreign affairs and were determined
to convert the United States into a society planned and stabilized
by direct action of its national government. The most important
and destructive aspect of this program, the abandonment of the
gold standard and the devaluation of the dollar currency, was,
as it had been two years before in Britain, designed for the same
purpose, of raising prices and encouraging re-employment. It
succeeded to some extent in this; but recovery was thus made
to hinge upon non-co-operation in world economic affairs and
upon complete freedom in determining future currency policy,
which seemed to threaten every foreign country in the world.
Hull, limited, obstinate, and out of touch with the New Dealers,
supported a British proposal for a World Economic Conference
in the summer of 1933, to try to reverse the spiraling demolition
of the remaining bases of international co-operation. But such an
effort depended upon Roosevelt's willingness to make commitments about the dollar, and this, in the middle of laborious
negotiations in London, he stunningly announced that he would
not do.

At the time it was felt that Roosevelt had pulled the carpet out
from under the rest of the world and of its own delegation to the
conference, and his decision was certainly a baleful and rather
frivolous assertion of America's determination to solve its problems in isolation. But it is possible to see now that the Conference could not have accomplished anything much anyway; its
purpose was a tentative restoration of a world which was being
blown to bits. The most important contributor to that prolonged,
ineffably destructive explosion was the man who had become
Chancellor of Germany a month before Roosevelt became President of the United States.

THE COMING TO POWER OF THE NAZIS

The Second World War seemed, when it was breaking out and being fought, to be so much Adolf Hitler's war that it became difficult for later observers to recognize that Hitler himself was an expression of something basically wrong with the articulation of political power in the world. When the old system was working more vigorously—although never better than imperfectly—before 1914, Hitler would simply not have been permitted.

There were people who saw the inner nature of Hitlerism. There were more indeed in the years just before and after 1933 than there were to be later, for the success of the regime was to lend it an importance, a sort of meretricious dignity, a place in history, that attracted the most sophisticated theorists and the most ponderous analysts to weighty and cosmic interpretations. Only in very recent years have some historians come to see Hitlerism with clarity as a movement of muddle-headed racketeers moved by occasional inspiration and well-advised by technicians. This was indeed how it was seen in 1933 by people in Germany who were threatened by it, by a large body of journalists (especially Americans, whose professional blending of tough shrewdness and good-hearted sentimentality gave them an especially useful insight), and by some scattered diplomats like Sir Horace Rumboldt, British Ambassador in Berlin, whose dispatches on what was happening in 1933 stand up today as evidence that contemporary judgments of current events *may* be as wise and complete as those of a later generation of historians.

Whatever else Hitlerism was, it was most conspicuously and most eminently Hitler. His odd genius and odd limitations were alike symptoms of a personality that was certainly psychopathic. Most of his leading associates—a malevolent cripple, an elephantine one-time drug addict who dressed up in costumes, a sadist, a paranoiac—were also obviously unsavory and abnormal. Some large adjustment of imagination is needed to understand why the Germans confided their nation to such leaders. This puzzle has been subject to the attentions of learned men who have elaborated cosmic explanations of the most portentous sort. The whole history of Germany was, for a long while, seen as a sort of road leading toward Hitler. This telic view of history, natural enough, not only violated the most elementary of historical purposes, to recreate the past with something like fidelity, but defeated its own purposes by making it seem that anything in German history, from the second century A.D. onward, that did not actually contribute to Hitler's rise to power was either transient or insignificant. When the past is studied as "background" to something in the present, it is usually misinterpreted and always distorted.

Any reasonable explanation of the Nazi success must be plural. There were, undoubtedly ancient and deep traits in German culture and society that predisposed Germans to submit to arbitrary authority, believe lies, flourish in a state of overorganization, and tolerate or admire the use of force whether on the majestic scale of national armies or the small but effective scale of brutality by gangs. There are these traits in any society. In Germany they may have been stronger, and they certainly existed in a particularly explosive combination. An American psychiatrist, Richard M. Brickner, shortly after the war wrote a book called *Is Germany Incurable?* in which persuasive evidence of group psychosis—or at least serious maladjustment—was advanced. It was certainly true, too, that the democratic republic set up in 1918 had proved singularly ineffective in establishing itself. It was not much admired, even by its own politicians and statesmen, because it had been born under the star of national disgrace and (conservatives argued) treason by socialists. It was in practice an attempt to salvage most of the cherished traditions of the German empire, which had, after all, been a remarkably imposing and substantial regime, while fitting them in to a not very well-conceived democratic constitution. The old elements were unassimilable. The fortresses of the old order were largely untampered with—the officer corps, the universities, the civil service, the proprietors of industry. Their representatives held high office, and sometimes worked to sabotage the state. The republican leaders, the moderates, and the moderate socialists, professed in some cases to deplore them, and sometimes fought bravely against them; but mostly they felt at home with them, as if they were part of the preordained moral and civil order.

Then came the Depression. Germany was especially affected by it, and not only because its suffering was so grave, though it was that, certainly. In 1932, some 43 per cent of the workers were unemployed in Germany. Production fell by almost half. Mortgages were being foreclosed. Banks failed. But it was much more than a bad economic crisis. It was also a social and psychological crisis, and in ways that were much more devastating even than in Britain or America or France. This was true for two reasons, among many others. The first was the heritage of the terrible inflation of 1923. This induced a sense of seismic insecurity among all classes, and particularly the lower middle class and professional groups for whom security and position—what would in the jargon of the midsixties be called "identity" and "status"—were particularly important. White collar workers, schoolteachers, minor officials were even more terrified by an economic collapse which threatened the symbols and salaries to which they clung than were their counterparts abroad. They had seen what had happened in 1923. And resolution not to allow 1923 to be repeated made it almost impossible to alleviate the crisis. The cast-iron determination to maintain, at all costs, the gold value of the currency was an obstinate and in some ways irrational product of having seen the old marks disappear into basketsful of worthless paper. Heinrich Brüning, the last Chancellor who had any respect for or belief in political freedom and international co-operation, watched the economy deteriorate helplessly because he thought it was politically impossible to devalue the mark. But devaluation was what saved Britain and the United States and, later, France, and in none of those countries —or indeed anywhere else in the thirties—did inflation proceed to inordinate lengths. Moreover, as the example of Britain had shown, the devaluation of a foreign currency placed a very heavy burden on any economy that did not itself devalue. The intensity of the Depression in Germany was to an important extent the result of the shock of 1923.

The other key factor in the destruction of the German republic was political. Economic crisis, particularly the unemployment which was its most appalling element, produced political extremisms seeking desperate remedies everywhere. Their spokesmen said—and they were certainly correct in principle, although their specific proposals were often crazy—that the Depression was institutional and therefore unnecessary. The crisis *could* be mitigated by strong measures by the state. If inhibitions against state action were swept away, and if the vested interests that protected the existing financial and industrial institutions were overborne, the worst effects of the breakdown would be relieved. To take an obvious example, and one which the Nazis effectively exploited, many farmers faced with ruin might be saved if mortgages were suspended. (It was the sanctity of mortgages that produced the nearest thing to insurrection in the United States.) But the honoring of debts was indispensable to the banking system, and was a fundamental requirement of anything but a thoroughly revolutionized and controlled society. The necessary measures would require drastic action—the coercion of powerful people; they therefore could be carried out only by a revolutionary and highly authoritarian state—and one whose leadership commanded not only acceptance but passionate devotion. Authoritarian revolution was, then, the necessary condition for survival. Or so a great many people—a majority of Germans, probably—saw it.

But there was no agreement on the necessary nature of the revolution, and it was this fact, as much as anything, that permitted the Nazis to gain power. In general, two sets of revolutionary attitudes prevailed. One consisted largely of nostalgia for the old days of grandeur and security, before 1914, and was associated with the defunct monarchy, Army officers, businessmen, and the like. The disciplining of workers and the destruction of a chaotic democracy were for these groups matters both of expediency and of sentiment. The second attitude conceived solutions through a workers' revolution, the destruction of capitalism and the bourgeoisie, the establishment of the dictatorship of the proletariat, and the application of Marxist-Leninist prescriptions to the economy. The first point of view was represented, politically, in parts of the Peoples Party and the Center Party and, unanimously, in the Nationalist Party; the second in the Communist Party. Both grew fast after 1929, but the Nationalist appeal was, necessarily, to a numerically small (but powerful) group of people, so that growth of the Communist Party was much greater.

The two points of view were irreconcilable; indeed, the growth of each was in some measure accounted for by people's obsessive fears of the other. But the strange mission of Hitler was to reconcile the irreconcilable. Not, to be sure, to convince hardcore Communists or Nationalists of the acceptability of National Socialism, but to appeal to the uncertain hordes as the fringes of each and—more especially—to pre-empt the citizens who found neither of the alternatives entirely acceptable. The Nazis borrowed what was most popular from each of the other revolutionary, authoritarian movements and stole the center of the stage. Like the Italian Fascists, they were in their ideas conflicting, inconsistent, and flexible to the point of nullity; as a movement, Nazism was a racket, not a revolution. But intellectual nullity permitted effective appeal to revolutionaries and reactionaries alike.

The name of the party was, after all, the National Socialist German Workers' Party, and the name provided a precisely accurate description of its propaganda line, if not at all of its real character and aims. The Nazis were attractive to "little people" —not, for the most part, to industrial workers, who remained loyal to the old Marxist parties, but to others, dispossessed and frightened, who hated communism but also hated and resented the financiers and aristocrats and capitalists who they thought were arrogantly manipulating them. The early Nazi program was extremely leftist in many points; the most often reiterated of all the economic demands was the popular one to outlaw the tyranny of "interest" which, if it meant anything, meant preventing banks from demanding repayment of loans.

The radical social and economic demands, so clearly directed against the still-entrenched governing classes from imperial days, were a serious embarrassment to Hitler as time went on. The republic was rocking, but short of general revolution no party could come to power without the approval of the President, von Hindenburg, and of the army and the conservatives who surrounded and dominated him; and no party—at least not the Nazis—could prosper without some financial support from the only people who had money. In this, at least, the German experience resembled the Italian.

In 1932 it began to look as if Germany were ungovernable *except* by either the Nazis or the Communists, the only parties with a broad base of popular support and sufficiently energetic leadership to restore order and save the country from utter economic collapse. Hitler saw quite clearly which side his bread was buttered on: the more "socialist" of his colleagues, notably the radical brothers Otto and Gregor Strasser, were expelled from the party. The radical program was played down. A deal was made with the leaders of Rhineland industry to provide money, and promises about private property were given. Hitler thus made himself acceptable to the people who nervously controlled the tottering German government and economy. The revolutionary appeal to idealistic youth, who formed the mass of the party, died gradually. As one historian has remarked, nazism, when it came to power, was a "curious compound of genuine radicalism and job-seeking."* But by the end of 1933 the revolutionary element was disgruntled, and in 1934 it was, at Hitler's orders, massacred.

Hitler, then, pre-empted both potential leftists and nationalists. He combined a fuzzy array of socialist-sounding slogans with an intense and explicit nationalism. It was nationalism of a new sort, borrowed in part from Mussolini but more largely from pseudo-scientists of the late nineteenth century and from German literature and myth. It included a quite ridiculous doctrine of racial purity, a preposterous application to people of notions about the superiority of thoroughbred domestic animals, combined with a great deal of nonsense about the superiority of certain "cultures." It was flattering to Germans to be told they were thoroughbreds of an inherently superior breed; it played on an old dislike of Jews, who were alleged to have infiltrated German society and to control, in sinister ways, German banking, commerce, and the press. But much more important, racist doctrines provided a sort of justification for the aggrandizement of the German nation. It had not only a *right*—this was something many, perhaps most, Germans vaguely felt—to dignity, expan-

* Alan Bullock, *Hitler* (New York: Harper and Brothers, 1953), p. 254.

sion, and the wiping out of the terrible wrongs and humiliations of the Versailles Treaty. It almost had the *duty* to dominate Europe and thus bring to other peoples the inestimable benefit of rule by morally, intellectually, and genetically superior beings.

The racism was a form of advertisement, but it appealed so profoundly to the hostilities of desperate men that before the war the Jews of Germany were ferociously persecuted, tortured, exiled, and murdered; and later, incredible numbers, between five and ten million, of racially "inferior" peoples—Jews, Slavs, and others, who were not engaged in military activities—were killed.

The sense of national renewal too was a sort of political advertising, but it convinced many Nazis themselves. The distinction between sincerity and hypocrisy is never very clear in the motives of any individual, and it is extremely rare in politicians, who must always possess strong convictions but must also adjust their convictions to the perception of needs. The Nazi leaders undoubtedly were in many cases dedicated German nationalists, but their dedication was blended in almost all cases with the central preoccupation, which was to gain, hold, and extend their power. There were a few eminent men of the regime who were genuinely seeking to serve the national cause out of visceral, not political, impulses; but these were mostly soldiers, like Field Marshal Erwin Rommel, or young men who rose to prominence during the war, like Speer. Hitler, at the end of his life, betrayed the reality of his career when he said, "The Germans were always unworthy of me." Mussolini, sooner, more frequently, and more openly, made like remarks about the Italians.

Contempt for the ruled is perhaps a common, perhaps even a necessary, ingredient for autocrats who rise to autocracy by their own efforts. Like those of many psychopaths, both Hitler's and Mussolini's beliefs were formed largely by reaction against the beliefs and actions of their enemies; this was, in a sense, a demonstration of the superficiality of their dedication. The same superficiality was betrayed by Hitler's surviving colleagues at the end of the regime: the most striking thing about the Nazi leaders in their last days was their inordinate eagerness to betray one another and to make deals with the advancing enemy in a scramble for power as unseemly as it was fantastic. The flames of

German national dedication in the Nazi regime were like burning alcohol spilled on a concrete floor; they were brilliant and terrifying but they were all on the surface.

Still, national dedication meant that international policy was the only sphere in which basic changes took place. The inward inconsistencies, or vacua, of Nazi political ideas, the fact that its verbiage was contrived almost entirely to secure and retain power, meant that there was to be very little real innovation in domestic policy, aside from dictatorship itself. As the most brilliant of Nazi Germany's recent historians has observed,* most of the structure and institutions of pre-Hitler society were taken over with little change, and continued to develop along lines already established. But the displays of nationalism, in both propaganda and policy, were spasmodically so extreme as to vary in kind rather than degree from their precedents.

The components of unleashed national mania were numerous and varied. One was, paradoxically, inertia. Germany, which was not made into a state until the 1870s, had for a thousand years been a congeries of competing and mostly feeble principalities, often dominated by foreign meddlers. "Particularism," the pull of local attachments and interests, was both strong and real. But for half the millennium there had been evident the perpetually frustrated but generally growing sense of the existence of a German nation and a desire to equip it with a central government. When at last this was accomplished in the nineteenth century by the statesmanship of Bismarck and the solidity and efficiency of the most important of the principalities, Prussia, the satisfaction of these strivings was incomplete, both ethnically and constitutionally. Germany remained a federal state, its constitutional and administrative power shared— though decreasingly—with state governments. And Germany remained unfinished. There were several million Germans beyond its borders, in Austria, Luxembourg, and Switzerland, and scattered in small regional groups or as landowning elites in many other places, in the dark corners of eastern Europe, in Bohemia and the Russian Baltic provinces. Then, in 1918, the number of *Auslands Deutsche*—"foreign Germans"—had been

* David Schoenbaum, *Hitler's Social Revolution* (New York: Doubleday, 1966).

forcibly multiplied. Alsace and Lorraine, by then heavily German in culture though not, perhaps, in sentiment, were restored to France. A few German towns were awarded to Belgium. Part of the province of Schleswig was given to Denmark. The vast amputations involved in the creation of Poland detached provinces that were not only German in at least a considerable minority but had long been incorporated in German states. The Saarland in the west, and the port of Danzig in the east, were administered as free states by the League of Nations. The situation of the *Auslands Deutsche* palpably violated the very principle of self-determination upon which the Treaty of Versailles, the frontiers of Europe, and therefore European peace, had rested. It confused the defenders of the system and, if they were at all altruistic, destroyed their moral defenses. As one Czech historian has pointed out, Hitler's most effective argument against the Versailles system was the very one upon which it had been based, the right of nationalities to union and freedom.

There was another, quite different aspect to Hitler's aims as set forth in his speeches, conversations, and writings but played down for a while after he took office. This was an apocalyptic dream of empire, whose ultimate achievement would be the conquest of Russia. It was based—like the Japanese dream in Asia—on the notion of the need for "space" for a crowded, productive, and gifted nation, naturally at the expense of inferior nations. Europe and most of Asia, it was directly said in *Mein Kampf,* must be under German control and must work to enrich the Germans. This notion probably owed something to "geopolitics," a doctrine of international relations and strategy that had grown up in Munich and was much discussed and admired in Nazi Germany. It was in some ways very old-fashioned, based on nineteenth-century assumptions about the ultimacy of national states and strategic competition among them. It was also up-to-date, since it revised nineteenth-century notions of strategy with reference to geography and power, and preached that the age of sea power had ended. And its core was the assertion that "he who controls the heartland [the Russian-Siberian continent] controls the world." It fitted admirably with the racist doctrine and with Hitler's wild German egoism; and it certainly fitted, if it did not form, his view of his ultimate and most formidable task, the reduction of Russia.

It has frequently been questioned whether he was indeed consistently moved by these visions and doctrines. Much doubt has been cast upon the consistency of his motives, of his drive to the east. But the evidence is very strong that, whatever his postponements and improvisations, he always had them in mind. He unquestionably dwelt upon them in his long, rambling expositions to his most intimate friends and advisers. And there is one almost incontrovertible piece of evidence: in 1941, when he had conquered France and controlled most of Europe west of the Soviet Union, with which his relations were moderately satisfactory, Great Britain was still holding out. German arms were frustrated in their assaults on the British Isles, which would represent a perpetual threat to German Europe until it was defeated. But at this juncture, instead of planning the destruction of Britain, he turned impatiently to the even larger project of an attack upon a Soviet Union whose principal aim was to be left in peace. It was his doom, and if he could not have foreseen the effectiveness of Soviet resistance he must still have known, with what powers of rationality remained to him, that the Russian campaign would be a most formidable and dangerous enterprise. Nonetheless, he undertook it, and provided evidence that his vision was stronger than his prudence—and, further, that it was a driving, dominating force in all his decisions.

It involved a new element, mythological in its odious grandeur, of something like a *Götterdämmerung:* either Germany won world supremacy, without which adequate Space could not be attained, or it would perish totally. This element was the key both to the psychopathology of the leaders and the power of doctrine: it exerted on listeners something of the same effect as a Wagnerian opera. The notions of Germans as gods, of Total Victory or Total Disaster, and of the Russian destination, were specifically set forth in *Mein Kampf.*

The book was a true clue to the absolute incompatibility of the Nazi state with any international arrangements based on reason, compromise, or law. But its very radicalism, by inciting incredulity, enabled Hitler to convince people that he really did,

after all, believe in reason, compromise, and law. Since practically everything that was done by Hitler down through the invasion of the Soviet Union in 1941 was consonant with the vision,
and often inexplicable except in terms of it, we may conclude
that historians who discount it as a serious factor are suffering
from the same myopic incredulity as statesmen like Simon or
Chamberlain.*

It is always slippery and usually misleading to speak of large
"trends" such as a persisting impetus to national unity and national completeness. History is much too complicated to justify
it, and it is beset with telic dangers that are involved in any
notion of direction—let alone destination—in human affairs. If
circumstance had been slightly different, quite different trends
would be picked out. There were other "forces" in German
history—the competing magnetism of association with east and
west, the very real and deep traditions of constitutional government, the religious division dating from the Reformation and
translated into new forms, the surviving remnants of particularism. But ther~ *was* undoubtedly also perceptible a trend toward
the completing of Germany, both through the creation of a
highly centralized governing authority, and by the expansion of
its jurisdiction to include all Germans. It was aggravated by the
indignities and losses of the peace settlement in 1919. Many
people realized this and thought to achieve European stability by
gratifying this desire. If it *had* been the sum of Hitler's aims,
they might have succeeded.

Another factor that made Hitler and his successes possible
was the moment in time at which he appeared. The progress in
communications and weaponry had reached precisely the point
where quick, successful attacks on neighbors might be conveniently contemplated. The airplane and the automobile, con-
joined, had diminished distance and permitted an entirely new
and very devastating development of an old tactical possibility
into a strategic program. The *breakthrough* had been sought by
the armies on the western front in 1914—in vain, because military
technology in those days had reached the stage of machine guns,

* (For a thorough discussion of the role of Space and Totality in Hitler's thought, see
Joachim Leuschner, *Volk und Raum* (Göttingen: Vandenhoek und Ruprecht, 1958).

barbed wire, and trenches, which made it less likely to take place and almost certain to be contained as a salient, mortally perilous to the attacker if it did. But the speed assured by motorized units protected by tactical air support reversed this situation: if a breakthrough of enemy lines did take place in the 1940s, the advance could proceed so rapidly as to defy all efforts to contain it, disrupting the defender's supply lines and denying him enormous parts of his territory. The airplane, moreover, could be used for bombing, at moderate distances, which could prepare and fortify the breakthrough by disrupting communications in advance. It was expected, in the thirties, that it could also be used with devastating effect against the economic capacity and the morale of the enemy.

All this reduced the ancient barriers of distance that had made quick, total victory so formidable a project in European history. Hitler understood that a series of such victories could be won, one by one, without putting the kind of strain on German society that had proved unbearable in 1918. What he failed, spectacularly, to realize was that the technique of the quick thrust would not work against powers with vast territories and vast potentials. The time when the conquest of Europe could be regarded as a closed-end project had passed. The portent of its passing was the inauguration of transatlantic commercial flights by Pan-American Airways in the summer of 1939. The airplane—to be followed by rocketry—had advanced beyond the point where it would enable one European region to subordinate the others, and was approaching the point where it would enable the world's vast, undeveloped arsenal of strength to subordinate all parts of Europe.

Hitler's book, *Mein Kampf,* was written while he was briefly imprisoned for taking part in the unsuccessful uprising in Munich in 1923. It was not simply a personal confession or a political pamphlet or a philosophy of history and society. It combined all three in random ways, but it was, further, a tract, for what it said at inordinate length was, "I, like Germany, have suffered humiliation and injustice at the hands of traitors and foreigners; but I, like Germany, possess an innate destiny and capacity to lead, and like all true Germans I have a special, genetic, claim to do so. I may and must violate conventional morality, but this is because conventional morality is the false and corrupting lie invented by Jews and Christians, and liberals and democrats, and capitalists and Communists, to enfeeble me and Germany. I, like Germany, know instinctively, and by definition embody, *true* morality. It is my destiny, and Germany's under my leadership, to convert this higher truth into political fact." The detailed prescriptions for this venture were mostly expressions of vulgar and rather badly informed prejudice; Hitler regarded Slavs as barbarians, the Latins as irredeemably bastardized with "Negro blood" and softened by humanism. (He had, however, a good deal of respect for the achievements of the Nordic-operated British Empire.)

Hitler's book was the assertion of a necessary connection between racial superiority, German greatness, and his own mystical destiny to refurbish it as a result of a sort of Immaculate Conception in the womb of Germania (he seems, quite often, to have confused his nature with Christ's) that most effectively stated and furthered his aims. *Mein Kampf* had other merits; to anyone at all sympathetic to it, its rantings seemed like inspiration—it is, indeed, remarkably clinging, in the way that religious scripture often is. No less useful to its author was the fact that it seemed, to anyone *not* sympathetic, to be so preposterously unreasonable as to show that he couldn't mean it. It is useful to a politician aiming at drastic action to be taken either intensely seriously or not seriously at all. Indeed, he managed to come to power largely because German conservatives, who put him in the chancellorship, regarded him as a fool who could easily be controlled while they used him as a popular figurehead whose large and disruptive following could be manipulated to consolidate their own aims—in effect, the restoration of the old empire.

HITLER'S EARLY ACTIONS

In the early days of Nazi power nothing appeared of the larger vision. What appeared, in external affairs, was an expression of the limited aim of redressing Germany's legitimate grievances. That the methods were peremptory frightened many people but gave to others a gratifying sense of drama, of justice restored by a *deus ex machina*. In the deadening atmosphere of the Depression, determined action of any sort excited respect and enthusiasm, and this fact beguiled Hitler's opponents and invigorated his friends.

The situation is sufficiently illustrated by the strange course of the disarmament conference, which runs like a dramatist's symbolic subplot through the larger perturbations of the early thirties. The disarmament conference was an example of all the things Hitler proposed to rescue Germany from: the heritage of Versailles and its child, the League of Nations; the hypocritical disarming of Germany; the meaningless and endless debates and negotiations of democratic statesmen; the inadequacy of parliamentary methods. Its course had unfortunately given grounds for the belief, from the standpoint of Germans and some other people, that it was both futile and sinister.

The existence of the conference, like many other confusing things in the early thirties, was a hangover from more optimistic days.

It had been long in the making. League investigations, preparatory commissions, diplomatic conversations, had all proved abortive. But after Locarno there had been more evidence of co-operation in spirit, if not in substance. Disarmament had begun to move and had finally eventuated in a full-dress international conference that met, under League auspices, in Switzerland in February of 1932. All the great powers, including the United States and the Soviet Union, were represented. From the beginning, enormous chasms separated their policies, reflecting accurately the basic contradiction of a world in which disarmament had to be procured through governments which had the duty and desire to define their own requirements for safety. These requirements were very different. The French argued—as they had been arguing since 1919—that disarmament could be achieved only by substituting an internationally controlled army for national armies, or at least subjecting national armies to stern international regulation and inspection; and that even then the size of national armies must be based on need and potential and that disarmament must be part of a strong international security system. It was a logical rather than an altruistic program, for France was in a position of relative weakness of potential while its frontiers were judged highly vulnerable and its responsibilities enormous. This sort of thing was flatly unacceptable to everybody else; most governments believed that they must be left independent of international control in this, the most vital of all spheres, if freedom was to have any meaning. The Soviet Union persistently proposed the complete and total elimination of all armaments, more as a propaganda strategy than as a serious policy. It was a meaningless notion; armaments are relative, and the nation with the largest number of bows and arrows would be in a position of aggressive superiority if firearms were totally suppressed. The British wanted to concentrate on limited and technical aims, notably curbs on "aggressive" weapons, although it was not clear exactly how these might be defined, and upon the size of reserves. This meant, in effect, the end of conscription, on which man-poor France depended heavily to provide a trained and mobilizable army of the necessary size. The Germans, governed now by Brüning, who was the last Chancellor not intending to subvert the free society, demanded "equality" as a prelude to disarmament. They felt obliged to do so because they thought that only an international concession of "equality" —the ending of compulsory unilateral disarmament—could prove to the German nation that the republic was capable of defending the nation's basic rights and thus saving the regime.

This immediately became the most important issue of the conference; the Germans argued that once the concession of equality had been made in principle, the basic element for stability in Europe, an internationally respectable government confirmed in its tenure in Germany, would be assured. The French wavered; it looked for a time as if it might be conceded. But they withdrew from their conciliatory position at the last moment. It has been argued that reactionary elements in Germany, then conspiring to get control of the government for the Nationalists, persuaded the French to withhold the step that might have saved Brüning with the promise of a co-operative attitude on the part of a more conservative and less shaky German government.

Brüning was dismissed in June 1932 by the President of the Republic. His place was taken by Franz von Papen, a schemer and a renegade member of the Catholic Center Party, who formed a cabinet, of extreme conservatives without influence in German parliamentary and party circles, but ardently supported by the President, which governed by presidential decree. The cabinet proved extremely weak; two national elections failed to show the slightest popular confidence in it but instead yielded increased representation for both Communists and Nazis.

In December of 1932, after endless negotiations and mutual threats, the principle of equality was agreed to by the leaders of the disarmament conference, in a formula that combined, without any indication of how it was to be put into practice, the leading features of the French and German positions: Germany was to have "equality of rights in a system which would provide security to all nations." None of the real issues had been solved; but the formula, if it had come six months earlier, might conceivably have saved the German republic.

It came too late; the last, footless effort to form a conservative cabinet, led by an ambitious Army officer, General von Schleicher, was demonstrating that no German government could exist that depended solely on the support of the President and his circle. Hitler took office as Chancellor at the end of January 1933. His appointment was manipulated by the Nationalists and their friends in the expectation that the Nazis could be outmaneuvered and controlled, in a cabinet in which they were in a minority. His first months in office were devoted to dispelling this illusion. Nazi control of the state government of Prussia, rigged voting, intimidation, flaming propaganda, and armed gangs produced, in still another parliamentary election, a plurality of about 40 per cent for the Nazis, and with some allies and many abstentions they succeeded in passing an act which enabled them—in effect—to do anything they felt was necessary to save the fatherland. What they deemed necessary was the sudden and brutal elimination of all the apparatus of a free society: state governments were immediately brought under Nazi control; all other political parties and all labor unions were summarily dissolved; all civil liberties were abolished; all opposition was quelled; summary arrests and informal lynchings by Nazi gangs were commonplace. Some of the conservatives clung to office so long as Hitler tolerated them, and almost all of them were acquiescent, although von Papen was led to denounce as illegal and immoral the destruction of the ancient freedoms of German politics.

These domestic operations occupied Hitler and his government during the first six months or so in office. Until September, the wrangling in Geneva continued in pre-Hitler patterns. Then the German representatives became brusquely unco-operative, and in October of 1933, when control at home was assured and when his quiescence in international affairs had not only assuaged the anxieties of some foreigners but had actually made a good impression, he announced that Germany was withdrawing from the League of Nations *and* the disarmament conference, and called for a plebiscite in Germany to ratify his decision.

The vote, unconscionably managed, was nearly unanimous. The Germans welcomed a decisive government that promised positive policies, one that was prepared to assert Germany's dignity and independence, and it seems possible that the management was necessary only to convert a large majority into near-unanimity. Abroad, the effect of Hitler's sudden action was of course shocking. It was made somewhat less so, in spite of its staggering abruptness, by several considerations which illuminated Hitler's luck and genius.

It might be supposed, in view of the campaigns which the German republic had already won to secure respectability and equality, and especially in view of the ruthless thoroughness with which the Nazi regime was extirpating its republican enemies and flaunting slogans of "Aryan" superiority and German destiny, that no rational person would view the assault on the only two important bodies working for world peace as a step toward improving the chances for it. Many people throughout the world did take an appropriately skeptical and gloomy view of Hitler's action, but many did not; for now whole flights of blackbirds came home to roost.

For one thing, it seemed to many people that both the League and the disarmament conference were approaching the verges of absurdity. Even Anthony Eden, the strongest internationalist in the British government, remarked that "the conference was becoming a sham." The internationalists had shown themselves quite unable to deal in action, and the Manchurian episode had disillusioned some even of the more ardent supporters of "collective security" (the name given to forcible efforts by an international organization to maintain the existing order of frontiers and power relationships). For such people Hitler was merely ratifying an action which history, as it were, had already taken. Moreover, in the same breath with which he announced Germany's withdrawal from these futile bodies, he guaranteed his eagerness to assist in the building of new agencies for international co-operation to assure peace, agencies to be based on new foundations and wholly detached from the Versailles tradition with its dangerous, unjust, and futile effort to build peace on the unrealistic assumption that Germany could forever be treated as a criminal held in thrall.

Further, the old burden of guilt about the treatment of the defeated Germans, and the hardships to which they had been subjected, now began to affect international affairs, particularly through British opinion. There was, it appeared, much truth in German assertions, reiterated long before Hitler came to power, that peace could be built only upon an acceptance of full German equality in the community of nations, and thus upon the revision of "the Versailles system." The League, Hitler said, was nothing more than a way to maintain the permanent subjection of the defeated powers. He privately told the British ambassador that he would require a "certain expansion" to the east. But Simon, the Foreign Secretary, evidently didn't take it seriously. Such revisions would mean war; the Germans most dedicated to them had found it prudent to be silent in public about them, at least until German power was built to a point where war might be contemplated with some confidence of winning it, and this was still a long way off. Thus, a degree of delusion existed in the widespread British reaction to everything Germany did in the next few years. The sense of fairness, both plausible and creditable, prevailed over conflicting perceptions of the nature of German ambitions and the nature of the Nazi movement.

The German initiative opened chasms in Britain. Neither the National Government nor British opinion was in a state where any spirited and united action could be expected, and the inevitable result of fear of war and a concentration on internal affairs, combined with a general dislike of Hitler and his methods, began to create rifts within the British governing groups. Those who felt that peace required acceptance of Germany's rights and good intentions clashed more and more fiercely with those who felt that Hitler was a shameless aggressor who must one day deliberately start a war. Negotiation confronted resistance. As individuals lined up, with increasing passion, on each side, both inside the British government and in Parliament and among influential people generally, the machinery of British policy-making began to go to pieces.

The cabinet was generally, although not at all unanimously, disposed to negotiation; the division in it was reflected in the existence of two ministers who were supposed to deal with foreign affairs, the Foreign Minister, Sir John Simon, and the Lord Privy Seal, Anthony Eden. Their reflexes to Hitlerism, if not their day-to-day conduct of affairs, were precisely opposed. And the negotiators found themselves more and more suspicious of the permanent and professional staffs in the administration. Many diplomats, many Foreign Office experts, many intelligence people, were certain that Nazi Germany was unconversable, unassimilable, and that peace could be kept only by determined resistance. The people, on the other hand, who felt that peace could not possibly be kept except by trapping Hitler into the network of traditional international relations, grew more and more to distrust the professionals, and in the end the foreign policy of Great Britain was being secretively conducted by the Prime Minister and a clique of friends not only without the professionals but actually against them.

For the most powerful men in Britain and France the initial reaction to Hitler was drowned in preoccupation with domestic economic problems. Insulationism extended to more than recovery programs; it extended to human souls and grand strategy. Britain was depending for its safety on its navy and its empire.

France had begun, in the twenties, the construction of a "wall," a system of presumably impregnable fortifications along the German frontier, named for the war minister who had presided over its inception, M. André Maginot. The Maginot Line was commonly taken as the symbol of a defensive mentality, especially in the high command of the French Army, which had learned in 1914–18 the lesson that French manpower was precious and that offensives cost hideously in casualties—but had failed to learn the lesson, as armies usually do, that the experiences of the last war will not be repeated in the next. The Line was, in some measure, exactly this; but it was also a symbol of an effort to shake off the unbearably heavy responsibilities of governing a Europe that did not wish to be governed. It is important to note that an unshakably *defensive* attitude already existed before September 1933.

Two months after his announcement, Hitler specified his conditions for a return to the international organizations. They involved an army 50 per cent bigger than Versailles allowed, no inspection or control, freedom to arm it as the Germans wished, and no account to be taken of the Nazis' private armies, the Sturm Abteilung and the elite Schutzstaffel (known usually as the SA and SS), or of civil aviation. The Saarland was also to be returned at once. These were apparently presented only because it was deemed wise to present *some* terms. They were immediately and predictably rejected by the French. But the Italians, Belgians, and British, the other signatories of Versailles and Locarno most immediately concerned, temporized. The Belgians realistically observed that it was foolish to argue about what the Germans were going to do, since they couldn't be stopped from doing it except by another invasion, which nobody was prepared to consider. The British went further; they expressed eagerness to "negotiate" the German demands, and tried to do so. It was the first symptom of the determination to build a fortress out of paper. The effect was merely to oblige the Germans to engage in long but doomed conversation; more cogently, it annoyed the government of France and much French opinion, which supposed that the British were betraying them to the very evil they had so long dreamt of, a resurgent

German military power capable of attacking France.

An attempt to stabilize the situation had been made by the Italians even earlier. Mussolini, involved in his own extremely grave economic problems, had put forward his own answer to the unreality of the League and the rest of the Versailles system in 1932, when he proposed a four-power pact, designed—not altogether fancifully—to confide the policing of Europe to a sort of renewed Concert of Great Powers: Italy, France, Great Britain, and Germany. In an odd way this coincided with the dictates of insulation; it would limit the commitments of the powers, provide a flexible and realistic leadership, work Germany into a position where it would have to agree to accept existing frontiers, and also serve the purpose—very much on the minds of western statesmen in a period of boiling social unrest —of isolating the Soviet Union. It would create a genuinely "European system," independent of, and able to defend itself against, the isolated superpowers, America and Russia. There was, naturally, consternation and outrage on the part of the smaller powers, in particular the eastern allies of France, at this suggestion of domination by the great. But the faith in documents oddly persisted; a much watered-down version of the four-power pact was actually signed in June 1933, after the Nazis had taken power. It was taken as a token of Hitler's intentions to be respectable, and this faith survived to some extent the shock of the following autumn.

Alarmed by the reactions of their small allies, the French set out to strengthen the system of alliances in eastern Europe which "contained" Germany. The British were intent on a different purpose by 1934. They were much impressed by the beneficent achievements of the Locarno pacts, and British policy in Europe after Hitler's rise centered on an attempt to extend the principle to Germany's eastern frontier. The Eastern Pact, as the project was called, or the "Eastern Locarno," would bring the Poles, Germans, and Russians together in a solemn assurance that they would not try to change the map, and this would be underwritten by the western powers. Neither the Russians nor the Germans wanted to have the map remain as it was. In fact, the long-run determinant of all German foreign-policy making since 1918 had been to avoid precisely that, and Hitler, while he might possibly have signed such a pact, would never have meant to adhere to it. Anthony Eden was sent east in the spring of 1934 to try to prepare the ground for the Eastern Pact, but he got nowhere.

The situation of Poland, moreover, had changed. The Poles had reacted very strongly against the four-power pact, since it seemed so obviously intended to erect an executive directorate that might change things instead of the French alliance system that was designed to prevent change. Any change in eastern Europe could only be to Poland's national disadvantage, and the Polish nation, recalled to vigorous life after more than a century of tortured coma, was in some ways quite as virulent in its nationalism as Germany.

The situation of Poland had always been both crucial and agonizing. The Poles were a numerous, highly civilized, Roman Catholic, people who occupied a large expanse of flat terrain whose frontiers, ethnic and geographical, were shifting and uncertain. In the eighteenth century their vast state had been compressed, and then squeezed to death, by the advance of the adjoining autocrats—Habsburgs, Prussian Hohenzollerns, and Russian Romanovs. They had been ruled, or misruled, by foreigners from 1792 to 1918, and for most of that time the heartland of Poland, Warsaw and its surrounding provinces, had been in the hands of the Russians, who made themselves extremely unpopular as oppressors. The peculiar tragedy of Poland lay in this: it was between two bigger nations; and while the heartland was solidly and unanimously Polish, the territories around it were all more or less shared with foreigners. All of these territories became Polish after 1918, and Poland's problem was essentially, from a national standpoint, the reverse of Hitler's. Since the Germans and the Russians both wanted to despoil Poland, and the Poles realistically understood that (whatever the differences that divided them), they would be perfectly prepared in favorable circumstances to unite to do so, for their own safety had to depend upon their own ingenuity.

The domestic situation of Poland did not help. The Polish nobility, as nearly feudal as any in Europe, had associated itself with the Polish national struggle in the nineteenth century and had thereby succeeded in salvaging its manors and prestige, so that free Poland was extraordinarily retrograde in its social system and its politics. The government, born without any past of working institutions, functioned badly. It was led by an ex-socialist, a heroic fighter for freedom, who had been made Poland's first marshal and first president. Marshal Pilsudski had been an able and patriotic if not very adventurous statesman, but by 1934 his mind had failed. (Poland shared with Great Britain and Germany on the eve of Hitler's rise the curious distinction of having a senile chief executive. It was significant of the kind of helplessness of European nations then—as it was to be, more specifically, in France after 1940—that they found it convenient to be governed by mindless national heroes. The substitution of figureheads for leaders argued a desperate effort to put national unity and stability above all other considerations and led, of course, to disaster.)

The effective force in the Polish government in 1934 was the Foreign Minister, Josef Beck, one of the "colonels' junta" which had taken control in 1932. Like most of his colleagues and many of his fellow-nationals his fear and dislike of Russia, fortified by a dread of bolshevism, slightly outweighed his fear and dislike of Germany. Witnessing the decay of the peace-keeping efficiency of the Versailles system, he had decided that Poland must live by its wits, which meant trying to buy off, or play off, the colossal shapes of nemesis. In January 1934, he negotiated a nonaggression pact with Germany. Taken together with a similar understanding with the Soviet Union and with a proud confidence in the Polish cavalry, which was correctly thought to be the best in Europe (it was the only cavalry left in Europe) he thought this contributed to safety.

Many Frenchmen thought the Nazi-Polish pact was a betrayal of the alliance system they had built up to contain Germany and guarantee peace in Europe, and its signing was a preface to a gradual decline in French reliance on eastern alliances and a further rapid rise in reliance on the Maginot Line, the French Army, and dependence on Great Britain. In fact, the German-Polish pact did not indicate any real change in Polish policy, or any disposition to abandon the French alliance. The Poles thought of it simply as a safety device, a necessary supplement to the basic security arrangements. But they did tend to exaggerate the reliability of Hitler's promises, just as they exaggerated the role of horses in twentieth-century war. They were beguiled by the fact that, after a season of absolutely venomous Polish-German relations since 1918, they had found a German leader who seemed anxious to demonstrate his good intentions. They did not fully understand Hitler's attitude toward the first Polish initiative, which was to seize the opportunity to silence the noisiest of his neighbors and disarm their suspicions and therefore their hostility. This misunderstanding arose from his total lack of respect for any of the trappings of traditional diplomacy, such as treaties, and from his ineffable inconsistency. In some ways he did at the moment want Polish friendship, and convinced the Poles of it by suggesting an anti-Soviet alliance. The appearance of cordiality was enough to fill gloomy western observers with suspicions of a Polish-German bloc, but its real importance was to give Hitler a diplomatic success that allowed him to consolidate his domestic position and prepare for rearmament.

Within a year after Hitler took office, therefore, the situation in Europe had changed drastically. There were plenty of signs for those who hoped that things would get better. The first faint indications of economic recovery were now noticeable in Britain, and the Nazi recovery program in Germany and the New Deal in the United States looked as if they might be going to work. The insufficiencies of the Versailles system were now so conspicuous that many people were willing to admit that its collapse was a way of clearing the scene for the construction of a better European order. Hitler himself had said so; Hitler was talking and, if in rather disruptive ways, sometimes acting, peace. Moreover, it was generally understood that German military power, however rapidly it might be built up, was so far from matching that of France that there could be no real danger from Germany for a long time to come. These considerations were what influenced Beck in Warsaw. They were fortified by the observation that Germany's isolation was almost as complete as ever. The "Little Entente" was solid. The small and thoroughly encircled "revisionist" countries, Hungary and Bulgaria, were helpless. The Italians, despite a certain ideological affinity, were certainly unlikely to assist Germany. Italy, no supporter of the Versailles system, was nevertheless still playing respectable diplomatic ball with the British and French, and it was felt that Mussolini's extreme aversion to having German power installed in Austria would prove an absolute obstacle to any serious Italo-German co-operation in the furtherance of German expansionism. The Nazis were already putting pressure on the Austrian government, of a sort that suggested the ultimate aim of union, and this seemed certain to force Italy's alignment against a resurgent Germany. It was even hoped, by people like Anthony Eden, that the League of Nations might now be reanimated, and collective security converted into a real instrument for maintaining law, order, and the frontiers of 1919.

The next year, from February of 1934 to March of 1935, which was to be relatively free of international crises, was to see major efforts made to devise new ways of solidifying Europe and assuring its stability. None of them worked, and their failure was followed by overt and drastic indications that the old European powers were being made helpless by their imprisonment in the shams and decencies of a dead age.

5

The Politics of Passivity

A year after Hitler took office, even the most passionate of his enemies had few grounds to fear him
as an immediate threat to peace. Nations with
strong reasons to oppose any aggressive German
action included almost all of Europe, and their
combined power was so hugely greater than that
of Germany that any possible effort to act on the
more ambitious prescriptions of *Mein Kampf*
seemed ludicrous. Moreover, Hitler's domestic
position was not secure. Despite the demolition of
parties, unions, and the federal system, some of
the powerful institutions in Germany still eluded
the full control of the Nazi Party. The most important of these was the Army, whose stiff-necked and
conservative officers, while they tolerated the
regime and welcomed Hitler's plans for rearmament, generally disliked intensely the man and his
cronies, whom they regarded as vulgar adventur-
ers. The officers were much exercised by the fear
that the vulgarians' leveling might extend to the
replacing of the army by its powerful, party-spon-
sored competitor, the armed rank and file of Nazi
youth in the Sturm Abteilung, which was far larger
than the Army, had played a conspicuous role in

the rise of the movement, and whose leaders ardently wished to see their organization become the German National Army. This tug of war between the Party, steadily consolidating its control of most of German life, and the most ancient and majestic survivor of the traditional Germany, was to occupy Hitler's attention for a long time.

What Hitler's Germany provoked was not fear of immediate war but alarm at his unseemly deportment, which was causing "the situation to deteriorate"—a quasi-technical phrase which meant, in effect, that things were changing in ways not arranged by diplomats. Foreign governments explored means of constructing a new equilibrium that would save them from having to take the initiative or engage in other exhausting exertions.

The event that determined the form and outcome of these defensive efforts was the violent disorder that took place in Paris in February 1934. This arose, strangely enough, from the revelation of shady transactions in connection with a bond issue intended to finance a public pawnshop in the town of Bayonne, in the southwestern corner of France.

The financial affairs of a minor municipality produced effects of cosmic magnitude, including a drastic change in the foreign policy of the Soviet Union and world communism. It happened so because the world order—the "situation"—depended primarily upon France, a France seriously enfeebled and distraught by the war, already badly affected by depression, and deeply divided by conflicting judgments as to what form of internal organization and what kind of foreign policy could save the nation. The strain had simply been too great, and when an unsavory small-time financier named Stavisky embezzled the pawnshop bonds he had been marketing, the fabric of France began to rip.

There were indeed peculiarities about the affairs of the pawnshop that justified concern. After the fraud was made known and Stavisky arrested, he died in prison; he was supposed either to have killed himself or to have been murdered. He was found, or believed, to have had the protection of people in high places in Paris, who allegedly had gotten a cut of his ill-gotten proceeds or were being blackmailed by him. The matter was sordid enough, and it was riotously exploited by those who hoped to discredit the regime as hopelessly corrupt. Some of these people were old-time rightists, including the strange monarchist party, tiny but intellectually potent, called Action française, which had been born out of a similar sordid scandal forty years before, and which ever since had been acting as a gadfly to the French Republic, which it viewed with philosophical contempt and nihilistic loathing. Its program had provided some of the prototypes for Mussolini's fascism. It was the model and progenitor of many later attacks on democracy. Action française had been joined in February 1934 by other organizations, more or less explicitly fascist, whose following, mostly veterans and university students, believed angrily that French democracy was incapable of efficient government, social progress, civic morality, and economic recovery. Other people sharing this view were on the left. The Communist Party ardently supported the attack on the government, and so, less ardently, did the Socialists. It looked like a real opportunity to overthrow the Third Republic with its constantly shifting governments and policies, its squalid gangs of trafficking politicians, its paralyzing party structure. On the sixth of February Parisian rioters, largely but by no means exclusively young people, turned out. They came very close to seizing the parliament house and other public buildings, which were held by the police, with difficulty and luck, at the cost of casualties on both sides.

The protesters had, in truth, a good deal to protest against. The state of France was unedifying. The Third Republic seemed increasingly to be presiding over an atrophying social and economic system; it appeared to embody all that was worst in a rotting nineteenth-century liberalism. France was in some respects exceedingly backward. Its social security and public-welfare arrangements were practically nonexistent. Its labor unions were unable to achieve collective bargaining. Many of its businessmen were devoted to quill-pen methods of business; French production, distribution, and financing were frequently antediluvian. The legal and administrative systems were frozen in their Napoleonic forms. And there was a rigidity and mustiness about the structure of society as a whole which was alleged to reflect the inordinate influence of a few magnates. The Bank of France, a private institution, controlled the credit of the state and much of the private banking, and it was alleged that this control was exercised in the interests of a crusted capitalism and served the interests of a very few plutocrats. Reformers spoke bitterly of "the wall of money" which was supposed to imprison innovators who reached high political office, and of "the two hundred families," the two hundred directors of the Bank who were supposed to control most of the economy. The claims of politically influential groups, in particular peasants, to protection by the state had been too generously met, and France had developed piecemeal a rigid system of economic controls, subsidies, and tariffs that suffocated enterprise and hindered change. All this, taken together with the unedifying and undoubtedly corrupt record of many politicians of the Republic, certainly justified strenuous efforts to remake the country.

But there were also strengths in the Third Republic and the nation it governed. The Republic had survived the First World War and brought the country, at inestimable cost, to victory. It had survived the scarcely less harrowing test of inflation and had restored the currency and the credit of France. In the twenties a degree of industrial construction and expansion quite as remarkable as Germany's had produced a new physical plant for some French manufacturers: a vigorous and modern industrial establishment coexisted with a stale and static economy of small shops. In contrast to Britain, unemployment had fallen to zero in the years just before the Depression. Moreover, while social justice might be harrowingly meager and the attitude toward taxation and welfare legislation archaic, France had much the most even distribution of income of any considerable industrial nation. Most important of all, the Republic had succeeded in preserving liberty under law to a degree spectacularly greater than in three quarters of the continent. And the Republic still, despite the maddening immobility of its politicians, assured the indispensable ingredient of democracy: it guaranteed free voting to all adult males, and so preserved the *possibility* of peaceful change.

The assault upon democratic institutions by groups who found them inadequate or repulsive and who were united on the basic rottenness of the society had historical precedents which were important in what followed. At the end of the century, the same Republic had been attacked by a comparable union of radicals and socialists with clericalists, military men, and monarchists. It had been saved because the leftists, while hating the "bourgeois republic," concluded (at the instance of the leadership of the founder of the French Socialist Party, the revered Jean Jaurès) that it secured liberty and made change possible and so was preferable to what its rightist opponents would install in its place if they got the chance. In the Dreyfus Affair had been born a lasting, if very conditional, respect for democratic institutions by much of the French left. It had brought the Radicals to power and led to drastic reforms. The leaders of the Radical and Social-ist parties remained thereafter dedicated to republican ideas, although the Socialists refused to take office. They had a long tradition of "nonparticipation" in the bourgeois regime, which they thought would be corrupting.

A more recent and compelling lesson for the left had been furnished by events in Germany just before the appointment of Hitler. There the end of the Republic seemed to have been decreed by the refusal of the Communists to support it, or even to abstain from violent efforts to destroy it. The German Com-munist Party had stood true to the belief that anything that weakened the bourgeois regime and precipitated its collapse would serve their purposes by providing what Lenin had called "a revolutionary situation." German Communist bands had quite literally linked hands with Nazis in protest demonstrations and resistance to the police, while exchanging deadly vitupera-tion with them in print. Even more conspicuously, they had attacked with virulence the Social Democratic Party, the largest of the parties supporting the German republic, calling the Social Democrats "social fascists" who blinded the workers to the need for revolution. Since the formation of the Third International, the Communists everywhere had logically seen their first, most dangerous, and most abominable enemy in their competitors—socialists, radicals, and advanced liberals. They had expected the Nazis to destroy them, which indeed happened. But the history of nazism in power showed from its first weeks that Communist power and organization were the first, and quite defenseless, victims of the state apparatus once it was taken over by determined anticommunists. The German Communist Party, the largest and most promising outside the U.S.S.R., had conceived, if it had not bred, its own fate. The historical pendant to the Dreyfus Affair seemed not only symmetrical but perfect.

The specter of a French rightist dictatorship was opened by the February riots, and therefore the Communists and other leftists who had taken part in them abruptly shifted their attitude. Further riots took place a week later, led by triumphant fascists and monarchists who thought their hour was at hand. In bizarre anachronism, the elderly pretender to the throne of the Bourbons waited eagerly in Brussels for a call to rule France. But this time the Communists fought on the side of the police to save French democracy, and the revolution died in brawls between last week's comrades-in-arms.

The effects on everyone concerned were immense. The cabinet resigned. The deputies who made ministries saw the need for something a little more dignified than usual in the way of ministries. A retired President of the Republic, an ornamental figure of some eminence, was installed as Premier. Gaston Doumergue, who was over seventy, had followed the common French political path from fiery radicalism to conservative immobility. (His choice was another example of the singular tendency of constitutional regimes in interwar years to try to shore themselves up by confiding their destinies to national figures of advanced age and doubtful intellectual vigor who were supposed to evoke unity by sheer respectability. The appointment pallidly presaged the politics of last resort that led in 1940 to Pétain.) Doumergue was too dim and too closely associated with the least-inspiring traits of the Republic to be a satisfactory figurehead; he was in office for only eight months. But he brought with him into the foreign ministry Louis Barthou, a man of intelligence and stamina, who had far-reaching effects on French policy.

There were even more far-reaching effects on French fascism and communism—and, through them, upon fascism and communism throughout the world. From then on, both proliferated, aided by the deepening depression and the advancing domestic paralysis of the Republic.

More and more fascist or quasi-fascist groups were organized, and old ones grew bolder and louder. They were united only in animosity to the Communists, to Socialists, Radicals, liberals, and true conservatives (typified by Doumergue) who wanted to save the existing order, and to Jews, foreigners, internationalists, democrats, and bankers. All taken together were seen as representatives of what some of them began to call Pluto-Judeo-Bolshevism, a term invented out of desperation for an enemy that seemed to them real but exasperatingly undefinable. Some of the groups, like Action française, appealed to the monarchist and nationalist tradition but were very twentieth century in their emphasis on lying and paramilitary organization. Some were conspicuously reactionary, like the peculiar Cagoulards (Hooded Ones) who combined the methods and appearance of the Ku Klux Klan with the interests and outlook of the National Association of Manufacturers. Of another sort was the Croix de Feu (Cross of Fire) led by Colonel de La Roque, which started out mainly as a veterans' movement directed against the "sell-out" of national interests by the flaccid republic. Jacques Doriot, once a firebrand of the extreme left, organized the Parti Social Française, which (like the British Fascist Party organized by the rather similar Oswald Mosley) combined leftist social programs with fascist organization. A group called the Franquistes preached a peculiar racist doctrine that distinguished between Frenchmen of superior Germanic (Frankish) stock and those of inferior Latin stock. It was, perhaps, evidence of the strength of the traditions of individual liberty in France that these groups remained divided and had uninspiring leaders, in contrast to Italy or Germany where similarly disparate elements had been forged into iron unity by demagogues.

Many of the antidemocrats imitated—and some were sponsored by—Italian fascism and German nazism. But they were troubled by the crucial inner contradiction of fascism as an international movement. While they imitated Mussolini and Hitler, it was perplexingly unclear whether to co-operate with them. Italy and Germany were the traditional enemies of the Ultimate

Value, France, and the aims of fascism and nazism could not be achieved except at France's expense. Most French fascists ingeniously squared the circle by envisaging the fascist International as a comradely crusade against communism. In the end, they remained divided under the authoritarian regime that replaced the Republic in 1940. But in the thirties their purpose was to exploit fear of war by asserting that only Jews and Communists favored it and that the safety of France lay in accepting Nazi ambitions in central and eastern Europe. They thus grew after 1934.

The Communists found themselves in a position at once similar and opposite. Because of what had happened to the German Communist Party, and because the Soviet Union justly apprehended itself as a likely victim of attack by the Nazis, the Communists now became the most ardent opponents of domestic and foreign fascism. Before the French crisis there had been no open indication that world communism had doubts about the prudence of denouncing as equally evil all non-Communist groups. It is true that as early as May 1933 *Isvestia* had commented on the Nazi regime, saying that enemies of the Versailles settlement (which Communist orthodoxy had previously denounced as imperialism) were to be regarded automatically as imperialists. But in December 1933, the Executive of the Third International was still insisting that the world capitalist order was disintegrating, that anything that speeded its disintegration (like nazism) was helpful to the Communist cause, and that Socialists were "social fascists." On February 2, 1934, the seventeenth Russian Party Congress renewed the traditional attacks on the Versailles settlement and said that nazism was a "favorable" phenomenon, indicating the disarray of the bourgeois world.

The Nazi-Polish pact of 1934 had alarmed the Soviets, but had not altered their line. After the February riots in France, however, the French Communist Party urgently argued the inexpediency of co-operating with fascists to destroy democracy, or of attacking the communists' principal potential allies, the Socialists. They were ordered to return to orthodoxy, and in April 1934 denunciation of "social fascists" again appeared in the French

Communist press. But in Moscow, now, their arguments were being listened to. The French party was permitted to make an electoral alliance with the Socialists in July, and throughout the world Communist parties began to change their line. Enthusiastic support for all parties that supported democratic governments and opposed nazism was suddenly voiced. This second Russian Revolution was ratified, a year later, by the Seventh Congress of the Communist International, but long before that Soviet foreign policy had begun to reflect the change.

The interests of the Soviet Union, forced by the circumstance of living in a world of national states to behave like one, demanded an anti-Nazi coalition of nations and parties alike. A very ancient logic operated; now that Germany was strong (and seemed to have found a friend in hostile Poland) Russia entered into friendship with Germany's potential enemies. Nothing more was heard about Socialists being "social fascists." Communists urgently appealed to the good will of all who loved democracy and freedom to co-operate with the workers in a "Popular Front." Patriotism had always previously been regarded as an opiate administered by capitalists to make the workers forget their true interest. Now it appeared in neo-Marxist mythology as a peculiarly proletarian virtue: the fatherland (any fatherland) was being betrayed by monopoly capitalists who, in Marxist thought, had created international fascism for their own lugubrious purposes, to guarantee markets and exterminate the workers' movement.

This reversal of policy had very far-reaching effects indeed. It implanted democracy and patriotism permanently in the Communist lexicon of favorable terms, and—for example—led the American Communist Party into idolatry of Abraham Lincoln and political support for Franklin Roosevelt. It led to a new program: communists tried to form electoral alliances with socialists instead of murdering them in the streets. Most of all, it justified and attracted the consciences of almost everybody in the world who had been unfavorably impressed by Hitler's activities in Germany. For left-wing intellectuals, especially, but for genteel liberals too, communism became respectable. It was, for a while, the conscience of the world; and nazism, for those who had a conscience, became a cosmic villainy. The ultimate villainy, indeed. Judgment Day appeared at hand as the world's intellectuals devoted themselves, with singular lack of historical perspective, to disseminating the belief that the final climax of human diabolism had appeared. The effects of this beguilement were long-lasting. Not for thirty years would the last western radicals abandon their sympathy for Soviet communism and move beyond its stuffy dogmas to more daring creeds.

So there were two revolutionary movements in the world, antithetic, and each much strengthened by the diabolistic fears the other generated. Both promised something new and revolutionary in the way of moral and social good. To people who disliked them both, they still seemed to be what an American national hero of limited prophetic powers was later to call Nazi Germany—"the wave of the future." Both exploited the horrors of the Depression; both proffered (despite their militancy) paths to peace as well as prosperity and morality. To a very large extent, both benefited from fashion and publicity. Fascism and communism were enormously rich news sources; they were novel, exciting, and photogenic. People like to commit themselves to mass movements and always have. They also like up-to-date and faddish things and always have. They like a sense of participating in the exercise of power, by conspiratorial meetings and throwing stones at public buildings. They like to wear power's petty trappings—uniforms and badges, and its sado-masochistic emblems—guns and leather belts, and always have. In the world of the thirties, such impulses flourished, heightened by the intense boredom that accompanies poverty as it does affluence.

Events in France precipitated this polar conflict because France was the kingpin of the world political system and yet so divided as to make it seem at once necessary and possible to get control of it. It spread, and helped to paralyze free societies everywhere.

THE BARTHOU POLICY

The immediate result of the riots was Louis Barthou and his robust attempt to rescue peace, and France, from Hitler. The

BARTHOU'S PLAN FOR AN ANTI-GERMAN COALITION

effort was essentially defensive. Barthou planned no adventures. And the strange fate of the policy showed that France was too small and passive a base from which to organize defense of the international order that Hitler was shaking. It needed allies more powerful than itself, whose interests were often incompatible. Most vitally, it needed Britain, and British policy and disposition opposed, although ambiguously, the very measures that France now pursued.

The program upon which Barthou embarked resembled the one that fifteen years later, when applied by the United States to the Soviet Union, was called "containment." It involved a principle as old as time, which after World War I was called the *cordon sanitaire.* It sought to build a diplomatic and defense bloc around Germany. It was hoped to invoke Rumania, Greece, and Turkey as well, thus surrounding *all* the "revisionist" countries, including Hungary and Bulgaria. The task was made more difficult because of the need to add the Soviet Union, which was feared and hated by all the other governments of Europe, especially those of countries on its borders which had profited by its territories in 1918, and by the bumptiousness of Italy. But it was hoped that urgency would prevail over these and other difficulties.

Barthou set out, therefore, with a more coherent and measureable purpose than any other western statesman of the thirties, and he was remarkably successful. His first steps were trips to Warsaw, Prague, Bucharest, and Belgrade, and in these, the capitals of the older French allies, he received encouragement in all save Warsaw, where the Poles were complacently content to rely on their recent nonaggression pact with Germany and extremely unwilling to envisage anything in the way of further commitments to France (which would annoy Hitler) or association with the Soviet Union. But he was encouraged by the favorable attitude in Britain, and by a more or less spontaneous Balkan Treaty that lined up Yugoslavia, Rumania, Greece, and Turkey against Bulgarian restiveness. Then he went to Moscow, where he found a receptive frame of mind.

Things moved quickly. In September 1934 the Soviet Union was received into membership of the League of Nations, with a seat on the Council, which embodied the idea of the directorship of Great Powers. Treaties of mutual assistance—which meant in practice alliance—were negotiated between the Soviets and France and the Soviets and Czechoslovakia. Thus, the Soviet Union was to be integrated rapidly into the system of French security alliances, which was in effect a system of world government that would permit the French to relax.

There remained to arrange a more reliable commitment from Britain and Italy, and to strengthen the connection with Yugoslavia. The king of Yugoslavia, Alexander III, was invited to pay a state visit to France. Barthou met him at Marseilles, and on October 9, 1934, as they drove through the streets, their car was approached by a Croatian terrorist, and they were both shot dead.

The execution of Barthou's policy now fell into less competent and less honest hands. His successor, Pierre Laval, was unscrupulous, and deeply suspicious of the Soviet Union. But he was determined to woo Italy. The Italians were in a mood to be wooed, but they required, as it were, a dowry from France; Laval was prepared to provide it, and by doing so he destroyed the anti-German front.

The background of the disastrous Franco-Italian negotiations was occupied largely by the Austrian Republic, and Italian distrust of Germany's intentions toward it. The Italians had every reason for alarm, even for outrage. In June 1934 Hitler had gone to meet Mussolini in Venice, to the accompaniment of blaring ideological trumpets. To the world, it looked like the fruition of a natural affinity between aggressive dictators, and the publicity confirmed this inference. But actually the meeting had gone rather badly. Mussolini disliked his guest. Not much is known about what they said to each other (Mussolini spoke German, or thought he did, so no interpreters were present; and no minutes were kept). But while Hitler was favorably impressed with Fascist Italy, Mussolini was by no means pleased by what he suspected about Nazi Germany and its expansive tendencies, having in mind not only Austria—he was determined that no great power should be installed on the northern Italian frontier —but also the considerable German population in the Italian province of Alto Adige, which had been taken from Austria in 1918.

Mussolini was not only apprehensive; he was also jealous of Hitler's achievements and fame—a fact that was to play an important part in what happened next. And he had always regarded the Germans as barbarous.

Proof of barbarism was forthcoming a few weeks after the Venice meeting. On the night of June 30—"the night of the long knives"—Hitler disposed of his enemies, and quite a few of his friends, too, by massacre. He caused the murder of the leaders of the Sturm Abteilung—the Storm Troopers, who had helped to bring him to power—along with a number of incidental victims, including the previous chancellor, a scheming general of redoubtable ambition named von Schleicher. But the principal blow was at the Storm Troopers, and it was undertaken among other compelling reasons to assuage the fears of the Army, which (rightly) thought the paramilitary outfit and its unpleasant commander, Ernst Roehm, were planning to substitute the new "people's" army for the old one. The butchery, which was extensive—some careful historians estimate that more than a thousand were killed—did eliminate most potential opposition to the dictatorship, and it removed the principal obstacle to co-operation with the Army. It also made a bad impression on Mussolini.

A much worse impression was made on July 25, 1934, when the Austrian Nazis rose, attempted to seize the government, and murdered the Chancellor (whose wife, as it happened, was at the moment a house guest of Mussolini's). The event seemed to demonstrate very graphically that the Nazis were prepared to go to unconscionable lengths to extend German boundaries to include all German-speaking people.

In fact, the unsuccessful Nazi coup in Austria was probably the work of impulsive Austrians. There seems to have been no direct instigation from Berlin, although there may have been advance knowledge. From the point of view of German-Italian relations, however, it was temporarily catastrophic. The murdered chancellor, Engelbert Dollfuss, had been something in the way of an Italian puppet, and the Italian Legation played a considerable role in advising him (and, when the crisis came, in frustrating the Nazis). The advice had been, for the most part, ill-judged. Dollfuss had been trying to stabilize a troubled and depression-ridden country through a dictatorship based sketchily on the Italian model. The democratic republic which he destroyed had seen the rise of internecine party politics, and the parties were equipped, as in Germany, with paramilitary troops. Dollfuss had dissolved all these but his own. Then, in February, he had dissolved the Austrian Social Democratic Party, which controlled Vienna and had made it a laboratory for daring and salutary social reforms. This was achieved at the cost of a brief, horrifying civil war, which ruined the most powerful group in Austria that was dedicated to Austrian independence. Dollfuss had destroyed, in short, the only possible domestic counterweight to Nazi power.

But a foreign counterweight existed, in the form of Italy, and on this Dollfuss, and his successor, Kurt von Schuschnigg, relied exclusively. The reaction of Mussolini, and the controlled Italian press, after the Dollfuss murder, certainly gave grounds for supposing that Mussolini would never allow Austria to be surrendered to the Germans. Italian papers burst into an anti-German rage, in which the epithet "a nation of pederasts and murderers" was not the least favorable. There was vehement expression of fervent determination to resist German expansion at all costs.

The internal Italian situation was also serious, owing to the Depression and the extreme rigidity of a regime which showed neither imagination nor resource in dealing with it. Unemployment was disastrous. Even if official figures were accepted, one out of seven of the Italian labor force was out of work, and official figures were certainly underestimates. The fact was that Italy's social and economic situation, beneath its paper wrapping that pictured breathtaking innovations, was singularly retrograde. Its program for the Depression had been one of retrenchment; the Fascist government behaved as if the salvation of the Italian lira were more important than the salvation of the Italians. The boiling social troubles that had broken out in France were suppressed in Italy by the iron lid of Fascist party organization, but a regime that based itself on the importance of glory now felt constrained to produce some.

It was with this background that Laval approached Italy.

He was the classical type of French politician who had trod the road from the extreme left to the respectable, slightly corrupt, and very immobile right. He believed in deals; his "fundamental desire was to keep international relations in the realm of . . . subtle negotiation."* He was a "realist," which meant that neither consistency nor honesty seemed to him an expedient component of political manners. He had no sense of the world scene outside of France's borders and needs, any more than he had scruples about other people's territory. In January of 1935, after long conversations between the two governments, he went to Rome to apply himself to the task of completing a Franco-Italian understanding designed to guarantee Germany's containment.

The two governments, both distraught by domestic and foreign problems, seemed to have similar needs, and in a way they did. But there was a fatal difference, unrecognized by either. The French needed safety. The Italians needed both safety and glory, and needed them quickly. It was the difference between a mature but uninspiring regime on the one hand and a new and tinselly one on the other. Laval was met with one major Italian condition for agreement.

Mussolini cherished ambitions for an expanded overseas empire, for a revived Roman empire in fact, and the combination of classical precedents and nineteenth-century lusts led him to insist, as an immediate *hors d'oeuvre* to the meal of glory, upon the consumption of the Empire of Ethiopia. He asked for French support in this venture, and got it.

THE BREAKDOWN OF BARTHOU'S POLICY

The annexation of Ethiopia seemed to many people outside Italy a project not only brutal and untimely but grotesque, and this view was what wrecked the anti-Nazi front and led Mussolini to join hands with a Germany that he disliked and feared. His attempts to get Ethiopia led foreigners to try to outlaw him

---

* David Thomson, *Two Frenchmen: Pierre Laval and Charles de Gaulle* London: Cresset, 1951), p. 51, quoted in George W. Baer, *The Coming of the Italo-Ethiopian War* (Cambridge: Harvard University Press, 1967), p. 70.

as an aggressor, and this attempt led in turn to a German-Italian understanding that undermined all future attempts to "stop Hitler." Italy, whose importance as either an ally or an enemy had always been consistently overrated by everybody in Europe, generated enough of the atmosphere of power to breed exaggerated hopes and fears.

Laval, interested in nothing but Europe and wholly free from any concern for international morality, was not at all opposed to the extension of Italy's influence in eastern Africa, though he may have thought it silly. But he may have been enough of a Frenchman to understand the subtle but powerful historical drives that led the Italian dictator to become dedicated to a project that to most people appeared gratuitous.

The reason for the Italian interest in Ethiopia was one that could scarcely be understood by non-Italians. The young kingdom of Italy had established itself on the fringes of Ethiopia— a disorganized and highly fluid state without defined frontiers— in the 1870s and 1880s. In the 1890s it had judged that an assault upon the Ethiopian empire would lead to its disintegration and the establishment of an Italian colony in most, or all, of its territory. Instead, it was found that the heartland of Ethiopia had great cohesiveness and something like a Western national consciousness. An Italian army was slaughtered in 1896 at Adowa, which became the first successful attempt of a non-European people to stem and reverse the onward movement toward Europeans' world control. The incident had been traumatic; it horrified the adolescent Mussolini, for example, and seems to have impressed many Italians with an ineradicable need transcending generations to prove their national manhood by erasing this "scar"—the word was used by the most flamboyant of Italian nationalists, d'Annunzio. For forty years, successive Italian governments had sporadically schemed and dreamed, but without effective action.

By 1933 several urgent preoccupations coincided. Pushed by a friend, an elderly general named Emilio de Bono, who apparently wanted a war with Ethiopia for the sole purpose of giving himself personal prestige as its commander, Mussolini began seriously to toy with the idea of seeking the necessary glory through the obliteration of the scar of Adowa. Rather desultory military preparations were commenced in 1934. In December of that year, before they were ready, or even before Mussolini had made up his mind, an incident took place in the good old way. The Italians had several years earlier occupied an oasis called Wal Wal, in the appalling desert of southeastern Ethiopia. The Ethiopians felt it necessary to assert their sovereignty. They attacked the Italian force and were driven off. Then the Emperor of Ethiopia, Haile Selassie I, one of a series of remarkable men whom his dynasty had produced, appealed to the League of Nations over the heads, as it were, of the Great Powers. The Italians made up their minds for war and hastened their preparations.

It was at this juncture that Laval had arrived in Rome. His meeting with Mussolini was a diplomatic success; indeed, it was a triumph. He got everything he wanted from Mussolini: agreement to join France in action to prevent further German rearmament and assure Germany's containment; agreement to maintain Austrian independence at all costs, and to collaborate with the Little Entente—Czechoslovakia, Yugoslavia, and Rumania—in doing it; surrender of the ancient and passionate Italian claims on Tunisia, which the French had seized from under the Italian nose in 1881. In return he gave up nothing that concerned France, apart from a slice of unattractive Sahara; the rest that he gave was given secretly. He agreed to Italian predominance in Austria. And he agreed to let Italy have a free hand in Ethiopia. This was arranged at a private conversation after a dinner party, and the exact terms of the bargain are unknown. It is clear, though, that while Laval probably did not explicitly approve an aggressive war against Ethiopia, he did agree to let Italy get control over it.

Seen as traditional diplomatic maneuvering, the agreement of January 6, 1935, was the high point of French diplomacy and hopes for the safety of the countries around Germany and the existing order in Europe. In pre-1914 terms, it was a masterpiece. But if peace meant gradual change through negotiation, respect for the independence of small powers, and support of the League, aggression in Africa was as bad as aggression in Europe.

It is conceivable that either point of view would have been successful in saving the world from another great war if it had been consistently translated into policy; but the two were irreconcilable, and the conflict between them was to erupt into paralyzing violence in Britain and France in the next year. Ethiopia's victory in 1896 had begun the erosion of Europe's poise. In 1935, Ethiopia's defeat completed it.

The breakdown progressed rapidly after one brief, misleading, final success for the anti-German coalition.

On March 9, 1935, the German government informed the other signatories of the Treaty of Versailles that a German air force, explicitly outlawed by the treaty, was already in existence. On March 16, the introduction of military conscription in Germany, similarly outlawed, was announced. The very contingency the containment policy was supposed to prevent had now occurred; Hitler was exploding the whole legal and material basis of the European order. In April, the Italians, French, and British met at the Italian mountain resort of Stresa and jointly issued a denunciation and a warning to Germany, and a solemn reaffirmation of the Locarno treaties. This was followed by stern reproaches for unilateral treaty-breaking by the League and, a little later, by the significantly timed signature of the Soviet guarantee treaties with France and Czechoslovakia. It looked as if the anti-German coalition were working, and the term "Stresa Front" became fashionable to describe its solidity.

But in fact it wasn't working at all. The reaction to Germany's announcement that it was going to disregard its treaty obligation should have been stronger, if containment was to mean anything. The reasons it wasn't were manifold. One was Hitler's ingenuity. He had chosen a good point on which to make an issue, for this was in both senses a *fait accompli:* everybody knew that German rearmament had already begun and had progressed to a point unknown but considerable; and everybody knew that it was impossible, short of invasion, to force a national leader to contradict himself on a point of national policy once he had publicly announced it. Nobody was prepared to invade Germany to restore as a legality something which they had already conceded as a fact. Once again, Hitler seemed to be doing nothing more than trumpeting a reassertion of national sovereignty, and once again his big stick was accompanied by soft words of enthusiasm for peace.

On May 21, he made a long speech about his devotion to peace, including emphatic assertions that he intended to observe the Locarno treaties and that he had no intention of interfering with Austrian independence. He specifically promised that German rearmament would be limited to "parity" and would offer no threat to his neighbors, and he offered to negotiate a naval treaty with Britain assuring Britain's paramountcy on the sea. All this made it difficult for the Powers to take decisive action of any sort; they themselves would have become aggressors. Initiative of any sort, especially aggressive initiative, was difficult for them. And it strengthened the hand of those, particularly in Britain, who thought Hitler's promises were genuine and that the path to peace lay through rectifying old wrongs and conciliating malcontents.

The British, their foreign policy still mainly in the hands of the Foreign Minister, Sir John Simon, had already shown ideas divergent from those of the French. They had in principle agreed repeatedly with the French program, and had indeed sent Eden, early in 1935, on European tours similar to those of Barthou and Laval. But what he was supposed to do was to change the containment policy into a general security system based on consent and treaties which would *include* Germany. The British aim was to extend the Locarno principle to every frontier in Europe, in particular those of Poland, which would be guaranteed by everybody. If Germany could be induced to accept such a principle, then (Sir John Simon reasoned) it would be unnecessary to worry about German rearmament, or about Hitler's periodic rantings about German destiny, or indeed anything else except the painstaking negotiation of further, supplementary treaties, for regulating armaments, commerce, international arbitration, and so on. The objective, often called the "eastern Locarno," was more general. It was a vision of general peace and security in Europe and (although Simon did not recognize the rest of the world in any substantial degree) the planet.

There were several things wrong with this, some of them inherent contradictions. The most important was that it was based on the erroneous assumption that Hitler regarded treaties in the same way that Simon did. It disregarded the fact, which he did not know but might have suspected, that the most important ingredient of German policy from times long before Hitler was the drastic alteration of the very frontiers which Simon hoped to lure him into solemnly guaranteeing. The "eastern Locarno" reflected a passivity which precluded its enforcement. It was also a vision incompatible with and disruptive of the French policy of encirclement, although they looked and sounded harmonious enough, and the French had agreed to support Simon's effort. Even if Germany had had the conversable and dependable government Simon hoped, to bring Germany into a European security system voluntarily would inevitably mean making concessions; and concessions were, in the last analysis, what French reflexes and French policy were designed to prevent.

And there was a more subtle weakness which was more intractable because it involved Sir John's personality and position. He had been installed in office, and left largely to his own devices in policy-making, because he could be counted on to keep things quiet while British recovery policies took effect. This fact, which harmonized with his own insular and rather complacent nature, showed itself in a particular kind of self-deception which was later graphically, if unknowingly, revealed in his memoirs. It is conceivable, as he thought, that Hitler might have been indefinitely prevented from moving to action from words about Germany's destiny and need for more territory; but this could have been assured only by some sort of balance of military power. It would have been true even if Hitler had not been so totally incapable of regarding his own solemn promises as anything more than words carelessly uttered for momentary purposes, since Germany had become again a Great Power in a world of Great Powers, where the intrinsic pressures of power pushing eternally outward could only be bound by initiative backed by perceptions of danger and expediency. And Simon was, above all things, unwilling to accept the imperatives of rearming Britain. It would cost too much. He later said that it couldn't be done because the Labour Party would have opposed it, and might have displaced the National Government on the issue, and charged Labour with something like treason as a result. But he acceded in this political competition to exploit the British voters' aversion to arms. He thought that "recovery" must take precedence and this confirmed the illusion that treaties could be substituted for airplanes, which cost more.

This state of mind, widely shared in London, was reflected in the events that followed Hitler's speech. It was leapt upon as providing a good beginning for the establishment of a general security system based on treaties, and negotiations were begun between the Germans and the British—the French were, inexcusably, not informed—for a German-British naval treaty. It was signed on June 18, 1935, and provided for a balance of naval forces on the ratio of three British units to one German. This was seen by Simon as a personal triumph, since it promised the indefinite superiority of Britain at no financial cost, while at the same time luring the Germans into accepting a new and reasonable restriction, freely negotiated, to replace the unenforceable and unfair disarmament clauses of the Versailles Treaty.

The French were completely taken by surprise, and they were outraged. In some measure the reaction was unreasonable. The French were almost as reluctant as the British to embark on an expensive program of rearmament, and indeed the British government's public pronouncement on its defense policy, on March 4, had been a good deal more vigorous than anything the French had said. But now they said that Britain's action was immoral and unacceptable. The French press was violent, and Laval was furious. Eden, a sort of high-level sales agent, was sent to pacify him, and confronted the entirely reasonable complaint that whatever the justification for the British negotiation with Hitler, the fact that it had been conducted without informing France was deeply troubling.

French policy had to depend on the co-operation of Britain, but Franco-British relations suffered seriously.

ETHIOPIA

The Mussolini-Laval agreement had laid the basis for Franco-Italian friendship, amounting to alliance, which flourished rapidly in the months that followed. Stresa was not its only consequence. Air and military conventions were reached between the two powers, and a quite unprecedented cordiality developed between two countries whose relations had been, at best, sullen. Laval was hysterically applauded by Fascist crowds when he went to Stresa. The French had succeeded almost too well in completing their iron circle around Germany. They rapidly became dependent upon Italy, as they had always been dependent upon Great Britain.

After January, plans for the war in Ethiopia proceeded rapidly. Once begun, they were difficult to reverse, for the mobilization of the Italian forces soon began to have exactly the effect that Mussolini had hoped. It provided a concealed and politically acceptable form of inflation; the expansion of the army reduced unemployment. Ethiopia itself held no economic attractions whatever for Italy, despite flamboyant assertions that Space was indispensable for a vigorous people. The propagandists talked in terms of lands for settlers from the crowded homeland, and of vast resources. But almost no Italians had chosen to go to the existing east African colonies, no Italian capital was available to exploit the conjectural natural wealth, and no Italian business concerns of any consequence were interested in Ethiopia. Still, the favorable economic results of military activity made it far more dangerous to abandon the quest for glory than it would have been to avoid it in the first place.

The only power that could have stopped it was Britain, and then only at an early stage. Mussolini was aware of this. On January 29, he had vaguely and preliminarily sounded out the British and gotten no reply at all. Simon, in keeping with his policy of keeping things quiet, which meant letting aggressors have their way, as he had done with Japan and Germany, was personally strongly inclined to let the Italians do what they wanted in Africa. Realizing Italy's intentions, he also realized that the British public would strongly oppose another affront to the League. He therefore made *no reply at all* to Mussolini's canvassing of British opinion. And the Italians got no clearer indication of British policy when the case was argued before the League, where Ethiopia pressed its grievances concerning the southeastern border and the Wal Wal Incident. The Italians were determined to keep the League from discussing it, the Ethiopians determined that it be discussed. The British held the ultimate power of decision at Geneva, and they supported compromises, arbitration, evasion, which did not strengthen the League or relieve Ethiopia but did mislead Mussolini.

The one real effect of the League debates had been to interest British public opinion, and to spread enthusiasm not only for the cause of the Ethiopians but for the League itself. The situation illuminated two facts which few realized: the League, as a world organization was not an entity in itself but merely the sum of national delegations—it could not save the world from Mussolini's imperial ambitions; but it was sufficiently influential to affect decisively the relations of European powers by involving the destiny of a small African state. Before 1914, the idea of a *world* system had had no reality. Now it did, but in ways incipient and inchoate.

There were, to be sure, people in Britain who had a clear notion of what ought to be done. One was Robert Vansittart, the Permanent Undersecretary of the Foreign Office—that is, its highest civil servant and administrative officer. Vansittart believed the central threat to peace and to British security came from Germany, and that the one thing that really mattered was to stop Hitler. He thought Italian aggression in Ethiopia was of a very different order of importance from the aggression that Germany might be expected to undertake. The one was romantically, although brutally, old-fashioned; it would, if successful, have no real effect on world politics. The other would destroy world peace and might destroy Europe, and Britain's independence. This was essentially the French, the *European,* view of world affairs. He therefore, like Laval, was prepared to buy Italian friendship by countenancing its egregious wickedness. But Vansittart had no decisive influence on the cabinet. For one thing, his position seemed (and was) immoral. For another, his was a singularly angular personality and he had always seemed (and was) irrationally obsessed by just the kind of wild hatred of Germany that engendered vindictiveness instead of peace in international relations.

The tide of public opinion was running much more in the direction of another but less bloody-minded dissenter. Anthony Eden's line, or at least the atmosphere he generated, was deemed neither so antithetic to the cabinet nor so dangerously vindictive as Vansittart's. Instead he appeared to be a youthful idealist dedicated to the League of Nations and to the principles of international morality and co-operation. His presence in the government seemed its strongest guarantee of respectability in progressive circles, and since the government was facing an election, this was important.

Eden was a sincere if rather ambitious and naive young man. He was also intelligent, although not very profound in his judgments. Very much a member of the ruling class and subject to their tradition, he had risen rapidly above the somewhat stodgy professional diplomatists. He did his best to try to sort out the conflicts between the evasive lassitude of his chiefs (MacDonald, Baldwin, Simon, and Sir Samuel Hoare), the bleak realities that he occasionally noticed, the genteel principles to which he was devoted, and the professional techniques required of him as a trained diplomatist. He tried it, with diminishing success, for a long time. It was not for three and a half years more, after the Ethiopian affair became a crisis, and after he had become Foreign Minister, that he concluded that his personal beliefs and purposes were hopelessly in conflict with the official purposes of the prime ministers and foreign secretaries he worked with.

The Foreign Minister after June 1935, when Simon was transferred to the Home Office, was Sir Samuel Hoare. His appointment was a peculiarly illuminating sample of the difficulty of trying to make world policy in the twentieth century with the cozy, cousinly, political practices of the nineteenth. Hoare was a gentleman, a Harrow and Oxford man known and liked by all his friends and relatives (who were the government of Great Britain). He had served in the Cabinet before and was, in the French term, eminently "ministrable." He had since 1931 been

Secretary of State for India and had worked himself into a decline in that exacting office. To him, depressed, exhausted, in ill health, his friends in the government offered the Foreign Office —insisted, indeed, that he take it, although he demurred—because they thought it would cheer him up. He knew little about Europe or diplomacy, but it was thought that the honor of being Foreign Secretary would reward his labors and assuage his melancholy.

Eden was of the same class, but he was a younger man, with experience in diplomatic affairs and a very different temperament. One thing that helped make popular the principles he seemed to represent was simply his freshness. But the principles coincided with a deep and politically important combination of currents in British life. The most basic was the notion of "decency," the diluted ebb tide of the Protestant ethic, which meant not the opposite of indecency, but aloofness from subtlety, single-mindedness, cruelty, or force. A "decent" foreign policy meant respect for foreigners, candor, and aversion from precisely such Byzantine rejection of ethical considerations as Laval was so notably guilty of.

There were more specific elements in the pro-League attitude of Eden which struck chords in national opinion. There was, for example, the legacy of the Labour Party, which represented a much wider section of opinion than merely its own constituents. This was quasi-pacifist and very high-minded, and was again affected by evangelical influences as well as by Karl Marx. The "Labour tropism," if one may call it that to suggest a series of general attitudes not consistently held in or out of the Party, arose from the vague feeling that a foreign policy dedicated to national purposes was "selfish," as opposed to one dedicated to the support of international organizations like the League. It was fortified by the feeling that capitalists liked armaments and even war, and that arms races were dangerous. It was further fortified by an economic theory, held to embody self-evident truths, that money spent on arms was money wasted, and must be subtracted from money spent on more worthy purposes, thus impoverishing the workers—a theory that was in the process of being disproved in Germany, and would be even more specifically disproved in

Britain a year or two later. The tropism included, very emphatically, the certainty that international relations must be founded on morality, and that aggression, the supreme expression of immorality, must be prevented or punished.

All these notions, coalescing, had provided the Labour Party with a platform that asserted vigorously that nationalistic policies and rearmament were dangerous frauds whose principal victims were the defenseless ordinary people of the world. As the developing disarray of world affairs intruded on British consciousness, the tropism became more and more evident. The League of Nations Union, a nonpartisan and highly respectable organization, sent out in the winter of 1934–35 a questionnaire asking five questions about basic issues in foreign policy. The results were announced in June 1935. More than eleven million people had replied, and by better than thirty to one they answered affirmatively the question, "Should Great Britain remain a member of the League of Nations?" Almost twenty to one they agreed that the League ought to use economic measures to stop aggression, and by more than two to one they supported "if necessary, military measures." The other three questions, relating to disarmament, produced five to one majorities in favor of it—by international agreement. The general flavor of the questions, and the public interpretation of them, was that an affirmative vote was a vote for peace against the fusty war-mongering of tradition-bound conservatives.

The Peace Ballot, as it was called, was undoubtedly impressive quantitatively, and, to people who saw the issue as "peace, decency and the League versus nationalism and rearmament," qualitatively as well. But in point of fact what was shown was a well-intentioned confusion on the part of those who answered. A quarter of the people who liked the League didn't want to have it use force to stop aggression. The innocence of this position was made apparent by the vote in favor of international disarmament which showed, at best, a pious wish that Hitler would go away. It seemed likely, as Eden himself observed, that many of those who did support military measures against aggressors did not understand that the burden of them would fall largely on Britain. In other words, action against the aggressor, whether by the

League or by Britain as an act of national policy, would involve a major British effort and would require a strong defense policy, and this many Britons could not accept.

The reaction of most of the Cabinet to the Peace Ballot was one of distress and annoyance. They felt the Ballot confused the issue, which it certainly did, and that it confirmed the alarm they had felt for some time when a by-election in London, two years earlier, had returned a pacifist Labourite in a normally safe Conservative district. Simon had been succeeded by Hoare, and Baldwin had replaced MacDonald just before the Peace Ballot results were announced. They were no more inclined than their predecessors to support League action that might lead to war, and they found the confused development of opinion to be mischievous. Reservations arose, too, from concern about overseas reactions. The ministers believed that Great Britain could not participate in any major military operation, such as League action against Italy might well turn into, without certainty of full support from the Dominions, which they were sure they could not count on.

They were wrong in their premises; Italy was a good deal weaker than they imagined. Hoare, on taking office, was sincerely frightened by the thought, which was absurd, that Italy might beat Britain in a naval war. But the calculation was, in a larger sense, an indication of the basic fact of world politics: Europe was trying to govern the world and had not enough power to do so.

The development of a strong public sentiment still had its effect—not in the way of determining the government to throttle Italy, but rather in the way of obliging it to seem to support the League. This, with increasingly vocal although still reticent policies, it did, throughout the summer and autumn. At the same time, it forced withdrawal from the moderately advanced position the government had taken on the need for rearmament in March. In the summer of 1935, alarmed by the possibility that the next election might go against them, intimidated, as it were, by public opinion and a Labour Party which seemed to be in harmony with it, the ministers were driven into the position of following the confusing precepts of the Peace Ballot.

They hoped for compromise. They hoped by tact to prevent an open split with France, which by the end of June was still supporting Italy and still fuming with outrage at the Naval Treaty. They believed that Italy's "traditional friendship" and fear of German expansion in Austria would prevent the Italians from going too far. What they did not know was that Mussolini was now hopelessly committed and was already, as early as mid-May, when the British support of Ethiopia in the League was noticeably hardening, beginning to adopt two fatal policies. One was to exploit, rather than to surrender to, Britain's opposition. The Ethiopian venture—still in the preparatory stage—was presented as a national crusade against the ancient and insufferable tutelage of Britain, a kind of Italian declaration of independence and greatness, and this did indeed begin to evoke a certain enthusiasm from some Italian opinion, hitherto apathetic about the horrid misconduct ascribed to the Ethiopians. Secondly, he began to try to patch up relations with Germany. Within a month after the proclamation at Stresa, Hitler found to his satisfaction that Mussolini was showing signs of giving up the role of keystone in the arch of German containment, to become a friend and comrade of Hitler's, in return for support of his policy in Africa. Hitler, cautious, nonetheless encouraged so welcome a development.

The lines were now laid down. The Italians and the Germans were beginning to draw together. The French and the British were drawing apart. The program of Barthou and Laval had been wrecked. Italy would go ahead, and Britain would berate it without stopping it. The remainder of the soggy saga was horribly prolonged, but nothing that happened changed the directions that existed in July. The League debates and negotiations dragged on. The British tried to buy peace by offering Italy some Ethiopian territory and giving Ethiopia some land in an adjoining British colony. The Ethiopians urged League measures to keep the peace, the Italians eluded them. In early October, the invasion began. It proceeded remarkably slowly, and not until the next year was substantial progress made against the forces of a thoroughly undeveloped state, one which Mussolini had said was falling into anarchy and civil war.

The slowness of the Italian Army (in all fairness, the terrain was impossible) aggravated a situation already very bad. The League of Nations, having stirred up much interest and feeling on behalf of its own efforts to save peace, immediately labeled Italy an outlaw when the invasion began (almost no one but the Italian delegate voted against the resolution). Then, at the instance of Britain and with the exceedingly unwilling compliance of France, sanctions were voted. This was the first time that international action had been taken to stop an aggressor that was a major power, and their adoption conciliated opinion in Britain about the intentions of the government. Considerable enthusiasm was generated. But the sanctions consisted of embargos of exports to Italy that Italy did not actually require. There were, in the first place, to be no military measures or suggestion of them. There was to be no embargo on oil—on the theoretical grounds that it would be ineffective anyway, since most oil resources were controlled by powers like the United States that were not League members (although the United States had shown some small indications of a willingness to co-operate). Exports of capital and of coal were outlawed, but these would not have an immediate or decisive effect on the Italian war effort. A stoppage of oil shipments would have. And the British never even considered closing the Suez Canal, which would have stopped Italy instantly. They feared Italy might attack British naval bases.

The fact was that the British were consciously decided not to take any action that would lead to war; and they hoped to avoid any action that would lead to the permanent estrangement of Mussolini—which meant, of course, any action that would effectively restrain him. Although the League had declared him a criminal, with Britain's delegate concurring, they hoped that he might be lured back into a co-operative attitude. In this they were much affected by the attitude of France, whose government found itself in the position of being simultaneously dependent on two incompatible friends. France was obliged to go through the motions at Geneva; for one thing, a large and increasing portion of French leftist opinion shared the British enthusiasm for League action. (The French faced elections too, although not for some months.) But Laval acted reluctantly and with reservations. He, too, still hoped to save the Italian alliance.

Behind British policy lay the General Election—the last to be held before the end of the Second World War—which took place on November 14, 1935. The National Government was obliged by law to hold elections before September 1936, but it could choose its time, and it chose well. Baldwin, a hearty fellow with a languid intellect, was temperamentally disposed to avoid boat-rocking; he was essentially a believer in negative action, but he was skilled at projecting a picture of safe and solid and shrewd English earthiness, and he was astute in his judgments on politics. He led a campaign based on the progress achieved since 1931 in recovery—it was, indeed, fairly impressive. Unemployment had been reduced, and trade, production, and housing, among other mild social reforms, had improved. He suggested, by inference, that the spirited rearmament program announced the previous March had been abandoned. And most especially, he and all the supporters of the National Government—by now overwhelmingly and almost overtly a Conservative government—were obliged to proclaim themselves the defenders of the League, of international morality, and of peace. Sanctions had just been adopted; the Italian aggression seemed to be bogged down; the popularity of the League was at an all-time high. The Conservatives, in short, pulled over themselves the cloak of precisely those opinions which the Peace Ballot had suggested were the dominant ones in British opinion.

It was an unconscionable, if partly unconscious, fraud, but it largely succeeded. A Conservative House of Commons was returned; the government lost seats, but it still had a majority of almost 300. The Labour Party gained—from 46 to 154 seats—but it was still far from winning. It had suffered from weakness of leadership. Above a second rank of able but somewhat fractious leaders, it had until recently been presided over by a very old and sick man, already marked for senility and death, who had been installed because he was a hero of the working classes and unions. He was George Lansbury, a doctrinaire and emotional pacifist who had held the Party to its intransigent, indeed vituperative, hostility to building up Britain's defenses. The Party

had found most of its electoral thunder stolen by the Conservatives; having been, for years, *the* supporters of the League and
peace, they now found that platform pre-empted.

As a result they suffered electorally, and faced a new House
whose membership was as conservative—as capitalistic, it might
be said—as any in history, and one in which friends of the Prime
Minister and his Chancellor of the Exchequer, a Birmingham
businessman of high ability, Neville Chamberlain, predomi-
nated. The friendship was political in most cases—the Commons
would resolutely support anything the government leaders did—
and in some cases ideological. They shared a passionate aversion
to boat-rocking, and to irritating Hitler.

With the election fought and won, the diplomatic situation
changed at once. It no longer seemed necessary to worry about
pleasing the electorate; what the government, notably the Foreign Minister, Sir Samuel Hoare, felt it prudent to do could now
be done. Indeed, throughout the autumn, at the time sanctions
were being adopted and unwillingly applied, conversations had
continued with the French about the possibility of making some
deal that would satisfy the Italians, ensure their gratitude, and
at the same time save something for the Ethiopians. These were
of necessity very secret, and their existence was not known until
many years later. They show a much greater consistency of
policy from the early days of 1935 when Britain had evaded a
commitment either to approve or disapprove the Italian venture
but had tried to bring it into the realm of diplomatic negotiation,
to the day in late December when Hoare and Laval, meeting
quietly in Paris, finally worked out agreement on a proposal to
be made to Italy. This provided that Italy occupy and annex half
of Ethiopia, but that the capital and the "heartland" of the
country should survive with a nominally independent government. This went beyond anything the British Cabinet had previously discussed, but it was not far out of line with the general
principles they had agreed on. The communiqué publicly issued
merely affirmed that the French and British had reached agreement on a formula for peace that they expected would be acceptable to the League.

The British cabinet (without Hoare, who had gone on to

Switzerland for a much-needed rest) rather reluctantly agreed to present the project to Haile Selassie and to Mussolini for their consideration. But the press had gotten hold of the story, and there was violent criticism in London. There was even more violent criticism in Geneva, where a sense of betrayal and danger convulsed the smaller European nations. The House of Commons, when it met, reflected the popular mood, and while Laval was still raging because the British had failed to back him up in his bid to save the friendship with Italy, Sir Samuel Hoare resigned, on December 18, and Anthony Eden was appointed to replace him. Once more the British government had adapted itself to the requirements not of policy but of politics.

The Hoare-Laval scheme, if the British had had the guts to prosecute the cynical course to its logical conclusion, might have worked. There is some indication that Italy might have considered it, and Ethiopia could have been coerced into accepting it. As a policy consistently followed in public, it might have survived the outburst of anger in London and Geneva. The clincher in the arguments of opponents was not really cynicism, but betrayal. Having conceded half a loaf to public opinion, the government could not then announce that it had really been intending all along that public opinion should starve.

Mussolini proceeded with his war and rapidly began to win it. The Germans, who had been cautious in approving him, and had indeed maintained an embargo on exports to both belligerents, had continued to show signs of increasing willingness to consider him a friend. Most Germans had no great faith in Italian military prowess. Most Germans remembered with extreme bitterness that Italy, their ally, had joined their enemies in 1915. But Hitler had always felt a strong affinity for the man who was, in some respects, his ideological schoolmaster, even though his feeling had not hitherto been reciprocated; after the failure of the last effort to save Mussolini for the anti-German cause, there was every reason for Hitler to cultivate him more eagerly for the pro-German one. Mussolini, now isolated from his old allies and embattled, was imprisoned in his own strident propaganda against Britain. In dispirited Geneva, it was agreed that sanctions could not be enforced.

Hitler's opponents were divided; the powers that had agreed to enforce the demilitarization of the Rhineland at Locarno were in full disarray. The last of the guarantees on which French security had been constructed was about to go down.

6

The Germans Move Toward Conquest

On February 27, 1936, ratification of the Franco-Soviet alliance was voted by the French Chamber of Deputies. It had been a long time in coming to a vote—it was almost two years since it had first been conceived, almost a year since it had been signed, and it had yet to be approved by the Senate. Laval had dragged his feet, giving rise to doubts and irritation in Moscow. The original purpose of the alliance was by now obsolete, for it had been seen as part of the general "front" against Nazi Germany.

But it had acquired, through attrition, a new meaning. It had been changed into a revived version of the Franco-Russian alliance of 1894. With Italy lost to the Front, 1936 began to look on the maps something like 1914—a Franco-Russian alliance joined to a friendly understanding with Great Britain and balancing German power supported by friends in central Europe and a link with Italy. But this appearance, while it comforted some Frenchmen, was in important ways misleading. Attitudes were quite different—the French, for example, had no Alsace-Lorraine to retrieve now, no vengeance to wreak, and no national will to do so. And the new regimes of Europe, Communist or Fascist, operated in ways entirely different from any in 1914, which had more or less shared the same kinds of morality and wickedness. This was the biggest difference: while Soviet Russia acted in some ways like a national state, despite the internal similarities and the continuity of national interests that linked Imperial and Soviet Russia there now existed a world-wide Communist movement, and the long and ramified antennae of Soviet power were dedicated to building the Popular Front against fascism. The diplomatic front had been ruined; the new ideological Popular Front seemed to be taking its place.

This difference conservative people clearly perceived. The Franco-Russian alliance was coolly regarded by the London government. In France, however, the left had brought down the Laval Cabinet in January 1935 because of its inclination to appease Italian fascism and its shuffling disinclination to support the League or execute the Soviet alliance. A caretaker government tolerated by the left submitted the alliance to parliament.

Hitler had long warned that he would regard the alliance, if it ever came into existence, as a threat—a deliberate and intentional threat—to Germany. The previous May, he had said the alliance would bring "an element of legal insecurity" into the Locarno treaties. In December of the same year he told Sir Eric Phipps, the British ambassador at Berlin, that the pending alliance had decided him to end all conversations for the Western Air Pact, which the British and French had earlier proposed to limit the expansion of air forces. There were other warnings. But warnings and threats were, as usual, ambiguous, and blended with assertions of devotion to peace. A week before the ratification, the Chancellor told a French correspondent that he had always been deeply devoted to France and the cause of Franco-German friendship, and that he had long looked forward to an eventual close understanding between the two countries.

On March 7, he reacted to the Chamber's ratification of the alliance. German troops entered the Rhineland region whose demilitarization had been provided for at Versailles and Locarno, and Hitler explained in a dramatic speech that the Franco-Russian alliance had invalidated the Locarno treaties (it was not a violation of them in any technical way, but psychologically the point had some merit, for Locarno had evidenced French faith in the possibility of a stable and friendly Germany, and the alliance evidenced the reverse). He also announced that now that he had reasserted German sovereignty over its own territory, he would be delighted to discuss a general settlement and Germany's re-entry into a reformed League of Nations. He proposed a new demilitarized zone, including French and Belgian territory as well as German and thus compatible with German sovereignty and dignity, and a lot of new nonaggression pacts.

THE IMPACT OF THE RHINELAND

It might have been—and indeed was—observed that Hitler's action changed very little. The demilitarized zone had been a sort of buffer for France; it protected the French frontier from surprise attack and, more importantly, provided an area through which French forces could advance to the heart of Germany without resistance. It was a built-in east-bound invasion road, as it had been intended to be. But in fact the road was impassable, for the French had lost the power to travel it. It was not so much a question of moral (or military) limpness as of moral (and military) feasibility. The French, like the British, had based their defense of the existing order on the principles of good manners, respect for other people's territories, avoidance of force. In the last analysis, they based them only on defense of their own borders. The universal and quite damaging excoriation of world opinion that had greeted France's Ruhr episode showed that any punitive expedition, even if entirely justified by law, would invoke dangerous reactions in Germany while placing France in the insupportable position of an aggressor before world opinion. So far as providing a convenient way to fight preventive wars or to conduct preventive operations went, the Rhineland zone was no longer important because preventive action had become self-defeating.

The contribution of the Rhineland to the defense of France should war break out was another matter; in that situation its strategic significance had to be determined by weighing the balance of power. But there, too, its importance was less than it had once been. If Germany became overwhelmingly strong, a few score miles of border land would not mean much, especially with the development of air power; if Germany were weak, it would not mean much either, since France would be able to cut through the German defenses.

But strategic realities, even to those who misjudged them (and many anti-Nazi people in the world did) were less important than what the Rhineland action showed about Hitler's methods and intentions. The most solemn treaty, entered into freely by the German Republic (in contrast to Versailles which, as Hitler kept saying, was a "dictated treaty") had been stunningly, suddenly, inexcusably violated. It had been the model for many workers for peace; it was associated with the whole sunny legend of "peace for our time" that had flourished in the later twenties. Spiritually, if not militarily, it was judged to be the cornerstone of France's safety. And—this was perhaps the most important of its effects on people who were not sympathetic to the new Germany—it suggested ineffable duplicity on Hitler's part. And it suggested, too, what rapidly became a myth and then a creed, a sinister timetable, a blueprint for world dominion. Hitler's hammer blows—the withdrawal from the League and the disarmament conference, the Polish Pact, the unsuccessful coup in Austria, the denunciation of the Versailles disarmament clauses, the Rhineland invasion, seemed to come at intervals so regular as to leave little doubt in the minds of many sensitive anti-Nazis throughout the world that everything had been planned from the beginning. The fact that Hitler was being remarkably successful in bringing off his outrages suggested not only planning but invincibility. There began to emerge the picture of an irresistible mastermind, and this was to play its role in the future. The Rhineland not only outraged his opponents; it also paralyzed some of them. Many who most feared Hitler supported the efforts of those who felt he could be negotiated with as a reasonable man simply because they feared he was indomitable.

All the facts were against this interpretation, but some of the crucial facts were not known. It was ignorance of them that

largely shaped the reaction of the French and British governments to the Rhineland invasion. Ignorance and fear were to be
decisive factors in shaping western attitudes in the next few
years, and it is worth exploring their nature and sources.

It is not perfectly clear what happened in London and Paris
when the message reached the governments that German forces
were entering the demilitarized region. They were certainly both
surprised and shocked, but their surprise was not nearly as great
as that of the public. They had suspected that something like this
might happen, in view of the ragings in the German press about
the incompatibility of Locarno and the French-Soviet alliance.
It had been discussed, rather desultorily, by the new French
Foreign Minister, Flandin, with Eden in late January. The very
desultoriness had formed, in a way, a commitment; Eden formed
the impression that Flandin was not seriously considering immediate resistance if the Germans acted. But nobody expected
the *fait accompli.* It is hard to see why they didn't, except that
they still reacted to Hitler as a congregation might react to a
drunken gunman in a church. They couldn't believe he would do
it. Until 1939, they never did.

The reactions in London were decisive—or would have been
if there had been anything left to decide. As it was, they were
illuminating. That morning, after Eden had received the German
ambassador who brought him the news, Baldwin said (and Eden
agreed) that *(a)* Britain would certainly not give military support
if the French reacted with force, and *(b)* France must be discouraged from reacting with force.* *(a)* was enough to secure
(b). This reaction was natural enough, quite aside from the current lack of Franco-Anglo cordiality. It fitted in with Baldwin's
insular reflexes. He rarely took positions on foreign affairs except
to try to keep them foreign. It also fitted in with the whole
tradition of British policy, an aloof and elegant substitution of
conversation and negotiation for substantial action. So Sir Edward Grey, Eden's prototype, had reacted in 1914.

The second set of reactions in Britain was more peculiar.
Opinion in general was confirmed in its belief that Hitler was an
irresponsible monster; but there was a concurrent feeling that

*Anthony Eden, *Facing the Dictators* (Boston: Houghton Mifflin, 1962), p. 385.

Hitler was only occupying Germany's own territory and that this was fair enough. Britain's civic morality cut both ways. Hitler was immoral; but Germany had been immorally treated, and the wrong done her must be rectified. And, as Eden told the Commons, the German action implied no threat of hostilities and therefore need not cause immediate concern. There was, moreover, distrust of France. Such views reflected both popular and official judgments, including that of the Labour Party, that everything must be done pacifically and calmly through the League of Nations. (Only three of the seven major nations of the world— France, Britain, and the Soviet Union—were still in the League. If it still meant anything at all, it meant not a world organization but an awkward form of alliance among them.) An even more striking and portentous appraisal of the situation appeared in the London *Times,* a newspaper that combined the dignity of a pulpit with the influence of a rabble-rouser. *The Times,* much encouraged by Hitler's promises of new Leagues, new nonaggression pacts, and new demilitarized zones, entitled its editorial "A Chance to Rebuild." It sympathetically viewed Hitler's fears of encirclement by Franco-Bolshevism and his desire to restore full nationhood in the Rhineland.

The Times was a most conspicuous monument of a gradually agglomerating body of opinion that was to acquire the label of "appeasement," a word which until then had meant nothing more than bringing peace. The morphology of this body of opinion will be considered in the next chapter. Here it is sufficient to note that it was taking definite and influential shape. But it was not, then or later, the most significant of the varying kinds of reaction to German initiative. The third and most interesting response was that of the service chiefs whom the government nervously consulted. They talked in large and lugubrious terms about the enormous military and naval preparations that would be involved should Britain be dragged into support for a French military expedition against the Germans. It would be, they thought, a frighteningly large project, for which Britain's defense establishment was scarcely prepared. In particular, it was said that the Navy would be embarrassed by a shortage of capital ships in the face of two brand-new German battleships, which, though small—almost miniature—were alarmingly efficient.

In France the response to the events of the morning of March 7 was a good deal more frantic and more divided, but it shared some features with the British. The cabinet at once considered the situation. Under the terms of Locarno, the guarantees by Italy and Britain could only be invoked after the League Council had certified a violation (in this respect, Locarno, with its internationalist spirit, had actually represented a restriction on French freedom to act, compared to the Versailles Treaty, although it had been universally regarded as providing greater security). This was what the French government agreed to do, and a Council meeting was immediately called.

It was realized by almost everyone, however, that this meant that nothing would be done beyond the issuing of protests against Germany's unilateral repudiation of treaty obligations. If there was one thing that had been demonstrated in the last year, it was that the League had no capacity to take effective action. The French sought to invigorate it, after having ganged up with the British during the past year to castrate it. Their decision was undoubtedly influenced by the knowledge that this was the only way, cumbersome and improbable as it was, that British support could be assured. They knew—and possibly had already been informed—that they could count on no support if they acted independently.

The question of independent action was nonetheless considered. The ministers were divided; of them all, only four were unequivocally in favor of it. (It is not completely clear which four; Foreign Minister Flandin later insisted he was, but a colleague contradicted him. He was the most important personage in the Cabinet, and he had considerable vision. But he had recently been injured in an automobile accident, and his arm was in a symbolic sling). It was fairly clear that if any military response were to be made, it would *have* to be made independently because it would have to be made quickly, before German forces became entrenched in the forbidden land to the point where their ejection would involve a major fight. The advance forces were weak, and French units, waiting on the border, could occupy most of the territory before they got there. It was thought by many people, including François-Poncet, the French ambassador at Berlin, that the Germans would retreat before a French counteradvance.

But whether the Germans would then back down or mobilize for a major fight looked questionable to the French ministers. Backing down would almost certainly, they thought, involve the collapse of the Hitler regime, and they doubted that it would collapse without a struggle. And this opened the prospects of both a Franco-German war and a German civil war, leading perhaps to either military dictatorship or to communism. The obvious course for the ministers was to consult the service chiefs, in particular General Maurice Gamelin, the commander in chief. Gamelin, consulted, was remarkably hesitant and indecisive, even timid. Startlingly, no plans whatever had been made for a campaign to prevent remilitarization. He said the Germans had a million men under arms, and a third of these were involved in the Rhineland operation.* Countermeasures would, he thought, precipitate major actions and a major war which France could not hope to win without allies. By the time Gamelin had finished his report it was certain that nothing would be done to stop the Germans.

All these calculations in London and Paris were reasonable. For the majority of citizens who feared war more than anything else, and who thought wisdom and restraint and good intentions could avert it, they were commendable and welcome. What was not fully realized by anybody outside certain inner circles in Germany was that the German service chiefs were acting exactly like their British and French counterparts. They had been dismayed when Hitler had first projected the occupation. They had attempted to dissuade him.

Hitler himself had been extremely anxious. He later admitted that if the French had marched, German forces would have had to retreat. The Germans had begun a year earlier to build an army of thirty-six divisions, and these were by no means ready for action in March 1936. The General Staff had been re-established publicly only in October 1935 (having theretofore lived an

---

*A detailed study of the French military reaction has been made by W. F. Knapp, "The Rhineland Crisis of March 1936," *Saint Antony's Paper*, No. 5 (London: Chatto & Windus, 1959), pp. 67–85.

underground and restricted existence). Armament was still short. The German generals, by temperament and training, loathed operations they were not fully prepared for, and Hitler's decision to march brought "the first head-on clash" with the generals, who were in a state "near panic."* Baron von Fritsch, the commander in chief, tried to argue with the dictator; he was snubbed and insulted and gained nothing but Hitler's hatred.

The hesitancy of the German generals was suspected abroad, at least by the Russians.† There have been assertions that the Army was prepared to try to arrest Hitler if the French marched, and while there is no solid evidence of an organized conspiracy to do so, there is no doubt that a willingness to destroy the regime accompanied many of the generals' anxieties about Hitler's audacity. But this did not affect Gamelin's judgment.

What is remarkable is that the military in all three countries (the same had been true in both Britain and Italy when the Ethiopian venture was being planned) were cautious to the point of timidity; that they consistently overrated both the determination and the power of their putative opponents; and that they drew back, as if by reflex, from steps that might lead to "complications." In Italy and Germany, it was impetuous civilian leaders (plus, in Italy's case, a single vain general) who forced war on reluctant Army men. This state of things obtained everywhere, with modifications, until after World War II broke out. It is one of the least understood and seemingly perverse aspects of the period. No complete explanation would be possible without giving a detailed history of European military establishments, but two elements of the situation bore particularly strongly in the thirties.

The first is the fact, increasingly noted by historians, that militarism is not at all the same thing as aggressiveness. Germany had always been militaristic in the sense that it had, since its origins, maintained large forces led by highly trained professionals with a strong, clublike tradition, and that the Army and the ethical virtues associated with it had enjoyed the admiring

---

*J. Wheeler-Bennett, *The Nemesis of Power* (New York: Macmillan 1954), p. 351, and Harold Deutsch, *The Conspiracy Against Hitler in the Twilight War* (Minneapolis: University of Minnesota Press, 1968), p. 30.

†Knapp, *op. cit.*, p. 77.

respect of much of the nation and had played an influential, sometimes decisive, role in its affairs. The same was true, with variations, in most European countries. It even affected Great Britain, where there was no conscription and the Army was small and not very noticeable. Still, it enjoyed a special and traditional place in society, and the Navy commanded general pride and prestige. Everywhere the professional Service people were like civil servants; they were at the command of a government of politicians (whom they often obstructed and sometimes distinguished from the mystical entity of "the nation," but never to the point of mutiny). They took an intense pride and pleasure in their own past, organization, routine, training, morals, and machinery. They formed, in short, a bureaucracy with some of the traits of a high-school football team and some of a masonic lodge.

Like any bureaucracy, the officers' corps was everywhere averse to the unusual and the unpredictable, and was disposed toward an intense conservatism, usually including retrograde views on morals and politics. Supremely, it disliked any change in its own organization, especially at the instance of amateurs and outsiders. Military men were, in short, defensive in their reflexes after 1918, so strongly so in France that the whole structure of French military policy was shifting to one based on the hope of holding attackers on the frontiers. The German Army displayed all these characteristics. What it wanted was money, men, and prestige, but it did not particularly want war. It might and did preach the warlike virtues, although after 1918 nobody dared to preach them as blatantly as before. But in fact the military minds tended to be less like the minds of crusaders than of brightly plumaged file clerks. What they disliked was not peace but pacifism, not tranquility but defeat. The hazards of war involved not only possible defeat but the certainty of changes that would disrupt their routines, tarnish their toys, and cause dangerous social upheavals including the dilution of their forces with outsiders. The fact was that armies in the thirties were even farther behind in their adaptation to change than they usually are —the touching confidence of the Poles in their cavalry was an extreme example of it. But they were not unaware that the age of the masses had brought threats to their traditions which war could only magnify. Navies and especially air forces were somewhat more flexible and professionally up-to-date in their outlook, but even the Royal Air Force of Great Britain, which was to prove the most adaptable and scientific-minded of all Europe's several fighting forces in the early years of the war, was still governed in the middle thirties by men so much struck with the offensive possibilities of modern bombers that they retreated into restricted defensive notions verging, at times, on despair. And the British navy, surprisingly, was by no means immune to underconfidence. In the summer of 1935, when war between Britain and Italy had seemed a possibility, the British Navy had been moved by a much-exaggerated fear of the Italian Navy and, especially, of the Italian Air Force. It was frequently said that the Royal Navy's defenses against air attack were so weak as to suggest that the capital ships might all be instantly sunk, and the Admiralty responded with horrified reflexes to the thought of losing a single ship. There were certainly some grounds for alarm that, in a world war involving Italy, Germany, and Japan, the Navy might be insufficient (although even in such a contingency the Admiralty's view was unduly pessimistic), but in view of what happened later, the fears in 1935 look merely neurotic. The advice of the naval advisers had been an important element in determining Britain's refusal to make a serious attempt to curb Mussolini, and one admiral (Lord Cunningham, in *A Sailor's Odyssey*) later went so far as to describe the attitude of his colleagues as "defeatist." What is interesting about this is not so much the British Navy's extreme lack of assurance as the fact that it was fully shared by the Italian Navy.

The second element in the timidity of armies, navies, and air forces was inadequate information. Intelligence was the nexus between the technique of soldiery and the making of policy. To know what possible enemies were thinking of doing, and how capable they were of doing it, was indispensable to keeping the armed forces of a state in condition to fight; but it was likewise indispensable to keeping ministers in a condition to conduct national affairs. Such knowledge is never more than relatively copious or reliable. Its accumulation requires luck and skill; its evaluation is a matter of high art. Secret information can usually be collected only by people who are by definition undependable and who may be double agents. It is invariably fragmentary. Information from one source is almost always in conflict with information from other sources.

Both in organization and evaluation, human judgments and therefore human fallibilities play a part. So do wide social and political influences. One of the disastrous defects of some European intelligence services, most notably the British, was that their form and tradition had been inherited from the romantic freebooting ways of nineteenth-century power and glory. This meant that Intelligence services in Britain were run like private satrapies, without much control, with internal schisms and warfare with competing bureaucracies. More seriously, they inherited Britain's nineteenth-century class system. Quite literally, the principal criteria for selecting a secret agent in Great Britain in the thirties were his ancestors, his boarding school, and his university. A gentleman was by definition loyal and courageous and devoted to old-time virtue.

This archaism would be incredible if it were not amply documented. But it was logical, consonant with the nature of bureaucracies at their most bureaucratic—that is, when they are removed from all outside supervision—and therefore least given to effective action. More, it illuminated the dangers of an old social system surviving in the age of ideology. For Britain's ruling gentlemen, far from being by definition loyal, courageous, and devoted to old-time virtue, were in the thirties much given to Marxism and sodomy. The British intelligence agencies harbored a number of Soviet agents. The fact, known because of the very public dénouement of their careers in the 1950s, is merely a part of the iceberg of extreme inefficiency in the information-collecting process.

If information is scrappy, invented, unreliable, or simply lacking, the people who are supposed to make decisions on the basis of it will choose those details that may happen to strike them, fortify a predisposition, fit in conveniently with battles of wits being waged with colleagues, or simply come from a source they trust. One of the most important springs of British policy from

1935 to 1940 was the persistent belief of many of its service and civilian executives that German and Italian military, naval and air power were much greater than in fact they were. In part they believed this because they wanted to. One characteristic illustration is the attention they paid to the emphatic, but in fact very ill-informed, assertions of Charles A. Lindbergh. Lindbergh, the Lone Eagle of the United States, was regarded as an unquestioned authority on air power, and after a visit in 1938 to Germany he gave the British leaders a fantastically exaggerated account of Germany's potential to destroy the United Kingdom from the air. Thomas Jones, a member of the inmost circles of the government, wrote, "Since my talk with Lindbergh . . . I've sided with those working for peace at any cost in humiliation, because of the picture of our relative unpreparedness in the air and on the ground which Lindbergh painted, and because of his belief that the democracies would be crushed absolutely and finally."*

That was two and a half years after the Rhineland episode. It was the climax of a process of moral attrition that had begun a year before it. The German announcement of remilitarization seems to have set off the cycle of defeatism. Baldwin, in particular, was apparently seized by a mindless conviction that Great Britain could be destroyed as a nation if it became involved in hostilities with Germany; beginning at least as early as Hoare's appointment as Foreign Minister, in June 1935, he seems to have warned repeatedly that Britain's foreign policy must be based on avoiding a war for which Britain was not ready. It was a curious proposition: no nation is ever "ready" in the sense that Baldwin used the word, and certainly Germany was not. The attitude of the political leaders in Britain seems to have involved chiefly a constant, myopic focusing on their own state of preparedness, an almost hypochondriac condition, and an extreme unwillingness to do anything to remedy it. A spirited rearmament program would be opposed by public opinion and the Labour Party (and might cost the Conservatives their majority). At the same time it would be construed by Hitler and

*Quoted in Jon Kimche, *The Unfought Battle* (New York: Stein and Day, 1967), p. 7.

Mussolini as an aggressive act that might lead to war.

The difference between the policies pursued in Italy and Germany and those pursued in France and Britain was simply that in the former countries the civilian governments paid little attention to the political judgments of the Service men. In the latter, they not only heeded them with despair, but outdid them in pessimism and uncertainty. This was in part because Italy and Germany were dictatorships, governed by men of great self-confidence and disdain for any sort of professionalism who were prepared to risk national suicide, while France and Britain were democracies led by politicians deeply apprehensive of war and accountable to the consciences of their constituents.

It has seemed desirable to discuss the Rhineland and its dynamics in some detail because immediately afterward it was seen as a turning point, a fatal episode after which Hitler could not have been stopped without war. This was a myth, not history; but it was a myth that made history. The story of the next three years (to the day) is a story of devolution, and the events that followed for a year and a half, until the devolution approached its dismal nadir, may be summarily dealt with. The rest of 1936, and most of 1937, were—for the thirties—outwardly relatively quiet, with the spectacular exception of the civil war that broke out in Spain that summer.

THE SPANISH WAR

The Rhineland was a study in the psychology of those who were uncertain how to deal with, or unwilling to oppose, Hitler. The Spanish war was a study in the psychology of the most resolute and vigorous anti-fascists. It was also a tragic illustration of the way in which the social and international conflicts of very advanced societies spread cancerously into regions to which they were largely irrelevant.

There was plenty of cause for conflict in Spain itself. In some respects, Iberia was like eastern Europe, and indeed like most agricultural regions touched by the export of technology and ideas from the centers of industry. In an intensely archaic setting, where ways of life and habits of thought were frequently and rather grimly sixteenth-century, there had appeared, in spots, modern industry and modern middle- and industrial-working-classes. And everywhere, transmogrified by the setting, there had appeared the ideas that flourished prolifically in France, Russia, Germany, and Great Britain. Anarchism flourished, a doctrine of violence against authority that was peculiarly congenial in a backward and oppressive society. So did Marxism and Leninism and reformist socialism. So did old-fashioned classical liberalism, and so did ideas of assertive national self-determination among the survivors—notably the Catalans in the northeast and the Basques in the northwest—of the innumerable tribal and ethnic mixtures that had gone to make up Spain. And so, with vigor, flourished the fortresses of the early modern era: a Roman Catholic church that was, in its higher reaches, sensationally reactionary and obscurantist and in its lower much touched both by the old community of parish priest and peasantry, and also by the newer ideas of Catholic democracy; a landed aristocracy that was still in some ways technically feudal and in almost all ways retrograde; and an Army, both monumentally inefficient and self-satisfied, which was recurrently disposed (like its brother armies in Spanish America) to rescue the nation from jobbery, confusion, and incipient rebellion (which certainly abounded) through the bracing expedient of military dictatorship.

Spain in the twenties had installed one of its periodic military dictatorships, this time set about with some tinselly adornments of modern totalitarian verbiage. Then the inadequate dictator had been dismissed by the king, Alfonso XIII, who was himself dismissed a year later in a burst of revulsion against the strangling traditionalism and unedifying decadence symbolized by the antique monarchy. (The parallels with Italian history at various times are very numerous, striking, and logical.)

This had happened, following local elections in which republicans won a large majority, in April 1931. A republic was proclaimed. All of Spain's discontents, sixteenth- and twentieth-century alike, rose to the surface. Regional centrifugal forces, embodied by Basques and Catalans, won concessions and were combated by adherents of fascism and the divine right of kings.

Absolutists rose. Fascists multiplied and also rose. A new right appeared, comparable to that in Italy, which clothed the landowners with the black, but up-to-date, cloaks of Catholic corporatism. Outrages became a dime a dozen, and so did martyrs. In February 1936 general elections were held, and the parties of the left—the Popular Front, now more or less united in electoral coalition and promising to carry out the inchoate reforms promised in the constitution—won a small majority in the parliament (although not of the popular vote) and formed a government. Dissent appeared in the majority parties, and insurrection appeared in the opposition. In late July, after long preparations, a group of Army generals in Spanish Morocco raised the flag of revolution and attempted to seize power from the foundering republic. It was expected to be a *coup d'état* like innumerable other *coups d'état* in Spanish history and to lead, after a few weeks of fighting, to another military dictatorship which would save the proud name of Spain and the security of the privileged classes from the threat of social change. This was not surprising: even in France there were men who were saying, in rather similar circumstances, "Better Hitler than Léon Blum."

The civil war lasted not weeks but years. Throughout its dreadful course it remained, basically and in its long-run effects, a bloody brawl among competing groups in a rather isolated society that had progressed toward modernity with notable unevenness. However, its prolongation and its importance to the rest of the world were largely the result of its taking place in a time when great ideological and national forces faced one another in the rest of Europe. Spain became—as it was often called—a cockpit and a microcosm of world war because of foreign meddlers, and of the echoes those meddlers struck in Spain.

Without foreign meddling, the Republic would probably have won. But that foreigners might not meddle was a condition contrary to fact. As early as 1934 Mussolini had been in touch with anti-republican leaders. At the outbreak of war he sent some planes to the rebels, variously called Fascists, Nationalists, and (after General Francisco Franco, who shortly emerged as their chief) Franquists. Italian aid steadily increased. Within weeks,

Soviet aid began to reach the Republic. The Soviet support encouraged a rapid growth of the small Spanish Communist Party (it had only six members in parliament) and earned the gratitude of all republicans. It helped convince their enemies that the loyalist cause was Communist (which many people vaguely thought anyway) just as Italian aid had convinced the loyalists' sympathizers that the Franquist cause was fascist. Neither was true. Still, the war was seen by most people who took world affairs seriously as a struggle between the two great ideologies of the future. This belief was the fruit of the Soviets' Common Front policy, which made friends of progressive minded people everywhere, and of Mussolini's adventurist policy.

The real reasons for Mussolini's meddling in Spain were (like most of Mussolini's policies) a mixture of impetuosity and a sort of cynicism which was as often as not based on unrealities. Mussolini wanted an ideological friend in Spain. (Conceivably, he imagined an eventual integration of a fascist Spain into the new Roman empire which was a recurrent fantasy with him.) More cogently, Mussolini was interested in Spain for naval reasons. The more friends he had in the Mediterranean, the less secure was Britain's control of it and the greater the relative strength of the Italian Navy, which was at the beginning of a vast building program. With the war under way, Spain became an admirable training ground for Italian military and air-force people. The aid Italy sent (at the end of a year there were 70,000 Italian personnel in Spain) was instructing the Italians in fighting methods. It also involved Mussolini in a draining commitment to a cause which looked more and more uncertain as the Republic organized itself for effective defense.

Like most of Mussolini's adventures, this was taken without the advice or approval of the king or other important Italians. Like almost all of them it turned from an ill-judged whimsy into a serious liability. Instead of strengthening Italy, the Spanish venture gravely weakened it. Spain became a bottomless pit for Italian men, money, and equipment. Hitler was much wiser; he limited his contribution to military advisers, a single air unit and a variety of German arms, sent largely for purposes of testing in combat experience, and he avoided associating himself with the

fate of the Franquist cause, although the German press de-
tachedly supported it. He saw the war for what it was, a drain
on the strength of all who became engaged in it. He was without
any quixotic illusions. A year and a half after it started, he told
his generals, "A hundred percent victory for Franco was not
desirable from the German point of view. Rather we are interested in a continuance of the war and in keeping up tension in
the Mediterranean."*

One effect of the Spanish War was to complete what Ethiopia
had begun: Mussolini became more and more needful of German
friendship. The two dictators had met, for the second time, in
May. The enmity of the year before had been erased by Mussolini's need for friends. By the fall of 1936, relations were increasingly cordial, and the solidification of something less than
an alliance but more than an understanding took place in October 1936 during a visit of Count Ciano, Mussolini's son-in-law
and foreign minister, to Berlin.

The term "axis" was applied to the alignment by Mussolini
when he referred to it the next month. This involved, in the long
run, the loss of Mussolini's influence in central Europe, which he
had sedulously constructed and which the Laval agreement tacitly supported. Tied now to Hitler and weakened by the military
and economic drains of Ethiopia and Spain, Mussolini would
have to co-operate with the Germans in central Europe, and
co-operation meant, in effect, abdication. The Axis was chiefly
a convenience for Hitler; it neutralized a possible opponent. To
the rest of the world, however, it looked quite different. It
seemed like the welding of a gigantic ideological bloc, much
fortified by their sinister doctrines of aggression. The dictators
were able to display whatever effects they liked, for they controlled their own publicity, and the pageantry and propaganda
that attended the Axis conveyed to the world that this was a
show of overwhelming strength rather than an expression of
Italian weakness and German calculation. The beguilement of
the democracies proceeded.

The democracies were behaving with notable incompetence.

* *Documents on German Foreign Policy* (Washington: Government Printing Office, 1949),
Vol. III, p. 172.

Opinion in France and Britain was divided, and in France the division was so deep and passionate as to threaten an extension of civil war across the Pyrenees. For this fact, the formation of a Popular Front government in Paris was, ironically, largely to blame. The May elections had been won by the newly allied parties of the Popular Front—Socialists, Radicals, and a significantly growing Communist Party (still small in France; but in the election their numbers in the Chamber of Deputies had gone from 10 to 73). The Socialists, with 159 seats, became for the first time the largest party. The new government, with Socialist Léon Blum as Prime Minister and with the conditional support but not the participation of the Communists in the ministry, was immediately faced by extensive sit-in strikes by workers who hoped that the socialist millennium was at hand. Blum negotiated, with skill and courage, an agreement that ended the strikes and provided long-overdue welfare and labor measures, including collective bargaining.

A Socialist-dominated government supported by the entire left met passionate fear and hatred from large parts of the middle class, which in France outnumbered the industrial working class and had been long accustomed to undisturbed and comfortable stagnation. They expected, or said they did, Red Terror, and they used all their financial resources to block, and in effect strangle, the putative social revolution. Their most violent spokesmen were the extreme right-wing fascist movements, who were, of course, zealously friendly to Franco in Spain. Since the government and its followers were naturally friendly to the Spanish Republic, the same dangerous divisions that were destroying Spain appeared in France in the summer of 1936.

For this reason, among others, the Blum government did not dare to intervene. Blum himself understood clearly enough the nature of the Fascist and Nazi regimes, although like many others he may have overrated their strength in 1936. He believed, however, that any policy of open support for the Spanish Republic might well cause both a civil war in France and a general war in Europe. Moreover, he was aware that he could not expect support for such a policy—or even in such a war—from Britain. He therefore tried to do what had been so often tried before, to keep things as quiet as possible. With the British, a policy of nonintervention was worked out, administered by a committee on which both Germany and Italy were represented. Nobody was supposed to send arms or other goods to Spain. The Italians openly and perpetually disregarded this, of course, while continuing to utter pious platitudes on the committee. Since Britain and France observed their own rules, the result of nonintervention was that Franco got all the aid that Italy dared to send him and the Republic was made entirely dependent on the substantial, though inadequate, flow of Soviet aid.

The British position and attitude were thus, in June, as they had been in March, indecisive and therefore controlling. The fact was that the Spanish war was an extremely complicated affair, internationally as well as domestically, and many points of view were plausible in Britain. There were a good many people, people in important positions, who were very pro-Franco. Franco was a gentleman, he was on the side of law, order, and business. He promised stability and respectability against the chaotic and inchoately leftist Republic. It was widely believed that a republican victory would lead to a Communist regime. Such people conceived, in some cases, of a greater danger to Britain from the establishment of Soviet power in the Mediterranean than from a possible extension of Italian power there. Therefore, nonintervention and benevolence to Franco seemed to them a necessary policy. This was the point of view of most people in the British government, including Anthony Eden, and of Winston Churchill outside it. The point of view might have been tenable had Mussolini not already been converted into an enemy.

The opposition, which included the majority of intellectuals and young people, passionately espoused the position that the Spanish strife was a straight battle between hopeful democracy and evil fascism, and a number of young Englishmen went off to serve, and die for, the Spanish Republic. But there were other attitudes which confused an issue already sufficiently confusing. Some people, regarding the matter as none of Britain's business, believed as Hitler did that the best policy was to let unsavory opponents fight it out. This was, incredibly, the view of the

British Prime Minister. He told Eden, who was trying to discuss Spain with him, "I hope that you will try not to trouble me too much with foreign affairs just now."* For people of this cast of mind, it sometimes even seemed to be to Britain's interest, as to Hitler's, to prolong the war so that both sides would be reduced to impotence.

This was, in effect, what happened. By 1939, when the war finally ended with the extinction of the Republic, Spain was so exhausted that even a sense of ideological affinity with Hitler could not induce Franco to give the Germans substantial aid in 1940. But the result, not altogether prejudicial to Britain's interest, was, so far as the government went, as unplanned as it was immoral. The fact was that neither France nor certainly Britain was willing to take a stand against the meddlers, on the ground that it might produce a general war, and this meant that they had no policy except the inadvertent one of allowing the Republic to be slowly tortured to death behind the thin curtain of nonintervention.

There was one minor but significant exception to the inaction of the British and the French. In 1937, pirates, in the form of unidentified Italian warships, began sinking British and French merchantmen entering Republican ports. To this, a direct attack and affront, France and Britain responded with firmness. A conference was called in September at Nyon, in Switzerland, and the law was laid down. The sinkings stopped abruptly. It was a most instructive incident, but no lessons were drawn. Indeed, the governments wished, apparently, to draw no lessons.

1937

From the point of view of France and Britain, it was indeed difficult to know what to do about Spain, and it seemed to many responsible people, like Blum, that there was no alternative to trying to reduce foreign intervention—"internationalization," as it was called—through embargoes and the nonintervention agreement. But the real problem was that, by 1937, the British and French governments, and parts of their population, had

*Eden, op. cit., p. 461.

come to think of the Axis powers as too strong to be resisted by force. An odd chemistry had taken place; until 1935, it had been common to hear in London and Paris that Hitler was too weak to justify strenuous policies. It would be years before German rearmament reached the point of becoming a real threat. By 1937 it seemed that the threat was so large and immediate as to make strenuous policies seem suicidal.

Not everybody thought so; the Communists (always more determined in their attitude than anybody else) and, after 1935, increasing sections of Socialist opinion, favored a determined resistance to the Axis and drew the now unavoidable conclusion that this would require French and British rearmament. The balance of power must be immediately seen to. In point of fact, in 1937 it was still strongly in favor of France and Britain; Hitler had told Ciano, in October of 1936, that it would be four years before he could contemplate fighting a general war. While Hitler tended to say whatever came into his head on matters like this, without really meaning it, it probably corresponded in a general way to the facts. But the curious fact was that the influential people in the west didn't believe this and, at the same time, they showed themselves remarkably reluctant to act upon their beliefs about dangerous Axis strength. French and British military preparations lagged.

There were good and bad reasons for this, but the most compelling one was undoubtedly the horror of war and the persistent belief that it could be avoided by negotiation. Hitler and Mussolini continued, at intervals, to give warm assurances of a desire for peace and good relations with France and Britain. There was no reason to believe that war was inevitable, and there was every reason to believe that an ill-judged opposition to the Axis might produce it. There were other reasons as well: financial considerations and the old, very deep-rooted feeling that armaments brought war closer. Parliaments, businessmen, and public opinions disliked them, and men like Churchill, and some of the Service chiefs in England who pressed for massive rearmament, were constantly denounced as reactionary warmongers. Resistance to increased taxes was very strong. In France there was another complication. There, a predominantly Socialist government was devoted to the principle that munitions-makers (including makers of military airplanes) ought for the sake of safety and prudence to be publicly controlled. Munitions-makers were believed to be—and in France were—sinister men. As a consequence, the Popular Front regime embarked on the nationalization of the industry. It is doubtful if the consequent disruptions were as serious as other causes in retarding French defense, and it is certain that the very left-wing Air Minister, Pierre Cot, who ran the airplane industry, was neither treacherous nor so inefficient as rightist critics insisted (Cot's responsibility for France's defeat in 1940 became an article of fanatical faith with rightists later). Still, the Popular Front program, the subsisting pacifism of many of its supporters, and the incredible loathing with which it was regarded by French business—in particular the organization of French steelmakers, the Comité des Forges—contributed to an inadequate build-up of a defense establishment already troubled by a combination of complacency and anxiety.

In Britain, something was done. It proved, in the end, to have been barely enough to be decisive. The planning for British rearmament had begun after the General Election of November 1935. Baldwin, talking about the plans in Parliament, made a remark that some regarded as infamous, to the effect that he could not have begun rearmament sooner because if he had, he would have lost the election. It was, perhaps, true; and it was certainly true that the Labour Party remained suspicious of defense spending for some time afterward. It was a remark which sufficiently defined Baldwin's character, however, and further definition followed. The pace was leisurely, the money appropriated modest. There were interminable wrangles among the services, and within each, about strategy. After the Rhineland occupation in March 1936, a much more vigorous arms program was decided on, but it provoked passionate opposition from both the Labour Party and the business community, which was to be taxed to pay for it. A new Ministry of Defense was set up, but it was placed under a singularly placid and incompetent politician, Sir Thomas Inskip. (It was said that there had been no appointment like his since Caligula made his horse a Consul.)

Commitments to France were lethargically discussed, and

Baldwin went so far as to tell the world that Britain's frontier was on the Rhine. Concern was still felt, however, in particular by Eden and by the man who was to be notorious as the archetypal appeaser, Neville Chamberlain.

Chamberlain became Prime Minister in May 1937, when Baldwin retired. He was a conscientious and highly efficient man; he was above all an administrator, and he understood that the rearmament effort, which had already been decided on, must be operated a good deal more energetically. He was firmly committed to a strong Britain and in no way shared the prevailing pacifist and defeatist views. Early in 1934 he had observed, "For the old aphorism 'Force is no remedy', I would substitute 'The Fear of Force is the only remedy'."* Five years later the remark would take on an acid irony, but it is true that he was, in both the MacDonald and Baldwin governments, much the staunchest advocate of rearmament, and in the election of 1935 he was passionately denounced by Labour Party candidates as a warmonger. In the spring of 1936, when as Chancellor of the Exchequer he presented a rearmament plan, he was accused of presenting "a sequence of war budgets" by the Labour Party chief, Clement Atlee, who would soon be denouncing him for his failure to stop Hitler.

At Chamberlain's insistence, improvements were undertaken, and an expanded arms program was decided on in the winter of 1937. Still, a year later the expenditures were under a billion pounds, while Germany's were five times that.† It was estimated that it would take a year for the Royal Air Force to "catch up" with the German, which three years earlier had not existed. It was not for another year that rearmament was wholeheartedly pushed in Britain.

The conduct of Germany in the year 1937 was relatively polite; the year saw no more crises made in Berlin. But what seemed to be happening on the surface of Nazi Germany was usually the opposite of what was really happening beneath the censorship, and this was true of 1937. For it was in this year, it now appears,

---

*Iain MacLeod, *Neville Chamberlain* (New York: Atheneum, 1962), p. 178.
†The figures are very difficult to calculate and much controverted. These are based on estimates in A. S. Milward, *The German Economy at War* (London: Oxford University Press, 1965), p. 7.

most important decisions were made, and for reasons not directly the product of ideology or even of ambition.

The matter is one for controversy; concerning it, the liveliest and most significant historical debate about the origins of World War II has developed. It is interesting that it recapitulates in some respects the historians' controversies about Bismarck's policies in the 1860s and later, and at least one of the principals is the same person, the brilliant and prolific Oxford historian, Professor A. J. P. Taylor.

The question is one of the motives, timing, and technique. In Bismarck's case, what was involved was the creation and consolidation of the German Empire through a series of wars in the 1860s; in Hitler's case, the prodigious extension of German boundaries after 1937, leading to the outbreak of war and to the eventual, short-lived, German dominion over most of Europe. The traditional interpretation has been, in both cases, that the two German leaders both worked to a schedule, brilliantly and almost completely conceived in advance, and executed in accordance with a timetable only slightly adjusted to circumstances. This may be termed the "blueprint" interpretation. It took shape, in both cases, as the events happened, and in both cases it was encouraged by the presumed blueprinters, who naturally found it to their advantage to be attired in a reputation, as the architects of events, that made them look infallible and irresistible. In Hitler's case, there was a good deal by way of logical inference and documentation to lend support to this theory. It looked at the time as if, with only a minor exception, Hitler's egregious ventures were always successful. (The exception was the Austrian coup of 1934.) And this in itself suggested long-range planning and superhuman insight. There was, it seemed, a logical procession, from internal consolidation and economic recovery, through rearmament, through elaborate diplomacy to divide and disarm opponents, to war planned for the moment when Germany's advantage would be not only optimal but almost total. The text and purpose of this program had been provided in *Mein Kampf,* with its assertion of Germany's destiny to rule Europe, its particular emphasis on the elimination of decadent France, its excoriation of democracy, its call for the destruction of barbaric, Slavic Russia, its program for supplying Germans with "living space"—a vast southern and eastern region to supply the Fatherland and its citizens with land and resources for developing their full potential for superiority.

After the war, when most of the German archives fell into American hands and were made available to the public, the records did indeed show a very careful series of plans drawn up in advance for the subjection of Czechoslovakia and Poland, and for the eventuality of war with the western Powers. The records showed some other things, too, that did not entirely square with the idea of a blueprint and certainly did not demonstrate any link among events in the way of a consistent plan integrating the achievements before 1937 with those afterward. But for people deeply impregnated with the myth of blueprinting these inconsistencies were generally explained away in terms of minor digressions.

The first major attack on the blueprint interpretation appeared in 1961 in a book by Professor Taylor called *The Origins of the Second World War*. In it, he rejected the notion of a blueprint and also the related notion of a great and highly articulated revolutionary movement with deep roots in the past and a deep harmony with major tendencies of the age, skillfully led by Hitler —the notion, in short, of the Nazi Third Reich as an altogether new phenomenon in the history of human organization.

He had already supplied a rather similar analysis of Bismarck's record of achievement in creating the Second Reich. Bismarck, he said, had been an improviser and an opportunist, without anything of an idea about what he was going to do next. He now said the same thing about Hitler. Instead of being the master of an entirely new and wholly unassimilable revolutionary movement, Hitler was merely a somewhat extravagant leader of an old-fashioned national state who behaved like other leaders of national states, in a world whose governance was their responsibility. The most notable avowed purpose of National Socialism, its fascist principle that the proper sphere of the state was to integrate all human activities into a highly planned and controlled system for serving it and the nation and race it in turn served, Taylor dismissed as a propaganda ornament invented for the old-fashioned political purpose of securing popular support. The appalling treatment of Jews and dissenters, the barbarous police system and concentration camps, he dismissed as irrelevant to German foreign policy. In international affairs, Hitler was a figure not basically different in motives and methods from Bismarck—or William II or the statesmen of the democracies. The British leaders, notably Chamberlain, who thought they could negotiate with him as with any other national leader, were quite right, although they did not do it very skillfully and did not have the courage to act on their convictions to the logical extreme, which might have proved successful and prevented the war.

Taylor's thesis was greeted with criticism, indeed with antipathy that verged sometimes on abomination. The part of his argument that naturally attracted most attention in England, the exculpation of Chamberlain and the appeasers from either evil intentions or fatuous self-deception, was denounced as both reactionary and wrong-headed. The claim that Nazi atrocities were or should have been irrelevant to the development of British foreign policy toward Germany was denounced as both incorrect and immoral. And it was pointed out that he disregarded some of the documents, in particular those that quite clearly showed careful advance planning for the destruction of Czechoslovakia and Poland and for war in the west.

Most of Professor Taylor's earlier books had been subjected, although with less indignation, to similar criticisms: his idea of history was sometimes said to combine brilliant and original insights, impressively broad learning in many fields, and superb prose, with a desire to shock readers, a tendency to lean on some sources of questionable reliability, and a casual treatment of evidence which did not support his judgments.

On this last point a most important scholarly controversy developed, in particular around the significance of a document called the Hossbach Memorandum. This was a record of a meeting Hitler, his ministers of war and foreign affairs, and the chiefs of the three armed services held on November 5, 1937, during the period of relative quiescence in Germany's international behavior. It had been made public during the Nuremberg trials, conducted by the British, Americans, French, and Soviets after the war, where the German leaders were prosecuted as criminals. It had generally been interpreted largely as one more item in the endless display of evidence for the blueprint interpretation, which was an inherent, if recurrent theme, in the prosecution.

Professor Taylor thought otherwise. He observed that Hitler engaged in his usual, off-the-cuff, ranting fantasies about eventualities. The eventualities he envisaged did not in fact eventuate (they included such possibilities as civil war in France and a Franco-Italian war) and he seemed to think that Germany's aims could probably be achieved without an actual full-dress war against either France or Britain. Taylor said that the meeting was designed mainly to secure the support of the men involved, all of whom had serious reservations about Hitler's activities anyway, for a rearmament program which was opposed by Hjalmar Schacht, the architect of Germany's economic recovery. His interpretation followed the account given by Hermann Göring in his testimony at the postwar trials of German war criminals.

This view, so strongly in contrast with the belief that the meeting recorded in the Hossbach Memorandum marked a further and decisive stage in Hitler's evolving plans for conquest, has been criticized from quite a different point of view by a later writer, Mr. T. W. Mason.* Mason's interpretation exactly rejects the notion that the November 5 meeting may be judged as the action of an old-fashioned national leader, to which the internal structure of National Socialism and German society was irrelevant. He agrees with Taylor on one basic point, that the meeting was basically concerned with rearmament, but he says that far from being irrelevant to plans for foreign policy, its importance lay precisely in the connection between the two. The meeting, he believes, was decisive because it evidenced that moment in Nazi history when the internal dynamics of German society and economic change led Hitler to the conclusion that territorial expansion, which *might* involve war with the west, was indispensable to the regime.

Mason is strongest in precisely the places where Taylor has

* "Some Origins of the Second World War," *Past and Present*, No. 29, December 1964, pp. 67–88.

been criticized as least convincing. He made a very careful study of the German economy (using research done after Taylor wrote) and concluded that, while no absolutely reliable conclusions can be drawn about the scale of German rearmament, it was assuredly formidable. He concluded that by the spring of 1939 the Germans were not only spending more than the French and British combined, but a very much larger part of the Gross National Product than either.

The German economy, in 1937, had reached the stage of what, in contemporary jargon, would be called "overheating." That is to say, something like full employment of men and resources had been achieved. This was the result of the remarkable effort at recovery from the agonies of depression that the Nazi regime had achieved, under Schacht's ingenious economic management. It was a striking sample of the Germans' capacity for miraculous recuperation, a quality amply displayed in the later twenties and to be displayed again in the forties. Recovery was, in the middle thirties, a world-wide phenomenon, but everywhere outside of Germany it was incomplete. In Germany it was, in certain ways, too complete.

It had been achieved, without open devaluation of the currency, by the manipulation of credit and public works, the most important of which was rearmament, which raised prices and soaked up unemployment, and by the even more intricate and original manipulation of exports and imports. By providing favorable terms for buyers of marks who had hard foreign exchange to offer, by forcing impoverished foreign governments to sell needed raw materials in return for German exports, German trade had been expanded, an adequate supply of raw materials had been secured, and the balance of payments held in equilibrium. All this had been done without heavy cost to the German population. It is true that real wages of German workers—which meant, in effect, the standard of living—were probably *lower* in 1939 than in 1933 for those who were actually employed. There were some unimportant scarcities of consumer goods. But many workers who had not been employed in 1933 now were, and this spectacular improvement was accompanied by elating intimations of further expansion—new roads, new cars, new cities. A life not merely good but excitingly new was promised by propaganda and evidenced by visible growth.

The underside of the miracle was not entirely evident, even to the most hostile opponents of the regime. It was obvious, of course, that recovery had been made possible by a centralized control, that economic stability and the promise of growth had been paid for in the total loss of political freedom. It was obvious that the endless bureaucratic manipulations had made impossible any return to a freely functioning international economy—trade was being "bilateralized," which in the long run was uneconomic. It was supposed that much of the reflation was the product of massive public spending on rearmament—the rather economically misleading phrase "guns instead of butter" was used to describe this phenomenon. But what was not evident was that some of the real economic problems of Germany had been hidden or postponed rather than solved. No real change had taken place in the depressed and inefficient state of agriculture, no technological revolution had been made in German industry. Only small changes had taken place in its organization and management (a fact that convinced Marxists of the truth of their belief that Hitler was an instrument of the capitalists). There had not even been any large expansion of total industrial capacity. Moreover, a serious shortage of foreign exchange impended. Deficits in exports had been made good with gold exports, and the gold reserves were exhausted. This portended a reduction of imports, which would eventually force reductions in both production and consumption. Schacht and German energy and ability had made the old machine to run at capacity. But now that there was full employment a rapid and shortly intolerable pressure on prices, wages, and imports would develop.

These could be met only by a large investment of capital leading to improvement in productivity and expansion of capacity, to the building of a new, larger, and more efficient machine. Otherwise, they must lead either to recession or, what remained politically unthinkable in Germany, inflation. But, as Mason points out, the problem was not understood, and no solutions were at hand. The Nazi regime faced—the first time that anyone in history had—a state of full employment of resources, and it was a situation that nobody, least of all Hitler, who was bored by economics, understood well enough to cope with. He concluded that the solution lay in conquests.

To Mason's argument may be added the fact that there were other pressures, similar but not wholly economic, which grew out of the nature of the Nazi state. The dictatorship, heavily equipped with bureaucracy of many kinds, was developing a sort of centrifugal force. The state and party employees, and the armed forces, had expanded partly in consequence of the effort to soak up unemployment, but partly for political and even spiritual reasons: the huge party structure was hierarchical not only in the figurative sense of being run from on high but also in the literal sense of constituting a sort of priesthood. The party associated the citizen in the mystical work of rebuilding and serving Germany as well as supplying jobs. It also stifled opposition by making individuals' positions and power depend on the machine. The apparatus was too big for the territory it governed, and bitter rivalries rose out of conflicting claims to things to govern. There was endless duplication of functions. This had already presented a grave problem in the rivalry between the Storm Troopers and the Army. The demand for more scope for the party, as for civil servants and the growing armed services, was strong. It was aggravated, too, by the extraordinary corruption and free-for-all empire-building within the cancer-growth of the Nazi state. The only way to solve jurisdictional disputes was to have more jurisdictions.

A recent and thorough German historian, Hans Adolf Jacobsen, has complemented Mason's thesis. His exhaustive and systematic researches have convinced him that the change that took place in 1937 was merely a development into coherent planning of intentions that had been Hitler's driving motive all along. He does not espouse the blueprint interpretation, but rather what might be called a *leitmotif* interpretation. He is less interested in the economic imperatives than in the psychological ones. But the general conclusion is the same: the mounting pressures and mounting power combined to make definite planning for expansion at once expedient and possible.

We may reasonably conclude that the visions of *Mein Kampf*

determined the direction of German policy and that economic stringencies determined their timing. Hitler's sense of personal destiny was the motive force of all the major decisions. He lived, to some extent, in fantasy, and he was already showing in sporadic ways the detachment from reality that finally turned Germany's difficult military situation, after 1942, into a madhouse. But he was exceedingly shrewd; he knew what lies to tell. He was certainly aware of the pressures as well as the requirements of his personal destiny.

While most of the particular contingencies and plans which he envisaged in November 1937 never developed, it does seem likely that he turned from improvisation to long-range planning at that time. His power, and Germany's, were now so considerable that he could force events to happen. They never did happen in exactly the way he foresaw, but he was quick at ordering the necessary changes of plan, and his subordinates were quick and skillful at carrying them out. It is plausible to suppose that from then on he made not a blueprint but a decision that the time had come to solve the Nazis' problems by territorial expansion, and this decision—informed, of course, by his own unchanging views about destiny, about control of the Eurasian heartland, about the racial inferiority of Slavs—was accompanied by the understanding that a European war might result from his policies and must be prepared for. He prepared for it by developing a machinery that could deal sharp decisive blows without straining the economy.

In the light of later analyses, a new reading of Hitler's memoranda to his Service chiefs suggests, then, a new hypothesis. He talks constantly of plans for a general war in all of them, but before November of 1937 the plans are defensive. In June 1937, when Hitler was detailing his program for the annexation of Austria and an attack on Czechoslovakia (there is no question whatever about these designs), he envisaged possible armed reaction from France and how to counter it ("The outbreak of war will presumably take the form of a surprise attack by the French army"*). But in November the tone changes, and by April of 1938, discussing how best to prepare for the forthcoming

*Quoted in Peter de Mendelssohn, *Design for Aggression* (New York; Harper, 1946).

war to destroy Czechoslovakia, Hitler rules out a surprise attack on the grounds that it would produce a hostile world reaction. And the minutes quote him: "Such a measure is justified only for the elimination of the *last* opponent on the mainland."*

The lull of 1937 ended almost immediately with the new year. Two things happened, aimed directly at preparing the way to larger revisions in the European order. One was that the German Army, the last institution in Germany, public or private, to retain its integrity and its independence, was humiliated and subordinated to Nazi control. Then Austria was annexed.

*Ibid., p. 40.

7

"A General Settlement"

$\mathbf{A}$T the moment when Hitler turned to expanding German territory vastly, and German power infinitely, for the fulfillment of his visions and of a Germany explosively bloated, there was taking shape in Great Britain a coherent policy and program for dealing with him. The days of Simon's maladroit attempts at disengagement were past. The days when Baldwin presided over a Cabinet of irreconcilables in the hope of satisfying everyone ended in the summer of 1937. The unhappy experiment of 1931, a Cabinet which agreed to disagree, was finished. The dissidents who had tried to "stop Hitler" were eliminated from high places, and Britain at last had a Prime Minister with a foreign policy, supported by colleagues sympathetic to his aims. The German ambassador contentedly reported to Berlin, "The present British cabinet is the first post-war cabinet which has made agreement with Germany one of the major points of its program."*

By the end of 1937, it was London's decision that mattered to the world. The French, frustrated in

*Quoted in Martin Gilbert and Richard Gott, *The Appeasers* (London: Weidenfeld and Nicolson, 1963) p. 65.

188

each of their successive efforts to build a policy, were driven from covert and into open dependence on Britain. They could not fight alone; they had drifted under the dominion of British policy. Moreover, Blum's Popular Front government, disintegrated by perplexity and obstruction, had gone the way of all republican ministries in France, and its successor, under the Radical Party leader Camille Chautemps, an old-time "pure" politician, had neither the imagination nor the authority to try to lead the world. France still seethed, although Blum's vigorous measures against disorder had repressed its outward shows. A growing body of opinion, often led by tired conservatives who had once been the loudest practitioners of jingoism, or by leftists whose pacifism outweighed their dislike of dictatorship, was ready to make deals with Hitler to save "the French race" from extermination; to become, if necessary, a junior partner in a fascist Europe. There was still great vitality in France; the Socialist Party was swinging to an emphatically antifascist position. More and more Socialists were willing to take up arms to defend French democracy. The Communists were more strident than ever in their demands for ecumenical antifascism, and much of the French intelligentsia viewed their resolution with enthusiastic cordiality. But the fact was what it had always been: France could not act alone; and France now was alone.

At least for practical purposes. Italy was estranged. The United States, despite Roosevelt's occasional denunciations of dictators, was still determinedly isolated, and indeed in 1936 had passed the Neutrality Act, designed to keep America out of the next war by forbidding the sort of loans which popular myths held responsible for getting it involved in the last. The Soviet Union, suffering severely from Stalin's fantastic purgings, was regarded by many people as militarily impotent. Poland still had alarmingly cordial relations with Germany. The Little Entente could certainly not provide a counterweight to a ferociously rearmed Germany.

So it was in London that the tune was called, and in London conversation—among the people who mattered—centered on the question of how to avoid paying the piper. During the thirties, British policy was first influenced, and from early 1938 made, by a group of people who shared like opinions, listened to nobody who disagreed with them, and tried to replace or bypass the people in the government who did. Indefinite in composition, the group was definite in creed and power.

It was known at the time as "the Cliveden Set," from the name of the house near London that was the home of Lord Astor, the owner of *The Times*, where some of its members often met. It appeared to some of its antagonists as a cell of conspirators. Marxists and friends of the Soviet Union felt that its guiding principles were a hatred of Communism and a determination to save by any means the capitalist system in Britain. It was even said that the Cliveden Set was conspiring with Hitler to try to get him to attack the Soviet Union while leaving Britain alone; the theory was extravagantly elaborated. It was at one time suggested* that the Munich Conference in 1938, where Czechoslovakia was dismembered to satisfy Hitler, was a prearranged humbug, and that the crisis preceding it was alleged to have been deliberately engineered to frighten British opinion into glutting Hitler's territorial appetite by raising the specter of a war which the British leaders had not the slightest intention of engaging in.

The name "Cliveden Set" was misleading, and there is not the slightest evidence of such an Anglo-German conspiracy. There was no cell; the members of the indefinite group had no regular meetings, and the most important of them rarely went to Cliveden. In fact, many of them rarely saw one another at all. But it was true that *The Times*, with its owner, its editor, the germanophile Geoffrey Dawson, and much of its staff, was the most powerful public voice of the appeasers. Deep hostility to the Soviet Union and communism was a reflex; they certainly disliked the Communists, at least as much as they disliked the Nazis. But while most of them were members of that part of society called "privileged," their anticommunism was not the driving force of their policy but rather one aspect of a view of the world which was for most of them an indivisible whole. They were a sort of anachronism, a microcosm of Britain's ruling class, Conservatives or conservative Liberals, highly educated, accus-

*Most persuasively by Professor F. L. Schuman, an American political scientist, in *Europe on the Eve* (New York: Knopf, 1939).

tomed to power, inclined to a sort of corporate autocracy. Even those who opposed appeasement shared the clubby instincts of the caste.

The membership was varied in origin and personality, but some of the more influential appeasers were heirs of Lord Milner, a highly efficient administrator and imperialist. In the early years of the twentieth century, he had tried to put together a sort of technocratic elite for the Conservative Party, training bright young men for leadership in an age of specialization. Intellectuals, or at least academics, were prominent among them; several, notably Dawson, were members of All Souls College. This was a singular institution, an Oxford college that had no undergraduates and provided fellowships and fellowship for mature scholars who mostly moonlighted in important outside jobs. All Souls, for example, also contributed Philip Kerr, the Marquis of Lothian, a Scot of ancient lineage and Catholic upbringing who had become an ardent Christian Scientist. (Extreme religiosity appears here and there among the appeasers.) He was full of spongy ideas for moral betterment, and he was much esteemed by the government leaders. He was for years Secretary of the Rhodes Scholarship Trust and was made Ambassador at Washington in 1939. Another important personage was Tom Jones, a Welshman closely associated with All Souls although not a member of it; he was private secretary to both David Lloyd-George, the Prime Minister in World War I, who retained a good deal of prestige in the thirties (and who visited Nazi Germany and liked what he saw), and to Stanley Baldwin. Jones, like many of the others, was by reflex and training a germanophile and something of a francophobe. Unlike most of them he was positively sympathetic to many aspects of the Nazi regime.

Baldwin, who resigned in May 1937, had had the instincts of appeasement, rising mainly out of insularity and sloth. Instincts congealed into a creed under Neville Chamberlain. The other principal ministers were Lord Halifax, who succeeded Eden at the Foreign Office in February of 1938; Sir John Simon, the one-time Foreign Minister, who knew even less about economics than about diplomacy but became Chamberlain's chancellor of the Exchequer (he later became Churchill's Lord Chancellor, a somewhat surprising fact indicating the tribal quality of British political leadership); Sir Kingsley Wood, Secretary of State for Air; and Sir Samuel Hoare, of the Hoare-Laval deal, after 1937 the Home Secretary. An important sidekick was Sir Nevile Henderson, whom Chamberlain sent to Germany as ambassador to replace Sir Eric Phipps, who was regarded as anti-German. Henderson was a man of very limited intelligence but wholly unlimited eagerness to remain on friendly terms with Hitler and Hitler's Germany. Another was Sir Horace Wilson, Chamberlain's most intimate associate. His official position was that of adviser to the Prime Minister on industrial affairs. Wilson was a pigheaded man who thought he knew more about international relations than the diplomats and was strongly sympathetic to the dictators. Chamberlain, who distrusted the Foreign Office, often sought and took Wilson's advice and used him as an emissary.

All these men, and the others of the group, shared a peculiar moralistic outlook. They abominated war (Simon, indeed, had opposed World War I) but they rather admired strength. They were passionately patriotic and in old-fashioned ways both chivalrous and insular. Foreigners seemed remote and rather unreal to them. They loathed violence and cherished human life— Chamberlain was unable to sleep when he heard of the sinking of a British vessel soon after the war broke out, obsessed by the conviction that the blood of the victims was on his hands—but they countenanced the appalling brutalities in Germany without a tremor. Dawson actually approved of the Nazi Blood Purge of June 1934. Most of all, they believed in the rightness of German-British friendship and its feasibility (although Chamberlain personally loathed Germany and Germans*) and in the efficacy of personal contacts as a means of securing peace.

They were fond of visiting Hitler and coming home with loud, ingenuous assurances of his cordiality and sincerity. Lord Lothian in 1935 reported without skepticism that Hitler had "explicitly" said to him, "What Germany wants is equality, not war; that she is prepared absolutely to renounce war."† Lord Halifax, a very experienced, very sensitive, and in many ways a very able

---

*Iain MacLeod, *Neville Chamberlain* (New York: Atheneum, 1962), p. 206.
†Quoted in A. L. Rowse, *Appeasement* (New York: Norton, 1961), p. 32.

statesman (who sometimes had conscientious doubts about appeasement), came away with confidence in Hitler's sincerity. He was one of those most determined to abandon the sterile formulas—Versailles, Locarno, the League, and anti-Nazi Front—and to form a wholly new policy to meet a new situation. He was so determined to reach agreement with the Germans that he was led to believe that good sense and friendly feelings might be enough to achieve it. Like all the appeasers, he believed in the efficacy of personal communication. For all his intelligence and experience, he represented the limitations of a patrician outlook in a world of vulgarians. Aristocratic and aloof, he and some of his colleagues gave evidence of a curious snobbery: if English gentlemen and statesmen were prepared, graciously, to trust Hitler, then Hitler could not resist trusting them. In fact, Hitler loathed him. When they met in November 1937, Halifax had mistaken the Führer for a footman. The dictator saw in the English gentleman the embodiment of aristocratic pretension and thought him a hypocrite and a liar; but Halifax thought Hitler a sincere, if crass, fellow, and suggested that Britain would countenance German expansion in central Europe if it were carried out in a decent and orderly way. He thought, in short, that Hitler could be wooed by reason and refinement.

It was characteristic of what happened on such visits. Again and again, influential Englishmen expressed confidence in Field Marshal Hermann Göring, Hitler's second-in-command, commander of the German Air Force. He was a psychopath, an arrant and brutal sensualist, a liar and a traitor, a wild egoist, an appallingly incompetent strategist, technician, and administrator, and a man of unparalleled greed. But he was of aristocratic background, and English gentlemen were sure they could deal with him and trust him. On the other hand, they fawned on, but disliked, Joachim von Ribbentrop, the social-climbing champagne salesman whom Hitler had sent to Britain as his ambassador. In London society he was regarded as gauche.

Behind these archaisms lay fear. Reasonable fear in statesmen is by no means discreditable, and the fear of appeasers had its sources in reasonable anxiety. The twentieth century was rapidly approaching the point where it might fulfill itself by exterminating humanity. Appeasers made an excusable mistake in timing —they believed the point had already been reached. In 1908 H. G. Wells, in *The War in the Air*, had prophetically described aerial extermination. In Spain, the fighting, which was on a relatively small scale, had reached at times the verges of extermination. The destructive potential of aerial bombing was correctly (but prematurely) anticipated, and it was a dogma of the Royal Air Force that there was no defense against heavy bombers. The airmen believed that the German air forces had achieved superiority and that this meant that they could bomb as they pleased. "They could not be prevented," Tom Jones wrote, "from laying the great capitals level with the ground."* The group was genuinely and deeply concerned about the prospective massacre of the British nation by bombing. And intimidation was contagious. In March of 1938 a very influential jounalist of leftist sympathies, editor of *The New Statesman*, told Hugh Dalton he thought "to plan armed resistance to the dictators was now useless. If there was a war we should lose it."†

Behind fear lay a sort of insular lethargy. Their credulity, supported by shreds of intelligence but not the real facts, was adopted without skepticism, almost with relief. The appeasers, and some of the Service people themselves, quite clearly *wanted* to believe in German invincibility. Wishing to spare their nation the unutterable horror of a science-fiction war, they mistook their class death-wish for a national will to survive.

Logically, the appeasers regarded Chamberlain not merely as their most important spokesman but with an increasing reverence, which fortified his own conviction that he was, as Eden bitterly remarked, "a man with a mission to come to terms with the dictators."‡ Chamberlain lent himself to the view that he was a messiah because he shared it. His was an odd personality. He was a lovable man to his friends. His views on social problems were humane and progressive. He had been a tough and extremely able administrator and financier in previous Cabinet posts. But he was on one hand shy, hypersensitive, sentimental,

*Quoted in Jon Kimche, *The Unfought Battle* (London: Weidenfeld and Nicolson), 1968, p. 7.
†Quoted in Gilbert and Gott, *op. cit.*, p. 119.
‡Anthony Eden, *Facing the Dictators* (Boston: Houghton Mifflin, 1962), p. 635.

and dependent, and on the other prodigiously obstinate and self-righteous. He deeply resented criticism, and thereby invited it—and so enclosed himself more and more within the circle of his admirers. It was characteristic that while he regarded Hitler as "half-mad," he still thought that he could manage him. Iain MacLeod, his most sympathetic biographer, has suggested that he was traumatized by the loss of a beloved cousin in World War I.

The essential clauses of the appeasers' creed tended logically to evolve toward a simple conclusion: "If you can't beat them, join them." Some were openly in favor of an alliance with Germany. Dawson, lectured by Professor Rowse on the increasing power of Germany, said, "If the Germans are so powerful as you say, *oughtn't we to go in with them?*"*

It was logical that the appeasers should, then, vigorously reject anything likely to annoy the Nazi regime. The year 1938 opened with an incident that was a telling illustration of this fact and of many others to come. It was a secret proposal by Franklin Roosevelt for a world conference to consider world tensions. Officially, all he was planning to suggest was a meeting of all nations to discuss great problems such as disarmament and international trade. Actually, he was hoping in this way to assert the prestige and leadership of the democracies by taking the initiative and to smoke out the dictators by forcing them to show their hand, possibly through refusing to attend the conference. Roosevelt's views on world affairs were changing, as were those of many other people in the United States. The Americans were better informed by their journalists about Nazi Germany than the British, and revulsion was strong. Roosevelt shared this; he understood, in fact exaggerated, the solidity of the Axis; and he saw the prospect of a domino process in Europe which would leave the dictators dominant on the Continent and perhaps in the world. But most Americans, however anti-Nazi, remained resolutely opposed to active participation in the affairs of Europe, which they still regarded as a nest of vipers, and determined never again to be involved in what they thought of as "Europe's wars." Roosevelt's proposal was designed partly to

*Rowse, *op. cit.*, p. 28.

educate them about the role of an America whose own safety
was tied to that of the rest of the world. Education required a
kind of ecumenical fuzziness that could make it seem compatible
with high-minded isolation. Still, the proposal was epochal; it
inaugurated the long, slow business of leading the United States
to exercise the power it possessed and whose disuse was leading
to chaos.

So the proposal was seen by Anthony Eden, who had long
tried to engage American concern in European affairs. So it was
seen by the British ambassador at Washington, Sir Ronald Lind-
say, who wrote of it, "I have long held that the best chance of
averting disaster is to range not only the United States Administration but also United States opinion behind the objectives of
the democratic governments."*

The attitude of Chamberlain and his friends was very different.
He thought Roosevelt's suggestion naive, meddlesome, and dangerous. It was aimed at the very purpose that Chamberlain
wished to avoid, the smoking out of the dictators' aggressive
aims. He disliked the embroilment of the strange Americans in
Europe's private affairs as much as he did that of the still stranger
Russians. He was himself confident that tactful and detailed
negotiations between Britain and Italy and Germany could produce fecund agreements ensuring stabilization of the world
situation, and he saw Roosevelt's proposed conference as interfering with them. Eden, who was vacationing in France, was
summoned home, but before he got there Chamberlain had sent
off a very curt refusal to Washington.

The results of this episode (wholly unknown to the public at
the time) were extensive and illuminating. Roosevelt was annoyed; his efforts to build a new policy and new American attitudes were frustrated. Two years were to pass before they were
effectively resumed. Eden, similarly annoyed and frustrated, resigned. He resented the way the Prime Minister was conducting
a personal foreign policy and circumventing the Foreign Office
and the Foreign Secretary, as well as being greatly distressed by
the unwisdom of his policy. Hitler and Mussolini presumably
concluded that the resignation was a sign of the determination

*Eden, *op. cit.* p. 624.

of the British government to avoid putting obstacles in their path and were emboldened. Most profoundly, the incident illustrated a basic element in appeasement and in European history: there was ample recognition of the weakness of Britain as arbiter of world affairs, but there was also a strong aversion to abandoning the old ways of European supremacy.

THE BEGINNINGS OF GREATER GERMANY

So far the Germans had done nothing beyond recovering part of what they had lost in 1919.

Following Eden's departure, Chamberlain pressed, with renewed confidence, for the first of the series of agreements that he expected to achieve a "general settlement"; that is, a voluntary renunciation by the dictators of their ambitions, a destruction by words of the thousand-year-old European dynamo in which the ambitions inherent in European national states were held in balance by the countering ambitions and power of others. Britain had no ambitions except for serenity. Consequently, it had no power either, for power in the European system was the armature of a strong sense of national destiny. And Chamberlain had no intention, either, of calling a new world into existence to redress the balance of the old.

The negotiations with Italy for a general settlement in the Mediterranean, pursued ever since the Hoare-Laval agreement had failed, had not been very prosperous. The League had affably abandoned sanctions, but Italy had withdrawn from the League and proclaimed its king the emperor of Ethiopia. Britain had no leverage, except the offer to "recognize" this state of things or to offer a reduction of its naval strength in the Mediterranean. But early in 1938, things began to move. Mussolini was nervous, frightened by the possibility of irretrievable estrangement. Chamberlain, working not through the Cabinet, the Foreign Minister, or the diplomats, but through private contacts (including his sister-in-law, who paid a friendly call on Mussolini), succeeded in reaching what he hoped was a general agreement in April 1938. It was, he thought, a triumph; the Italian reign in Ethiopia was "recognized," agreements about the level of naval

armaments and bases and abstention from inflammatory propaganda were reached. Italy was given the right to relatively
greater naval power, and if they had meant anything at all, the
agreements foreclosed a measure of British strength in the interest of conciliation for its own sake. This was precisely what
Chamberlain wanted. Believing in his personal mission and im-
bued with faith in the forms of the old order of treaties and
settlements, he supposed that this piecemeal dealing with spe-
cifics would eventually entrap the legions of the new Roman
empire within a network of limitations on their action. The network was a cobweb.

While the attention of the British Prime Minister was entirely
occupied with this project, Hitler was moving in new directions,
necessary prefaces to larger projects which made meaningless
the general settlement with Mussolini.

In early February, he attacked the independence of the German Army. Unthinkably difficult at any earlier stage in German
history, this was now feasible. The Nazis controlled the state
apparatus, they had the huge Party organizaton to back them,
and, in the past, especially in March 1936, Hitler's judgment had
been spectacularly right and the Army's spectacularly wrong.
These facts inclined more and more officers to a feeling that,
willy-nilly, they must accept his leadership—even his deity. But
most of the higher officers distrusted and disdained the vulgar
and irresponsible dictator who, they thought, would lead them
into a war they could not win.

The commander in chief was a very old-line type, the haughty,
sardonic Baron Werner von Fritsch. It is said that he and other
old-line generals objected to the marriage of Marshal von Blomberg, the Nazi Minister of War, on the grounds of the social
unsuitability of the bride (she was a lady of low degree and a
former prostitute). Hitler had attended the wedding, and the
generals' objections represented precisely the classic, cliquish
aloofness and condescension of the German officer corps which
Hitler, a former corporal, a petty bourgeois, and (in this sense)
a democrat to the point of mania, could not abide. He took an
ingenious revenge, by using forged documents showing that
Fritsch was a homosexual (which was not true; the culprit was

an inferior officer with a similar name). Homosexuality, a very common form of self-expression in Germany, was tolerated in private but loudly deplored in public by Hitler and the Nazi press. He had in the past exploited the disgust it excited to get rid of people whom he disliked, notably Ernst Roehm, the leader of the Storm Troops, whom he had had murdered in 1934. Now the Army's chief was dismissed on the same charge, along with sixteen other members of the high command.

There was involved, of course, much more than questions of morals and manners, or Blomberg's outrageous wife. To men like Fritsch it was horrifying to see a vulgar noncommissioned officer and his odious gang in charge of the destinies of *their* state. Hitler now punished the insubordination of the haughty Army. This he had long projected. Detailed planning for the reorganization of the armed forces had begun a year earlier, and starting with a directive on June 26, 1937, Blomberg had worked out plans for a unified command. The scheme was based on a detailed analysis of the possible wars it might be necessary to fight and envisaged much-strengthened co-ordination of all aspects of the national effort. The plans now began to be executed, and Hitler himself assumed the office of supreme commander in chief of Army, Navy and Air Force.

Blomberg also lost his job in a shake-up and was put into retirement. This may have been because the old-line officers detested him (and Hitler could not liquidate the entire officer corps). But it has been plausibly suggested that his oblivion resulted, ironically, from his having sided with Fritsch against Hitler's projects for expansion at the Hossbach meeting.* The high command was drastically shaken up and henceforth staffed with loyalists, many of them Nazis.

The purge was accompanied by similar renovations elsewhere. Baron von Neurath, the Foreign Minister, a comparable hold-over from the era of monocles and dueling scars, was kicked upstairs, and his place was taken by Joachim von Ribbentrop, the vulgar ambassador at London. Ribbentrop was a typical product of the Nazification process, an ambitious *arriviste* of humble origins who had been adopted by an aristocratic family, thereby

*Laurence Thompson, *The Greatest Treason* (New York: Morrow, 1968), p. 33.

acquiring the "von," (a preface indicating ancestors as an American DDS indicates dentistry) after which many Party dignitaries still insatiably lusted, despite the official contempt for the trappings of the monarchical past. He had good looks and some charm, and no discretion. He had been a successful salesman; now he became a courtier who, as the French Ambassador François-Poncet noted, "hurled thunderbolts of flattery at Hitler."* He enjoyed with equal gusto the panoply of traditional diplomacy and the purging of traditional diplomats. He was mainly a mouthpiece for Hitler, although his wild ideas sometimes influenced his boss. Under his direction the diplomatic service was, if not exactly cleansed, gradually reorganized to put new men in high positions and most of the old ones in harmless posts. In Germany, as in Great Britain, the professional diplomats were becoming irrelevant to the making and execution of policy. Increasingly, it was done by the political chief of state aided by private advisers and emissaries. It was a clear example of the way in which the inexorably growing national state was eating those parts of its apparatus, diverse and pluralistic *imperia in imperii,* that had been at once its servants and the restrictors of its despotism.

Hitler, freed of generals and ambassadors, was now, like Chamberlain freed of Eden, able to prosecute the plans he was dedicated to. The first agendum was Austria. Austria had several claims to priority. It occupied an area of vital strategic importance: its territory outflanked the most substantial of the proposed victims on Hitler's southern and eastern borders, the Czechoslovak Republic. The Czechs had a large army, large determination, and large fortifications facing the German frontier. The least defensible, and quite undefended, part of the Czechoslovak frontier was in the south, facing Austria. With Austria in German hands, Czechoslovakia could be garroted: the country's neck was small; less than a hundred miles separated the German frontier on the north and the Austrian on the south. Britain and France would not fight to restore Austria after it was engulfed, and it could easily be overrun in a few hours, while the ponderous processes of democratic decision were just beginning.

*André François-Poncet, *The Fateful Years* (New York: Harcourt Brace, 1949), p. 232.

Therefore, it was safe to annex Austria as *preparation* for possible war in the west, without risking it. Further, Austria was German; it had only a meager consciousness of nationhood, and it had a big and growing Nazi party. It had a dictator, a client of Italian fascism. It had, in short, very limited claims on the sentiments of the democracies. It had, lastly, a large gold supply, which was urgently needed.

The way had long been prepared. Austrians, already in truth soft enough, had been further softened by flattering propaganda about jobs and glory in their natural homeland, Greater Germany. The Austrian Nazi Party was adept at the now familiar methods of its kind: huge protest rallies against the reactionary government, nonnegotiable demands, excoriation of the enemies of the German Race, passionate denunciations of police brutality, exemplary beatings of assorted enemies, hoarse unisons of thousands shouting in hypnotic rhythms for Nazi power. They were capable of seizing it, too, as the Austrian police found when they raided Nazi Party HQ in May 1937. The evidence of support from Germany was conclusive and copious.

There is no doubt whatever that Hitler had always intended to unite the two German states as soon as feasible, and detailed studies of alternative methods for doing so had been long in course. Definite decisions had been taken at least six months before. In the Hossbach Minutes, annexation appears as a decided thing, although Hitler's outline of his plans showed that he was considering an attack on Czechoslovakia first, or the two simultaneously. He was probably diverted from this strategy by the military, who cogently argued that Czechoslovakia before Austria would be strategically very formidable, while Czechoslovakia after Austria would be easy. In any event, congenial visitors in Berlin were freely told that the "liquidation of the Austrian problem" was planned for spring 1938. Marshal Göring, as Chief Game Warden of Germany, presided over an international sporting exhibition at Berlin in November and invited its more notable participants to dine at his shooting lodge. The guests were struck by a huge fresco, newly painted, which showed Austria as part of Germany.*

*Gordon Brook-Shepherd, *The Anschluss* (Philadelphia and New York: Lippincott, 1963), p. 7.

A former German Chancellor, von Papen, had been ambassador to Austria. He had carried out the official German policy of respecting Austrian independence while demanding complete freedom for the Austrian Nazis. (Sometimes he complained to Party headquarters in Munich about its illegal activities in Austria.) He had been led to believe that this was what Hitler really wanted; it was typical of the state of Europe that foreign policy and the men who were supposed to carry it out had become masks for the real purposes of the state. The old methods of intercourse disguised the new. As part of the diplomatic shake-up, he had been dismissed. Hitler resorted now to intimidation in place of guile. He instructed the army to *feign* troop movements, and spread rumors indicating a possible invasion of Austria. The intention was to put the Austrian Nazis in control of the government at Vienna and then engineer its annexation at the initiative of a Nazi-run Austrian government.

The Austrian Chancellor since Dollfuss's assassination in 1934 had been Kurt von Schuschnigg, an old-fashioned conservative, a devout Catholic, a patriot, pro-Fascist but anti-Nazi. On February 11, he was summoned to Hitler's residence in Bavaria, Berchtesgaden, to hear a ranting complaint, accompanied by threats, about the maltreatment of the Austrian Nazis. Hitler demanded that Arthur Seyss-Inquart, their leader, be made a member of the Austrian Cabinet.

Schuschnigg displayed unexpected obstinacy and resource. He was a man of exceptional honor and rigidity, he was shocked by his lengthy exposure to Hitler's maniacal rage (which had been, though no doubt real enough, deliberately worked up), and he knew that putting Nazis in his ministry would be fatal to Austrian independence. He evolved, instead, an ingenious project. Having agreed, or seemed to agree, to Hitler's demands, he announced on his return home that there was to be a plebiscite held to discover whether the people of Austria wished to continue to be independent. It was announced on March 9, to be held on March 13.

Hitler was furious, and he knew he had to act quickly. There was little doubt that the plebiscite, if held (Hitler alleged it would be manipulated by Jews and monarchists, two groups which he had come to know in his early youth as a resident of Vienna and which he hated most of all groups in the world), would show a large majority for independence. This would remove the pretext for annexation. He at once sent an ultimatum to Schuschnigg demanding that the plebiscite be called off and that the Chancellor turn over his office to Seyss-Inquart. He also ordered the immediate assembling of German forces to invade Austria, "to establish constitutional conditions there and to prevent further outrages against the pro-German population." Schuschnigg did announce that the plebiscite would not be held, although the President of the Austrian Republic for a while refused to appoint Seyss-Inquart. He did not agree until the marching orders had been given, and Seyss-Inquart became Chancellor a few hours before the invasion began. Seyss-Inquart's first act in office was to invite the Germans to cross the frontier. They did so at daybreak on March 12. That night Hitler made a speech at Linz, Austria, and the German army, unopposed, was in Vienna, with something like two hundred thousand troops in the country. It looked like a terrifying display of military efficiency, although in fact some of the motorized units had broken down on the way.

Schuschnigg and Miklas, the President, had forced Hitler to act before he meant to, and with a display of military power he had wanted to avoid. There was now a question whether this very overt act of aggression against an independent state might meet with opposition from France, Britain, and, most of all, Italy.

It did not. Italian-German relations were at the moment good, in sharp contrast to three years before. The aftermath of Ethiopia had led Mussolini progressively, although reluctantly, into dependence on Germany. The estrangement of Italy from the western democracies is most simply testified in trade figures. Italy was entirely dependent on imported coal. In 1933, 23 per cent of its coal imports came from Germany; in 1936, 63.9 per cent. The proportion fell slightly after the war in Africa ended, but never below 58 per cent.*

*Figures compiled by Elizabeth Wiskemann, *The Rome-Berlin Axis* (New York: Oxford University Press, 1949), p. 55.

There was another, very embarrassing fact that dictated Italian policy. Italy had defeated Ethiopia, but it had notably failed to defeat the Ethiopians. The major cities were occupied, and the imperial family was in exile, but Victor Emmanuel's new empire consisted of a few heavily garrisoned towns and roads surrounded by a country the Italians dared not enter. It was expensive to try to run it, a serious drain on Italy's insufficient resources. This had the painful and paradoxical effect of making Mussolini more reluctant than ever to envisage war especially with Britain, while at the same time forcing him into close friendship with Hitler, who he was sure was going to provoke one. Tergiversation, always the dominant feature of Fascist foreign policy, now took the form of silent writhing. Mussolini, however, had no choice but to present the German connection as a triumph of Italian diplomacy. Typically, he sometimes thought it was.

In September 1937, he had paid a state visit to Germany. There, amid lavish displays of pageantry and popularity, intensely flattering, he had signed the Anticomintern Pact which Hitler had negotiated with Japan, a piece of paper intended to persuade everyone in the world who disliked communism that the sole mission of the three aggressing governments was to resist it. Its effects were probably not large, and certainly they were not immediate. But a written document now fortified the Axis. Mussolini went into one of his spasmodic fervors of germanophilia. The Italians who had stayed at home, notably the cautious and anti-German king, Victor Emmanuel III, resisted such inane symptoms of Mussolini's infatuation as the introduction of the Prussian goose-step into the Italian army and the importation of anti-Semitic ideas, which were entirely at variance with all the past preachments of the Fascists and with all of Italy's traditions. The old wiliness that had led the Italian dictator to distrust Germandom was for the moment dissolved.

Hitler's hospitality along with Mussolini's needs paid dividends when Austria was annexed. Hitler, rather nervously, sent a hasty message to Mussolini saying that the state of Austria and evidence (entirely fabricated) of a plot by Austria and Czechoslovakia to threaten Germany made the occupation of Austria necessary. He promised in effusive terms that he would never concern himself with the several hundred thousand Gemans who lived south of the Brenner Pass, in the Austrian province that Italy had acquired in 1919. He waited anxiously for word of Mussolini's reaction—and at 10:45 the evening before the invasion it came, a better one than he could have hoped for. His emissary, Prince Philip of Hesse (who was married to a princess of Italy) called from Rome, and the remarkable conversation was recorded for posterity. Prince Philip reported that the Duce accepted the idea of Austria's annexation to Germany.

Hitler: *Then please tell Mussolini I will never forget him.*

Hesse: *Yes.*

Hitler: *Never, never, never, whatever happens. . . . I shall be ready to go with him through thick and thin, no matter what happens.*

Hesse: *Yes, my Führer.*

Hitler: *Listen, I shall make an agreement. . . . You may tell him that I thank him ever so much; never, never shall I forget.*

Hesse: *Yes, my Führer.*

Hitler: *I will never forget whatever may happen. If he should need any help or be in any danger, he can be convinced that I shall stick to him whatever may happen, even if the whole world were against him.*

More than five years later, when the whole world *was* against him, Hitler made good his promise. It was one of the few promises he ever kept and is exemplary both of the peculiar personal traits which made him genuinely respect Mussolini, while seeing his limitations and follies very clearly, and of the extreme state of sensibility in which he found himself on the day he had first ordered German forces to invade a foreign state.

There were second thoughts in Rome. Mussolini, in one of his moments of realism, spoke of Austria as a pill he had been obliged to swallow; anti-German elements were strengthened. It was during the hangover of this dose that he pursued the negotiations with Britain and signed the agreement on April 23, 1938, in a mood (which was recurrent with him) of "showing Hitler." Hitler was shown; he was furious. But the outward Axis was undisturbed, and in May Hitler came to Rome. The arrangements were even more lavish there than they had been in Gemany in September, although Hitler was not fully subject to their flattery. The visit was uncomfortable. The Führer stayed a week in the royal palace and was patronized by the king, who visibly loathed him and publicly referred to him as a psychopathic drug addict. But Mussolini, mercurial as ever and perhaps frightened by his show of independence, was again receptive, and their relations were better than ever. Hitler kindly referred in a speech to a restored Roman empire, which was the reference that would most gratify the Fascists.

The Axis pursued its course, inwardly undulant, outwardly superb. The fact was that, despite his brooding and his surges of spite, Mussolini knew that Hitler had more to offer him, psychologically and militarily, than ever Chamberlain did with his painstaking negotiation of details and his warships still patrolling the Italians' Mare Nostrum.

The British and French also reacted to Austria's end as Hitler hoped they would and were rewarded not with effusive gratitude but with contempt. If there were to have been any effective aid to Austria, it must have come before, not after, the invasion, and this Hitler's scheme and swiftness prevented. In fact, the British Ambassador, Sir Nevile Henderson, who shared Hitler's view that Schuschnigg was a dangerous monarchist intent on restoring the House of Habsburg to the throne of its ancestors, actually gave the Germans encouragement in the original plans and later lied about it in print. The invasion was not expected in London and Paris. Word of it reached Chamberlain when he was actually attending a banquet in honor of Ambassador Ribbentrop, about to depart to take up his new post as German Foreign Minister. The Prime Minister was put out; his patient efforts at better relations with the dictators deserved a better fate than this. In Parliament he contradicted Hitler's public assertion that the matter was none of Britain's business and said it was: Austria had been a member of the League. But Austria was now dead and it was, of course, out of the question to go to war to resuscitate it. Churchill, in the same debate, warned in his usual orotund and delphic prose about the strategic disaster involved in the uncovering of Czechoslovakia's defenses. But he was *so* delphic, and so much occupied with lamentations for the thralldom of beautiful Vienna, that he convicted himself, in the eyes of the majority who were not his friends, of egregious romanticism, of lacking any sense of proportion.

The French were occupied, at the moment of Austria's downfall, with a Cabinet crisis, as they usually were during Hitler's more outrageous coups. It developed from the Republic's familiar Byzantine domestic politics. The ministry of Camille Chautemps had just resigned. No new one had been formed. The caretaker authorities of March 1938, like those of March 1936, were unable to act. (It might have been recalled by the cynical that when in 1914 Austria-Hungary had begun World War I by attacking Serbia, the French Prime Minister and Foreign Minister had been at sea, on their way home from a state visit to Russia. A quarter of a century later the responsible governors of the Third Republic were again at sea.)

Austria, its motto ran, *Erit in Ultima Orbe:* Austria will exist at the end of the universe. Today it seems possible again, but it took twenty million lives to make it possible.

CZECHOSLOVAKIA

The crisis of Czechoslovakia which was to lead to the temporary erasure of that name from the map, following those of Ethiopia and Austria, began on February 20, while the Austrian crisis was still at its height. In a speech Hitler announced that the persecution of the German-speaking minority in Czechoslovakia was "intolerable" to Germany. And while nobody knew it, on April 21, 1938, Hitler and General Wilhelm Keitel, newly appointed chief of staff of the German Army under the Nazi dispensation, sketched out Plan Green.* Plan Green was the program for invading Czechoslovakia, and, although Hitler had apparently not reached a final decision, it was based on the assumption that invasion would be necessary and would be resisted.

---

*The German word *Fall* is usually translated "case," its literal meaning, and it does in fact include the notion of a choice among several eventualities. But it is more intelligibly rendered as "plan."

The occasion for it was given careful attention; nowhere in all the Nazi records is there a more suggestive detail than that Hitler thought at this time of arranging to have the German ambassador at Prague assassinated, to provide an "incident" as the excuse for invasion—ambassadors were not merely to be masks instead of agents for the new ways of managing affairs; they were to be its victims. The war was to be preceded by the internal disruption of Czechoslovakia, to weaken its resistance and provide grounds for German intervention. It was expected that Prague would be occupied within four days. Only by such quick action could European complications be forestalled.

The preparations for the invasion were to be completed by October 1, 1938. They began at once. (Two days later, Chamberlain, hopeful of a general settlement, signed his agreement with Italy.) Secrecy and surprise were found to be the most useful elements in making history; the fact was Hitler's richest legacy to the dictatorships that came after him.

The German planners worked quietly and with resolute competence. There was an endless amount of minute planning for eventualities, including such details as what would be said by the propaganda services if, by chance, the British Legation in Prague should happen to be hit by a bomb. The theme of assassinating his own ambassador kept recurring; Hitler was apparently fascinated by the idea, although it was in the end abandoned. Very careful consideration was repeatedly given to the possibility of intervention from the West, and Plan Red was developed to deal with it. But Hitler thought France would not intervene, and he flew into a rage (which frightened the generals) when he was told that if it did the German defenses in the west could withstand the French army for only a few days. (This was probably true; the so-called Siegfried Line, which many in the west believed impregnable, hardly existed.) He was sure that he could count on the divisions and disarray in the democracies to allow him another free *fait accompli*. There is some question as to how irrevocable the October 1 deadline was, or Hitler's decision to march. But the records are full of finalities; the contingent plans for *general* war (in case the west reacted) "must be fully assured by October first"; "It is my unalterable decision to smash

Czechoslovakia by military action in the near future."

The principal preparations, beside the melodramatically secret Army planning, were the melodramatically public operations of German propaganda and the Nazi Party in the German-speaking parts of Czechoslovakia. There were daily reports of sensational outrages against the poor Germans in Czechoslovakia. Persecution and murder were shown as a lunatic fad with the Czechs. The picture was drawn of a minority that *had* to be rescued from the brutal clutches of their bestial oppressor, a Czech state that, having practiced injustice for twenty years, had passed to violence and was approaching dissolution. Nobody outside of Germany believed all of this, but the point was being made; there were three million Germans inside Czechoslovakia who were denied their birthright, and Hitler was determined to do something about it. Even skeptical people had to take into account the "evidence" that there was something basically rotten in the state of Czechoslovakia, a rottenness that required fundamental reordering of central European affairs.

Czechoslovakia was indeed vulnerable, although the only thing that made it more vulnerable in 1938 than it had been before was the massive protest of its German citizens. It had been formed in 1918 when the Austro-Hungarian monarchy was losing control of its own provinces, put together by Czech nationalist leaders out of leftovers, provinces almost as diverse as those of its parent. It lay, fishlike in shape, about five hundred and fifty miles long and never much broader than one hundred and fifty, across central Europe. Within its borders lived peoples of six nationalities. The Czechs were dominant, but on the whole the minorities were more generously governed than anywhere else in central or eastern Europe. The state was fairly stable, impeccably constitutional, and more prosperous than any other east of the Rhine. Its existence depended, however, on general European acceptance of the Versailles settlement. Neighboring powers all had appetites for Czechoslovak lands.

There were Poles on the northern fringes, in lands that postwar Poland hankered for, and Magyars on the south, in some of the numerous areas that Magyar Hungary had lost and passionately wished to recover. And there were the three million German-speaking citizens—as against some seven and a half million Czechs. The majority lived concentrated in areas around the borders of the provinces of Bohemia, Moravia, and Silesia, many of them on the outer slopes of the Sudeten mountains that enclosed the Czech heartland on two sides. They had never formed part of a German national state; the Bohemian frontier with Germany was the oldest political frontier in Europe. They were not treasonably assertive in the twenties about their kinship with the Germans of Germany; but they were used to the traditions of the Austrian empire. In that empire the Germans had been dominant. Bohemian Germans had been brought up to regard the Czechs with more or less tolerant contempt, and they were accessible to the messages of their innate superiority and their racial destiny.

After 1933 a new party was growing among the Bohemian Germans. It was called the Sudetendeutsche Heimatsfront (Sudeten German Homeland Front). It was led by Konrad Henlein, an obscure young man, himself half Czech, who at first made no demand for union with Germany but concentrated his attention on righting injustices suffered by the German population in Czechoslovakia and fighting the competing German parties, mainly the Social Democratic and Catholic parties, and the Jews. At first the new party was not specifically Nazi, but after 1933 it rapidly became so. It was much aided by real though minor grounds for complaint against Czech rule (most of the officials and the police in the region were Czechs, for example) and by rumors and lies exaggerating them and, perhaps most of all, by the Depression. Czechoslovakia suffered from the economic crisis, and the unemployed Sudetens were as willing to listen to Henlein as their German brothers were to Hitler. (So were the British. Henlein was invited to speak at the stately Royal Institute of International Affairs and made a good impression.) In the Czechoslovak parliamentary elections of 1935, the Sudeten party won the votes of more than 60 per cent of the German-speaking voters in the republic and became the second largest party in Parliament. The other German parties lost as many as three quarters of their supporters. Thereafter, the Sudetens' energetic challenge to the state grew faster still. Support from Germany also grew. Money and advice poured in. There now began to be the kinds of incidents familiar in Austria, in which Sudeten Germans were subjected to Czech police brutality. They were mostly deliberately or indirectly provoked by the Nazis, but they provided documentation, lavishly elaborated, for the German propaganda ministry. There was, moreover, a simultaneous spreading of discontent among the Slovaks, who resented Czech overlordship.

There was, then, a convenient background for Berlin's intense interest after April 1938 in the welfare of the Sudeten people and the assertion that Czechoslovakia was going to pieces. Beneath this interest, Hitler's assumption that Bohemia must one day be part of Greater Germany was made urgent by the fact that Czechoslovakia, a heavily and efficiently armed bastion, must be reduced before other expansive programs could be undertaken.

The appeasers were perfectly content that Hitler should expand in central Europe. Henderson was actually urging them to *encourage* German expansion to the east as early as November 1937.* No one of Chamberlain's friends seems to have questioned the expediency of this policy, and some British and French leaders spoke and thought of seeking a "solution to the Czech problem." It is a very clear case of a situation where reality followed imagination. Efforts to solve the problem were nonetheless agonized and painstaking.

The gulf between the western efforts at a solution and Hitler's decision to break up Czechoslovakia decided the terms on which the European war would eventually be fought. It was widened by a curious incident in May 1938. Rumors, which were unfounded, reached the west of troop movements and an impending German invasion (the German preparations were in fact just getting underway and the German Army commander nervously warned that at the moment he could not possibly hope to defeat even Czechoslovakia alone). They reached Prague, and Prague, understandably edgy, mobilized. (It has been alleged that the Czechs themselves invented the rumors, but this is both unproved and rather implausible.) In any event, there was a crisis,

*In a memorandum, previously unpublished, which appears in Thompson, *op. cit.*, Appendix.

even more unreal than most crises in those times. Overt aggression was precisely what Chamberlain could not tolerate; his plan for peace depended upon keeping Hitler caught in the cobweb of negotiated settlement. Moreover, the French and the Soviets were both loudly protesting their determination to honor their alliances with Czechoslovakia, coming to its aid if Hitler attacked it. It was therefore of the first importance to the London government to prevent the rumored invasion, and a strong warning was delivered to Hitler by the British on May 21, 1938. It was answered (quite honestly) with puzzled indignation. It seems likely that Hitler's final decision to invade was made as a result of this incident. That was how he reacted to thwarting. In any event, no invasion took place at this time, but the British were alarmed by the Czech show of initiative and the German indignation. It was another, reverse, example of fantasy.

As early as March 1938, Chamberlain had rejected proposals, initiated by the Soviet Union, for British, French, and Soviet discussions about how to prevent German aggression against Czechoslovakia. He said, in effect, that Britain would probably never fight except to defend its own national and imperial interests or in the face of unprovoked military action by an aggressor —which he was sure could be avoided. The situation thereafter presented itself to him as a series of imperatives for his personal conduct; he had trapped himself. He must dissuade Hitler from unprovoked military action. He must restrain the Czechs from provocation and induce in them a readiness to make concessions, and to do this he must discourage the ardors of their protectors, the French and the Soviet Union. He knew that if France unconditionally honored its pledge of Czech integrity, Britain would sooner or later be involved in war. In effect, what this meant was simultaneously to find out what Hitler's demands were and persuade the Czechs to grant them.

The summer was spent in these pursuits. The Czechs were eminently reasonable, surprisingly so. Most of the leaders agreed that something had to be done to assuage the German minority, and they were willing to listen to advice. Advice was freely given. Heavy pressure was exerted by London on both the Czechoslovak government and on Henlein (with whom the British had direct private contacts) to negotiate with each other. Henlein was evasive and obstinate; efforts were made to get the Germans to make him behave more reasonably, but the Germans, while shrieking about the misdeeds of the Prague government, answered enquiries by saying that the matter was not their business; it was all up to Henlein. Privately, they were telling him to be as evasive as possible, to play for time until the Army was ready to attack. At the beginning of the crisis his demands had been formulated as self-government for the Sudeten Germans, and a pro-German foreign policy in Prague, but this formulation, it presently developed, was by no means final. In fact, the most awkward fact of all was that Henlein, and later Hitler, kept shifting their requirements. Eduard Beneš, President of Czechoslovakia, later said that at one point he had baffled Henlein's emissary by giving him a blank paper and telling him to write his demands on it, promising in advance to grant them. The story has been questioned; but it is true that the Henleinists were interested only in keeping negotiations going, not in settling the issue.

An elderly and frigid British Cabinet minister, Walter, Baron Runciman, President of the Board of Trade (the equivalent of Secretary of Commerce), was judged a suitable person to investigate the situation in Czechoslovakia and advise its government on a proper policy; he was accordingly sent to Prague. Both in private and public, Chamberlain and various of his confidants were letting it be known that Britain would under no circumstances fight to defend Czechoslovakia with its present boundaries, and Runciman's mission was quite openly intended to weaken Czech resistance. It got nowhere. Henlein was acting under Hitler's command, but Hitler still said that the matter was none of his business. There was, in effect, no way to find out what concessions could be made to satisfy them.

In London, the appeasers were working hard to frighten the British public out of sympathy for the Czechs. Early in September, *The Times* stunned its readers by telling the Czechs they should allow their country to be partitioned. But these activities availed not at all in quieting Hitler. His speeches grew longer and louder, and at the vast Nazi party convention at Nüremberg, on

September 12, he ranted interminably before hundreds of thousands of cheering admirers about the iniquities of Czech brutality and his intention to relieve the sufferings of its victims. The speech was inconclusive, because (as we know now) there was still more than a fortnight to go before the German marching orders could be issued. It conveyed, however, the likelihood of imminent invasion while not announcing its certainty, with the natural effect, in London, of encouraging an ever more fervent resolution to negotiate.

Europe believed that war was near. It seemed inconceivable that the French could desert the Czechs; their own interests provided unanswerable arguments against doing so, for the Czechs had some 30 divisions whose elimination would, in effect, decrease the strength of the French defense by 60—30 Czech divisions lost, 30 German divisions released to fight elsewhere.* In Paris, war hysteria collided with fascist demonstrations while preparations for defense against air attack were commenced.

In London, air-raid shelter trenches were dug in the parks, and Chamberlain spoke, in the odd, dry voice that moved so many listeners:

> How horrible, fantastic, incredible, it is, that we should be digging trenches and trying on gas masks here because of a quarrel in a far-away country between people of whom we know nothing.

But that was not until later in the month. In the fortnight between the onset of fears of imminent war and Chamberlain's reference to what sounded like a quarrel on another planet, the situation in both France and Britain had altered considerably.

Chamberlain had been thinking for some time about the possibility of a personal meeting with Hitler, although the plan had been considered in great secrecy and without the knowledge of most of the government or even of the King of Great Nutain (who complained that he was being kept in ignorance of high state matters). After the Nuremberg speech seemed to be the time to execute it. Hitler disliked the idea of the interview. He could not act before October 1, however. What he expected was

---

*The exact strength of the Czech forces and their efficacy is not certain. Churchill, a notably impressionistic authority, put it at 40 highly efficient divisions. A more careful chronicler put it at 30, half of them indifferently prepared. Other authorities say 36.

a warning, but he could not avoid meeting the Prime Minister as a delaying tactic. On September 15, making his first flight in a plane, Chamberlain went to Germany. There was much excitement throughout the world when the announcement was made. In Britain and Germany there was rejoicing. Elsewhere reactions varied from astonishment to consternation.

In the drama that now began to enact itself there is farce, tragedy, and shocking irony. Nothing was what it seemed to be. Chamberlain was acting on the belief that a German attack on Czechoslovakia was likely in a matter of hours, while actually Hitler was playing for time. Most ironic of all was what was going on in the German army. The reorganization of February 1938, with its purge of the important non-Nazi generals, had cowed the Army but had by no means converted it. The generals still suffered from their ineffable pessimism about their Army, and they continued to dislike and distrust Corporal Hitler and his harebrained strategies. From Walther von Brauchitsch, Army commander in chief, down, the majority of them were reduced almost to panic by the prospect that an attack on Czechoslovakia (itself, they thought, sufficiently speculative) would lead to war with France. And they were convinced it would.

They presented their doubts repeatedly to Hitler, but Hitler merely roared in answer. As a result, a core of organized opposition began to form. Von Brauchitsch excused himself—he was sympathetic, but he was a loyal soldier. The principal mover was the Chief of the General Staff, Ludwig Beck, an honorable officer of the old-guard persuasion. He and his fellow conspirators organized, and they went so far as to talk to Otto Strasser, the left-wing Nazi who had been purged by Hitler in 1933 and was living in exile in Switzerland. They told him they planned to take action (of an unspecified sort) if Hitler marched on Czechoslovakia. Emissaries were also sent to London, where Halifax and Chamberlain dismissed his reports without serious consideration.

The generals' plot is difficult to assess. There is no doubt that it existed, and there is no doubt that, if Hitler had launched a war, it would have been formidable. Whether or not it could have succeeded, the plotters could have disrupted the German invasion of Czechoslovakia and destroyed the prestige of the regime. But Chamberlain discounted all this, and instead determined to pursue his negotiations with Hitler.* Beck and his friends were appalled.

If the generals' plot was the most substantial irony in the situation, the most grotesque was Hitler's treatment of Chamberlain. At the interview on September 15, at Hitler's aerie in the Bavarian mountains above Berchtesgaden, he was baffled by Chamberlain's apparent willingness to concede everything that he had been planning—and apparently wanting—to take by force. He disliked categorical questions, and he was cautious and rather evasive when the old Englishman asked quietly for his terms. He stated them—without really thinking about it very carefully—as all the areas of Czechoslovakia whose populations were more than 80 per cent German. These would be annexed to Germany. The rest of the republic, he supposed, would then be split up among its component nationalities. Chamberlain had already made up his mind that the cession of the Sudeten areas to Germany would be "necessary." He agreed to Hitler's terms, and to try to persuade the British Cabinet, the French, and the Czechs, to accept them. The two would confer again, and Hitler agreed in principle (barring incidents) not to invade Czechoslovakia in the meanwhile. Chamberlain, having formed the impression that Hitler "would be better than his word," flew home. Immediately following the meeting, the Führer gave orders for the armies that were scheduled to attack Czechoslovakia to begin their final preparations.

At some point, Hitler had not merely decided that a war might be necessary but that it would be desirable. He was perhaps influenced by others—this had been Ribbentrop's line from the beginning. The plans for the invasion had been completed on August 30, when the date was finally decided on,† and this hard and final fact perhaps influenced him. A few days after the

---

*A good account is now available in the introductory chapters in Harold Deutsch, *The Conspiracy Against Hitler in the Twilight War*, (Minneapolis: University of Minnesota Press, 1968).

†Keith Eubank, *Munich* (Norman, Oklahoma, University of Oklahoma Press, 1963), p. 121. Eubank gives an excellent description of German military planning.

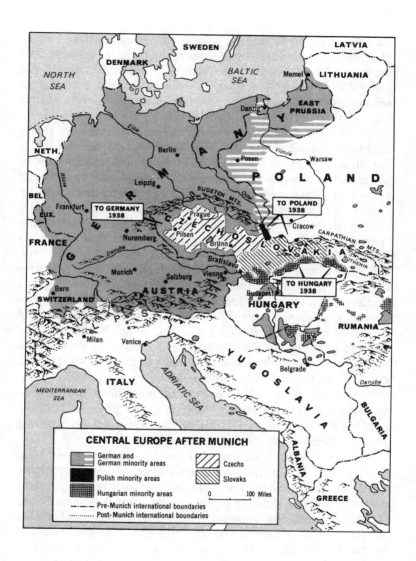

CENTRAL EUROPE AFTER MUNICH

German and German minority areas

Polish minority areas

Hungarian minority areas

Czechs

Slovaks

0   100 Miles

Pre-Munich international boundaries

Post-Munich international boundaries

Berchtesgaden meeting, he told a foreign diplomat that he
planned to start military operations against Czechoslovakia, and
there is evidence to indicate that he thought the time for a
general European war favorable, since he thought Britain's rearmament might alter the balance of power unfavorably in coming months.

After the first meeting with Chamberlain, however, Hitler
decided he could get anything he wanted out of him. He had a
very low opinion of the old man's talents and staying power.
Chamberlain thought, on the other hand, that he had achieved
a major success, and this complacency was strengthened by
clamorous acclaim. He had passed through screaming friendly
crowds in Munich on his way back. At home, less volatile
crowds showed that they felt deeply the moving spectacle of an
old man with an umbrella setting out to reduce to order, decency, and prose the wild mystery of Hitler's rhetorical sav-
agery. Even among the French, not generally given to
sentimental idolatry of elderly English politicians, there was a
tendency to tears in some circles and a disposition to see Neville
Chamberlain as a savior. They thought, as he did, that he had
stopped an invasion. His trip to Berchtesgaden, in short, made
him a symbol and created an aura that had nothing whatever to
do with the facts of policy and peace.

Within the British Cabinet he had no serious difficulty in
securing a large majority in support of his project. Then he
conferred with Edouard Daladier and Georges Bonnet, the
French Premier and Foreign Minister.

They had earlier been spirited enough in their professions of
loyalty to the Czech allies to frighten Chamberlain, but now their
resolution had weakened. It was subject to attrition by the British—when asked squarely by Bonnet whether they would fight
if France honored its alliance, Halifax ambiguously replied that
the British Cabinet ministers "are unable to make precise state-
ments of their future action, or the time at which it could be
taken, in circumstance that they cannot at present foresee."* He
did not wish to encourage the French to rashness. But French
policy was being reshaped by larger and more melancholy con-

*Quoted in Thompson, *op. cit.*, p. 113.

siderations than this. Frenchmen were obsessed by the general strategic situation of their country.

The crumbling of the French determination took place partly for a reason of the utmost significance which only much later came to light. Bonnet was to be regarded as a slithy politician and as a traitor who almost deliberately destroyed France as a great power. This reputation, based partly on his own unconvincing apologias, arose during the period after September 1938, when he became the most ardent French appeaser. But he was rather an excessive realist. His offense was to lose hope. He did not destroy France as a great power; rather he exaggerated the fact that it had ceased to be one. He was a trained economist and a former ambassador at Washington, and these qualifications helped him to see, as clearly as anybody else in Europe, that the only way to preserve a system which had depended on the fading illusion of French greatness was to invoke the power of the United States. In September of 1938 he acted on his certainty and secretly pled with Roosevelt for promises of military support in the war he knew would follow the honoring of the alliance with Czechoslovakia.*

Bonnet's reasoning was based partly on the pessimism of the French generals, much heightened by the horrifying tales spread that September by Charles Lindbergh about German air power, which reduced the French air force to the verge of tears. Lindbergh, after a visit to Germany, was convinced it was irresistible. He passionately sought to persuade the British and French that resistance was suicide. He presented fabulous figures (8,000 planes) on the German air force and German plane production. They were terrifying, although completely incorrect.

The logic of such a strategic situation was formidable. The Soviet Union had no common frontier with the beleaguered Czechs or with Germany, and the governments of Poland and Rumania, which lay between, were fanatically averse to allowing Red troops on their territories. France had no common frontier with the Czechs, and the estimate of German power and the strength of the Siegfried Line, much overrated by the French

---

*A very important study of this episode, theretofore unknown, was made by J. M. Haight in "France, the United States, and the Munich Crisis," *Journal of Modern History,* 1960, 32 (4), 340–58.

generals, seemed to assure that Czechoslovakia would be doomed and France itself threatened and its cities laid waste. It seemed possible that Italy and Spain would join Germany. Most significantly, *the French General Staff had made no plans at all to march into Germany to assist the Czechs.* Still, Bonnet had been willing to risk war if France could be assured of American aid.

It was out of the question. American public opinion, though more anti-Nazi than ever, was almost as far as ever from readiness to contemplate fighting again in Europe. For Roosevelt such a course as Bonnet proposed was politically unfeasible, nationally unthinkable, and technically impossible. The fear of war, the sense of central Europe being far away and irrelevant to national affairs, so potent in Britain, were a thousand times more potent in America. Roosevelt promptly rejected Bonnet's solicitations. There was then nothing left, the Frenchman despairingly concluded, except to follow Britain's initiative, and thereafter he exceeded the British in his zeal for a general settlement which would, if necessary, concede Hitler anything he wanted east of the Rhine.

Bonnet's chief was Edouard Daladier, who had succeeded Chautemps as Prime Minister. He was a Radical, but of a singularly stolid sort. Of peasant background, the son of a baker, he shared the French peasants' horrible memories of 1914–18, when peasant blood had paid the costs of French heroism. Like the British appeasers, he was insular and unimaginative; unlike them, he had the cautious skepticism of a small-time democratic politician. Like all Frenchmen, he was frightened and appalled by the continuing disarray in his country. Neither Bonnet, whose perception of needs was clear but too categorical, nor Daladier, whose perception was clouded by caution, could assert his independence of British suzerainty in foreign policy.

The other French ministers were divided in their views, and so was the nation. Much of the French press was stridently opposed to a strong stand; in some cases it was openly pro-Nazi. As one headline put it in April 1938, "Must three million Frenchmen die to keep three million Germans under Czech rule?" The French skill at epigram concealed a much more pertinent and difficult question: should an incalculable number of French lives be risked to prevent the Nazi state from dominating Europe? Bonnet and Daladier, informed men, might reject the false premises of the first question; the second they dared not answer.

They agreed almost without reservation that Czechoslovakia must yield its borderlands to Hitler. They had hoped to save the Czech fortifications, without which the republic would be defenseless—this was also Beneš's principal hope now. The fortifications were unfortunately in solidly German areas. (In any case, though no one knew it, the fortifications were exactly what Hitler was determined to get.) The French also insisted on a guarantee of the indefensible stump that would be left, and the British agreed, also with reservations, to consider this.

The titular great powers thus surrendered. The Czechs, however, boggled. The Czech people faced the terrors of the summer of 1938 with the same stoical and almost superhuman resolution, and their leaders with the same skill and patriotism, that they were to show in a no less terrible summer thirty years after. The government at Prague at first refused to agree to the Anglo-French proposals and prepared to fight. Beneš had no illusions, however. He was sure the country would be overrun, even if the French and the Soviets were forced to come to his aid. Still, he gave in only after forty-eight hours of threats, culminating on September 21 in an outright ultimatum. The French and British envoys told him categorically that *their* governments demanded his surrender. Beneš agreed. Two weeks later, when the Germans had won their demands, he would resign at German insistence.

On September 22, Chamberlain paid a second flying trip to Germany. He saw Hitler in a hotel beside the Rhine at Godesberg, a suburb of the sleepy university town of Bonn, which a decade later would become the seat of the German Federal Republic. On the Rhine, the Prime Minister found Hitler deplorably changed from the cordial, if evasive, host he had met in the Alps. Chamberlain had given him all he had asked for on the first visit. Hitler now haughtily rejected it; "It is no longer enough." Conditions had changed in the past week; the atrocities of the Czechs had become unendurable and must be punished. He was personally rude and abusive. Chamberlain was deeply offended, and himself grew angry. His vanity as well as his policy was affronted; he prepared to go home. But then word reached Godesberg that the Czechs had ordered general mobilization (in fact, Chamberlain had himself released them from a promise not to mobilize). The effect was to frighten Hitler; he was willing to have a war, but he could not fight one for another week. Temporizing was necessary. So he presented Chamberlain with a new set of demands, much stiffer than those he had casually proposed at Berchtesgaden. *Immediate* evacuation of the Sudeten areas by the Czechs was to be required. There were further reproaches; Hitler, now more gracious, extended the time limit to October 1, a date with a significance of which Chamberlain was wholly ignorant. Chamberlain dismally agreed to forward the new demands, but without recommendations to Prague; and for a second time, under sadder circumstances, he flew back to London.

By the time he got there, he seems to have become convinced that Hitler's terms must be accepted. But he was faced now by outrage in British public opinion and much stronger opposition in the Cabinet. Even Halifax felt that the Czechs could not be asked to make further surrenders. In France, on September 9, reserves were called up and military leaves canceled. This preface to mobilization was received stoically by the public. Hitler's Godesberg ultimatum had quelled the peace hysteria of the previous week.

The Prime Minister pursued with weary, anxious patience the terrible job of convincing his colleagues, the French, and the Czechs that the terms of the previous surrender were grossly insufficient. Viewed in retrospect, it seems incredible—Chamberlain's patient obstinacy, one old man forcing three nations to surrender to an enemy whose own generals thought that it could not survive a week against attack by the French Army. But this was known only to German generals. To much of the world it seemed that what hung in balance was the instantaneous destruction of Paris and London and the fifteen million people who inhabited them.

In London some opinions were hardening. Two members of the Cabinet offered their resignations, and even the *Daily Tele-*

graph, a paper of reactionary cast, called Chamberlain's policy "an abject and humiliating capitulation." It looked as if patience were not enough this time. The French Premier rebelled; summoned to London, Daladier pounded the table and insisted that this time France would not back down. He won, or seemed to win, his point. Chamberlain at last agreed to grant what he had so long refused, an unconditional guarantee to fight at France's side. And he also said he would dispatch Wilson with a message to Hitler warning him that if he would not accept the Berchtesgaden agreement, he must face war.

He also forwarded the Godesberg demands to Prague, where a frightened cabinet discussed them, but did not act on them. Time was very short. Hitler was now publicly threatening war; he was sure that it would begin as scheduled on October 1. He was tired of the interminable meddling by Chamberlain. Wilson in Berlin on September 27 was having a bad time. Chamberlain's letter was somewhat gentler than the French, and his colleagues, had intended, but it was enough to throw Hitler into a rage. He said that he did not care what anyone else did; he would have the Sudeten lands on October 1, whether the Czechs evacuated them or not. His imprecations, Wilson reported, were terrible to hear.

In London, Chamberlain despaired. He wearily believed that he had come to the end of the pressures he could apply to Paris and Prague. His final attempt to save the peace was an appeal to Mussolini to intervene with Germany, but he had ordered defense measures, and Britain prepared to fight. The Navy was mobilized. The distribution of gas masks to the population began. Women and children were being evacuated to the country. The government, guilty as it often was of projecting its own feelings, feared a mass panic, although there was never the slightest sign of hysteria in Britain, and called out troops to control the citizens. The lamps of London began to go out; the blackout, the gloomy shroud of war, impended.

Chamberlain was dismally recounting the failure of his efforts to the House of Commons when he was dramatically interrupted by a message to say that Mussolini had proposed, and Hitler had accepted, a four-power conference to discuss the crisis. It was to meet in Munich the next day. The scene in the crowded House resembled the streets of Pittsburgh when the Pirates won the Series. A member of the House shouted, "Thank God for the Prime Minister."

But it was neither God nor the Prime Minister but the Italian dictator who had postponed the war. The fact was astounding. To the democracies it seemed providential. To Hitler it was irritating. To the conspiring German generals it was a disaster. To Mussolini it was simply logical; he had received Chamberlain's appeal in a mood of extreme trepidation. Italy was, at the moment, sadly unprepared. The renewed euphoria of Hitler's May visit had subsided, and the strong germanophobia in Italy, plus calm appraisals of Italian fighting strength, made Mussolini dread as much as Chamberlain the possibility of hostilities in which he would be outclassed. His initiative was the one that Hitler could not disregard; once the proposal had been made, a conference must be held. And at Munich, on the following day, the extensive proposals for dismembering Czechoslovakia that Hitler had presented at Godesberg were written into a treaty and signed by the British, French, Italians, and Germans.

The Czechs were not consulted; they were ordered to accept it. The Germans reluctantly agreed to wait a week to complete the occupation of the Sudeten lands, but the frontier was crossed on October 1, in peace, by troops prepared to attack. Hitler had gotten that much, anyway, of what he wanted. He was able to tell Chamberlain an inspiriting lie. The Sudeten lands were, he said, his last territorial demand in Europe. Chamberlain believed him and began to consider the possibility of restoring some of the German colonies.

The British and the French yielded what the day before they had been prepared to fight for, with no compensation except that the surrender had been made "by negotiation" instead of in the face of armed attack, and that Hitler vaguely agreed to negotiate a guarantee of surviving Czech territory. (None was ever negotiated.) The most extreme territorial demands were granted: 50 per cent German provinces (to be determined by the authority of the pre-World War I census) were to be given to Germany at once. Other areas that Germany demanded were to be occupied pending plebiscites. (None was ever held.) The powers yielded to Hitler's threats, constantly repeated at the conference, that if he were not given all he asked he would immediately order an invasion—which the French and British were by then irretrievably committed to oppose by war. They yielded, one is tempted to say, because they were frightened by their own brief show of resolution in the previous days. Like Hitler, they could not refuse to attend a conference once it had been proposed, and once they attended it they could not reject a peaceful solution that was not much worse for the Czechs than the one they had pushed a fortnight before. And most of all, perhaps, they yielded because Munich seemed to provide machinery and a precedent for what Chamberlain was seeking, a general settlement.

The price was high. When the Czech representative was given the text of the agreement to read and was told his government must accept it immediately, he broke into tears. And it was not a precedent, nor a settlement. Nothing was settled by it. It forestalled nothing which would not soon take place anyway. Still, at the time it was regarded as epochal, and this misapprehension is part of its significance. Chamberlain returned to weeping mobs of thousands and impetuously plagiarized his brother Austen (and the Bible), telling them that this meant "peace for our time." Daladier, expecting to be greeted at Paris with all the vituperation that baffled French patriots are capable of, found instead something that looked like adoration. Hitler was at a new pinnacle of prestige, and henceforth even skeptics would believe in his supernatural powers. Mussolini had acquired a dazzling reputation as a man of peace and a maker of history. All these reputations were to have their importance in what happened next, for they guaranteed that Hitler's next initiatives would produce staggering disillusionment.

Even while these false reputations were being built, they were being dispelled. Chamberlain himself had doubts; two members of his Cabinet resigned; much of British opinion was dismayed. Hitler had no intention of observing the limitations Munich seemed to have placed on his freedom of action, just as Mussolini had no intention of fulfilling his pledges of unconditional support for Germany. The cynic, Daladier, as he drove in stolid embarrassment through the cheering Paris crowds, muttered to himself, "the idiots."

The Munich illusion was a complex one. The abstract ethics of the Czech crisis made judgments difficult: almost any price seemed fair for peace; the price paid was the sacrifice of Czechoslovakia, but also the liberation of three million Germans who in a large majority wanted to live in Hitler's Germany; to have fought to prevent them from doing so would have seemed —and in a sense *been*—absurd; the French and British certainly believed that Hitler *might* win a war. They were the victims both of illusions cast by Hitler's secret aims and methods and of their own overcautious military men.

What was significant about Munich, beyond the illusions, was not what was done by those who were present but the absence of those who were not.

This was a purely European conference in the traditional sense. Europe's great powers assembled—for the last time in history—to settle its chronic and incurable malady, the tangled affairs of central-southeastern Europe. Their agreement, with the events it gave rise to, was an almost conscious act of faith in the proposition that the old Europe was still in charge of its destinies and that the rest of the world had no influence on its fate. The United States and the Soviet Union were not there. This was the crucial fact about Munich. There is a certain symmetry in Chamberlain's rejections of America as an arbiter of affairs in January and of the Soviet Union in September. In one sense his judgment was correct; to the purposes he pursued the Americans and Russians were both irrelevant and unassimilable. Their presence would have wrecked his efforts and the settlement he sought. What he did not realize was that his purposes were impossible of fulfillment.

The situation of the future superpowers *looked* very different, for the United States did not wish, and could not be forced to, full participation in European affairs, while the Soviet Union seemed to be pressing with embarrassing zeal for just that. But the Soviets also dispensed illusions. In May, before Munich, the Moscow government was apparently certain that the western powers would not come to Czechoslovakia's aid. If they should do so, the Russians were calculating not to take a vigorous part in the war. Maxim Litvinoff, the Foreign Minister (he was still called "commissar") frankly told the Czechs that the Russians hoped that the west and Germans would fight it out among themselves, and that Soviet professions of support for their Czech allies were calculated to provoke such a situation.*

This was in its way a rational policy, the precise and cold-blooded counterpart of the appeasers' unformulated hope that the Germans and the Russians could be left to fight it out. Moscow and London both hoped to save themselves and leave everybody else dead and bleeding on the battlefield. The basic fact of the Soviet position, like the American, was extreme unwillingness to get mixed up in the European mess and—here Chamberlain's calculation was accurate—extreme military unreadiness. The Americans were by choice without an Army or Air Force. The Soviet regime had just liquidated, by execution or imprisonment, half of its Army officers.

The Soviet Union was, as always, of more immediate importance than the United States, because it lay within the formal boundaries of Europe, its forces alarmingly poised on the Polish border, and because of the ideology it embodied. It was Camus's plague, the armed and inimical alien at gates that were designed to withstand weapons weaker than his. But the ideology was in one sense also an illusion.

The Soviets in the years from 1935 to 1941 had acted with a just appreciation of realities and an intelligent, if extremely guileful, effort to control them, and the most basic of their realities was the safety of the Soviet state; between periods of outward devotion to the cause of world communism, the Soviet Union behaved like an old-fashioned national state intent on its own security, and it did so with more single-mindedness than most. The symbol of this phase was Litvinoff, a Jew who behaved like, and in some ways probably was, what today would be called a "Communist liberal." He was the Soviet representative at Geneva, whence he addressed the world, and his message was "Stop Hitler." But his show of friendly co-operation with the democracies was a cloak for a Soviet policy entirely devoted to

*Thompson, *op. cit.*, p. 89.

safeguarding Soviet frontiers. Litvinoff and the Soviet diplomats at Prague and Paris again and again repeated promises to aid the Czechs if they were attacked, but they did so in the hope of provoking a war between Germany and the west. And this was justly suspected. No one wanted the Red Army in central Europe or thought it could be effective in stopping Hitler.

In the prelude to Munich, Moscow was treated by the rest of Europe as if it did not exist, but the ideological illusion did exist and helped to discredit appeasement. The Soviets, profoundly skeptical of the democracies' intentions, had themselves no intention of being used by them. But they were much cleverer than Chamberlain. They retained the appearance of disinterested, even idealistic, antifascism, while Chamberlain appeared as a saboteur of their high-minded policy. The Soviets and everyone who admired them could see Munich as an anti-Soviet plot. The fact was that Chamberlain, unquestionably very anti-Communist and aware that the Red Army and Air Force were not only weak but in a state of dissolution, hoped that the Soviet power would go away, as he hoped that America would stay away; and this looked sinister to many people.

The rejection so stunningly embodied in Munich had the effect of confirming the darkest suspicions in Moscow, as the rejection of Roosevelt's January proposals had done in Washington. The superpowers were still absent. The ghosts of nineteenth-century Europe were to walk a little longer, a parody of 1914 was to be enacted, and the French and British and Germans and Italians were to be allowed to destroy what was left of their vitality as great powers without interference.

8

Politics Continued by Different Means

Iᴛ is an adage, invented by the German strategist Clausewitz, that war is a continuation of politics by different means.* The dictum took on a novel and peculiar irony in 1939. In that year, war formally began, but it closely resembled, so far as the great powers went, the political relations that preceded it. For a long time the Second World War was not much more than a legal fact. In the west, for seven months, nobody got hurt. France and Britain were temperamentally and therefore militarily incapable of fighting until they were attacked, and the date of the attack was set by Hitler's convenience. The initiative remained his; the declarations of war were merely formal protests against his policy. It was only tradition that made September 1939 look like a turning point.

Munich was a much more important one. Its principal effect, seen in perspective, was to confirm Hitler's autocracy. The German generals, who might have overthrown him if Munich had not taken place, were silenced by his dazzling success.

*There is an illuminating problem of translation involved in putting Clausewitz's famous phrase into English. *Politik* means both "politics" and "policy." The confusion of the two notions, arising from an old-fashioned idea of statecraft in which politicians, diplomats, and soldiers formed an interchangeable elite, is revealing.

His position was unshakable, and his opposition gloomily abandoned, or at least postponed, its plans. Munich also had great effects in Britain and France. In its aftermath, appeasement became more difficult to operate and to defend, and the appeasers shifted their ground. They did not abandon the defensive premises of their policies, but they were led to pursue them by different means, and public opinion in their countries, and in most of the world, was gradually consolidated into a strong anti-Nazi force.

The most important reason for this was not merely the terrifying evidence of an insatiable German appetite for territory and the shocking brutality with which Nazi and Fascist propagandists justified the predatory conduct of their masters. Whetting that appetite, provoking that brutality, was what had always been the worst weakness and largest anomaly of the system of European governance, the softness of eastern and southeastern Europe. There the new states made in 1919, with their unresolved nationalities, their savage ambitions, their aggressive but inadequate armies, their social inequities, could neither defend themselves nor convert themselves into replicas of western countries. They had the form, and the formal prerogatives, of traditional states like Denmark or the Netherlands, but they had neither the structural solidity nor the good manners.

Eastern Europe was the source of Hitler's strength and of the democracies' weakness. The notion of a German-dominated middle Europe was very old. Before the days when the smaller peoples erupted in molten chauvinism, when "Germany" was still a word associated with cosmopolitanism, it had a certain plausibility and respectability. Reason, as opposed to the mystique of the ultimacy of nationhood, undoubtedly suggested a benevolent overlordship. This was what a Czech patriot, Francis Palacky, had meant when he said a century before that if the Habsburg empire had not existed, it would have been necessary to invent it.

The need for a new centripetal force was even more obvious in the 1930s than in Palacky's day. It was heightened not merely by the ills of depression-ridden eastern Europe but by the brooding menace of the Soviet Union. Moreover, the very frontiers and policies that made a plethora of persecuted minorities una-voidable in the Europe of Versailles made it hard to justify the existence of countries like Czechoslovakia or Poland with refer-ence to the hallowed western principles of self-determination and the sovereign right of small powers to be free. The French and British, faced with the obviously unsatisfactory state of Czechoslovakia or Poland, could not conscientiously start a world war to defend them except on grounds of arrant strategic expediency, and among enlightened people strategic expediency was out of fashion as a reason for starting wars.

On the other hand, imperialism, dictatorship, and armed at-tacks on small nations were also out of fashion among enlight-ened people. Whatever they were inside, on the outside Czechoslovakia and Poland were sovereign states entitled to respect, if any kind of international order based on judicial con-ceptions—the only kind of order most people could imagine—were to survive. And the Germany of Hitler was very different from the Habsburg empire of Palacky's day. No rational person could suppose that its overlordship would be benevolent.

This conflict, which made appeasement unworkable, was in fact much more than an intellectual or moral dilemma. It was a practical one, and insoluble. Some kind of unity was necessary in eastern Europe, but the centripetal pull was (as events showed) almost precisely balanced by the centrifugal force of national feeling. Hitler invented, as if to meet Palacky's prescrip-tion, a new Habsburg empire. It failed to impose tranquility, just as has its successor, the empire of the Soviets.

The amorphousness of central Europe was amply illustrated, once the Versailles system had gone flabby, by what happened to Czechoslovakia after Munich. Both the Poles and the Hun-garians whetted—but did not satisfy—their appetites on an hors d'oeuvre of Czechoslovak territory. With Hitler's benediction the Hungarians took the adjacent fringe of eastern Czecho-slovakia, and the Poles annexed the important industrial center of Teschen. There were reasonable arguments for these transfers but equally reasonable arguments against them: Poland and Hungary acquired a number of Poles and Hungarians who had previously languished under alien rule; they also acquired a number of Czechs and Slovaks who would henceforth languish under alien rule. The dismemberment powerfully indicated that *no* frontiers in central Europe would be stable or satisfactory; and that the perpetually clashing ambitions there could be effectively used by a determined great power to assist its own ends. *Any* order in central Europe would depend on the authority and determination of great nations to maintain it.

There is no doubt that Hitler had from the beginning of his career intended to superimpose German dominion on eastern Europe. In the Hossbach memorandum he had specifically described the states formed in 1919 as the places where Germany must satisfy its urgent needs for growth. The appeasers, or some of them, some of the time, recognized and approved this. But the logic of their policy, if persuasive, was wrong. It was wrong for two reasons, both purely European in character. First of all, and most obviously, because Hitler was willing to fight Britain and France. In his jubilation after Munich he was sure he could beat them; in October he told Mussolini that he would be militarily ready to face them by September 1939. The keeping of the peace in terms of little Europe, while it might require the satisfaction of German needs along with a stable suzerainty between the Baltic and the Aegean, also required a balance of power. If Germany controlled most of central and eastern Europe then Germany would be too strong to be safe. As if by physical laws regulating the power relations of states, it would be drawn to threaten to use its vast superiority to force the western European states to give way to its needs. It was already doing so. If the western states were so weak as to give way, then they ceased to be states in the old sense. There were some people who were prepared to accept this, as Laval was in France. But they were not numerous, and the British appeasers were not among them. The limits of appeasement were, for them, set precisely at this point: Hitler's expansion would not be allowed beyond the point where it threatened Britain's capacity to defend its national existence. The limits were reflexive and unalterable, although their exact location might be debatable. The imperatives of traditional nationalism and sovereignty were much too strong.

The second reason that made it impossible to carry appeasement to the logical, if temporary end of allowing Germany to build a Mitteleuropan empire was a matter of conscience. Such an empire could be achieved only by a German regime so highly organized and so ruthless as to compel the loathing of all men whose consciences had been shaped by the ancient ethics of Judaism, Hellenism, and Christianity. What Europe was, in fact, was first and indispensably a moral principle, one that had for centuries been translated into institutional and more or less united imposition of certain forms of Christian doctrine. The will to save the outward forms of the European civilization—or system—arose precisely from the force of its inward morality. The two were inseparable, as ethics and institutions are always inseparable. The Nazi regime not merely embodied but flaunted a fanatical detestation of that morality as it had evolved into the Europe of bourgeois, liberal decencies. Hitler incessantly pandered to them, but it was his nature and need, and the nature and need of the miserable dominion he had built, to deny them. The fact that he was pandering became obvious; when it did, a second (but closely connected) limit was apprehended. A very deep historical logic led to the failure of appeasement. It failed because its chief architect, Neville Chamberlain, had conceived it out of the very morality that Nazism assaulted. The British and French were never able to fashion a new policy to replace appeasement.

Almost immediately after Munich, planning began in Germany for the occupation of what was left of Czechoslovakia. By December 17, 1938, the final decisions had been made. This was entirely unknown in London or Paris, but nonetheless a good deal of malaise, amounting to revulsion, was being felt. The growth of revulsion was fast but piecemeal. For a long time Chamberlain thought he had succeeded, despite a crescendo of disillusionment. Churchill had thundered in the Commons, saying, "This is only the first sip, the first foretaste of a bitter cup which will be proffered to us year by year unless by a supreme recovery of moral health and martial vigor, we arise again and take our stand for freedom as in the olden time." It would be hard to find a more accurate gloss for the theory of morality outraged. It began, in Britain, to look as if the ruin of Czechoslovakia were a sin that must be expiated. Halifax was dispirited, sometimes despairing. His faith in Hitler, so high a year before, was gone. But he and Chamberlain still thought in terms of a general settlement. Three months after Munich they were in Rome, trying again to negotiate with Mussolini, to ratify the agreement of April 1938. Chamberlain was delighted by signs of Fascist amiability; the Fascists thought the visit showed that England's governing class had lost the will to survive.

But Chamberlain's curious hopes looked more and more ghostly. On the seventh of November a Polish Jew named Herschell Grynszpan shot a junior official of the German Embassy at Paris. It was the occasion for an explosion of atrocities in Germany that seems, in retrospect, as if it must have been an expression of pure, irrational hatred and defiance. It was clearly arranged from on high. It served no practical purpose, since the Jews, in Germany now much reduced in numbers, impoverished and cowed, could offer no conceivable threat to the regime. It was certain to call forth anathema abroad, since it was not only public but ostentatious. The savage irrationality of the pogrom was proved by the fact that some of the German press said that the French and British governments had instigated the murder. Several thousand Jews were murdered, and the survivors were charged with a corporate fine of three hundred million dollars. It was quite accurately taken as revealing that the Nazis and their government were not merely intolerably cruel but psychotically unaccountable as well. The reaction of the world opinion to the pogrom was almost unanimous, and in its way it was final. The pogrom suggested to many people theretofore open-minded that Nazis were unappeasable.

A more specific and trivial incident affected France. There was a good deal of talk after Munich about a "general settlement" of colonial problems, which meant giving Hitler, and possibly Mussolini, some colonies to keep them happy. Hitler's dictum at Munich, that he had no more territorial demands in Europe, had raised the issue, never wholly latent, in a more focused form. The Italians, now committed to marriage with Germany, and under orders to enjoy it, zealously pushed the question. Mussolini roared, and (it cannot be known whether the incident was the spontaneous result of overenthusiasm or the consequence of an ill-judged order) on November 30 members of the Italian pseudo-parliament, the Chamber of Fascists, applauded one of his virulent harangues against France by shouting, "Tunis! Corsica! Nice!" It was a fateful shout.

French conservatism, alarmed by the prospect of a war that would kill its sons, diminish its bank accounts, and encourage communists and socialists to contrive the destruction of the social order, had largely supported Munich, as it had in some cases anticipated appeasement by supporting native fascist movements. But the logic of appeasement in France involved an interesting addendum. It was widely argued after Munich that France must no longer concern itself with European affairs, which it clearly could not handle. It must, as it were, stay out of Hitler's way. And this could be done by retreating behind the Maginot Line and rebuilding French greatness on the base of the colonial empire, to be developed by French skill and capital. It was not a new idea. Jules Ferry, with German help, had tried it in the 1880s, after the disaster of the Franco-Prussian War. De Gaulle was to try it after the disaster of World War II. Then came the Italian shouts. Tunisia was a cornerstone of the empire, and it lay on the Mediterranean next to Algeria, which was governed as part of France itself, a bastion of French power and a showpiece of France's civilizing mission which Frenchmen incessantly spoke of. But Corsica and Nice were worse. Corsica had been won in the eighteenth century and was a French county. Nice, a Riviera city of more than a hundred thousand, had been acquired as a sleepy fishing port from the Italian state of Piedmont in 1860, but it was by now entirely French. What was demanded in Rome was the annexation of parts of the French homeland. It had been to forestall exactly such demands that Frenchmen had acquiesced in appeasement and even for a short time shown enthusiasm for it. Now all except some dedicated pro-fascists were appalled and angry: the aftermath of their shouting in the Italian chamber was far, far beyond anything the Italian deputies could have dreamt of. Even Hitler had never breathed a word of seizing French territory. Indeed, he had specifically, and with an appearance of deeply moving sincerity, proclaimed that he sadly accepted, forever and ever, the loss of Alsace and Lorraine. (They were annexed to Germany in 1940.) The defeatist Bonnet continued his efforts to reach a friendly agreement with Germany, and Ribbentrop paid a state visit to Paris in December to discuss a commercial treaty. But the pogrom and the Italian shouting had been too much for the Parisians, and the German Foreign Minister had to be kept hidden from the public.

The two episodes, one vast and tragic and the other small and comic, were pieces in the picture puzzle of Axis aims and methods that was gradually being put together. In March, a whole section of the picture was put in place. Hitler annexed what was left of Czechoslovakia.

Its history in the intervening months had been doleful. It had suffered numerous amputations. Slovakia had been given self-government, and the Germans saw to it that a pro-Nazi government was installed in Bratislava, the capital. In Prague, Beneš and the men who had made a state were also gone, replaced, also by German demand, by a new government under a president practically nominated by Germany, Emil Hacha, who nonetheless worked to discipline the surviving Czech provinces into a state that Germany might respect. At Munich it had been agreed that the truncated republic would be guaranteed by all the powers—the only thing that the French had dared to try to salvage from the ruins of their policy. This guarantee, desultorily discussed, was never given.

But for a while the appeasers in Britain still had faith. In fact, they were seized by a mad, but psychologically explicable, optimism. Chamberlain was still so sure of his mission that he was also sure it was succeeding. He pursued inexorably the flitting, batlike specters of "general settlements," and Bonnet followed him. In March, Chamberlain stated his conviction that Europe was at last settling down to a period of tranquility. Hoare on the same day spoke glowingly of a Ten-Year Peace Plan, and of new riches, economic development to be undertaken as a Europe-wide project. He said that mankind might now look forward confidently to a Golden Age. Henderson, in Berlin, was sending assurances that a period of calm could be expected. The effect was to baffle increasing numbers of people outside of government circles. Even Mussolini was startled that Chamberlain had shown him, for approval, the draft of a speech he meant to give in Commons—an unheard of action by a foreign executive. The mystique of appeasement was becoming more and more difficult to defend.

PRAGUE

For Hitler, Munich had been makeshift, obstructing the march on Prague, on which he had set his heart. On October 7, a week after the agreements were signed and while German troops were still engaged in occupying the areas he had been awarded on the basis of self-determination, he began to make new plans. The usual judgments about ways, means, and timetables were solicited from the generals, and detailed plans were developed. The pretexts and politics were minutely considered and prepared for. It is not known when the date was chosen, but it was well in advance, and on December 17, 1938, three months before the event, Keitel, the Chief of Staff, circulated to the three armed forces a general statement announcing the forthcoming invasion and outlining the character and method. By March 13, friendly powers had been warned, and the operation began. The familiar pretext was to be the inability of the Prague government to maintain order, in this case the result of the complaints of the Slovaks and their efforts to sever their connection with Bohemia-Moravia (Czechia, the Germans called it) and their allegedly brutal repressions by the Czechs. (It is worth noting that for the first time the Nazis extended their solicitude to non-Germans.) The propaganda build-up, while shatteringly violent, was hasty and rather perfunctory. So was the showdown.

The Prime Minister of Slovakia, Father Josef Tiso, dismissed a few days earlier for sedition, was called to Berlin and ordered to secede. He was unaccountably reluctant to do so. Hitler angrily lectured him. Tiso returned to Bratislava and induced the Slovak parliament to declare independence. The next day, the president of the rump republic, Hacha, was summoned. He was received by Hitler, Keitel, and other dignitaries. The interview was long and gruesome. Hitler accused him of anti-German actions in words that recalled the very similar interview with Schuschnigg a year earlier, but now more hysterical. Hacha was told that invasion had already been decided, and the frontier would be crossed in a few hours. Hacha's choice was between acquiescence in the reduction of his country to a German colony and its utter destruction by German might. The threats were graphically and endlessly repeated. The President of Czechoslovakia fainted. When he was revived, the Nazis resumed their intemperate ravings.

On March 15, Prague was occupied. The German Army met no resistance, and that night Adolf Hitler slept in the palace of the Bohemian kings. The Czech provinces were annexed to Germany. Slovakia was made a German protectorate. The Hungarians occupied and annexed the easternmost part of Czechoslovakia, Ruthenia.

In considering the western reaction to these events, it must be kept in mind that the Führer had already coolly begun work on other projects. Poland was to be next; that had already been decided. But first, either as a preface to Poland or as part of an attack on it, came the Free City of Danzig. It had been self-governing since 1919, lying on the Baltic between the province of East Prussia and the Polish province of Pomorze, which formed the Polish Corridor to the sea, dividing German territory. It had a population of 400,000. Its reincorporation into Germany had been a prime demand of German nationalists since the early twenties; the governing senate had already been in the hands of a Nazi party majority for over a year. It was a tricky problem for everybody concerned. Danzig and the Corridor were the losses that the Germans had always most resented in the Versailles Treaty, and it was true that from both the economic and the ethnic viewpoint their separation was indefensible. On the other hand, Poland required an outlet to the sea, and there was nowhere else to provide one except Pomorze (West Prussia, the Germans called it) and no adequate port for Polish trade except Danzig. The Germans had, as they had had with Czechoslovakia, legitimate grounds for complaint. The Poles had legitimate grounds for anxiety.

The trickiest part of the problem was the Germans in other parts of Poland. Poland had been, more or less, a friend of Nazi Germany since Beck's pact of friendship in 1934, and Hitler probably hoped to keep it one for a while. As early as October, he began negotiations with the Poles looking toward the cession of a corridor-within-a-corridor and the annexation of Danzig, in exchange for guarantees of their sovereignty and a friendly welcome into the Anti-Communist Pact. But the Poles were both suspicious and overconfident. They were acutely aware that Poland, although it had many fewer German-speaking citizens than Czechoslovakia, had enough (some 750,000) to be vulnerable, and they knew enough not to value Hitler's promises highly. They wanted to avoid provoking the Germans, but they were not going to make concessions on Danzig and the Corridor that would be prefaces to further demands leading toward a Czechist fate. They agreed to negotiate, but the negotiations—friendly enough at first—were characterized chiefly by the fancy footwork of which the Polish Foreign Minister, Beck, was a master. He seems to have supposed he could walk a tightrope indefinitely. This was for a singular reason: the Polish military people were the only ones in Europe in the thirties who overrated their own power and underrated their adversary's—with, as it turned out, the least possible excuse.

For Hitler, the problem was that he could not afford to estrange the Poles out of hand. There was an absolute need to plan for the possibility of war with France and Britain if Poland was attacked.

So Danzig might bring the European war which he thought (although he was not sure) was eventually probable. Between intervals of planning the invasion of Bohemia, he mulled over the problem of Danzig, and instructed his officials to commence a press campaign about it and about the atrocities the Poles were committing against the German-speaking citizens of Poland. Two weeks after the occupation of Prague, detailed planning for war against Poland began. The date for action was set for not later than the first of September.

This was of course unknown in London or Paris, but no one could now avoid inferring that some such plans might be in the

making. Therefore, the reaction in the west to the German sei-
zure of Bohemia and Moravia was quite different from the reaction to anything that had happened before. There was no longer
any doubt about Hitler's appetite or the unreliability of his promises. It was not that appeasement was universally rejected, but
the voices opposing it were much stronger than they had ever
been, and even among its supporters there was an understanding
that it must be pursued by methods different from those of peace-
able negotiations and promises given and exchanged. The
change from promises to warning was not, however, instantaneous. Chamberlain was not unduly surprised. (Henderson, the
ambassador at Berlin, actually asked the Germans for arguments
with which to justify Hitler's action in London.) On the day of
the occupation, the Prime Minister addressed the House of
Commons in a manner that suggested he had expected something of this sort all along (which was not the case). The situation
had changed, he said, since Munich. While Britain had regarded
the guarantee of Czechoslovakia as binding, even in the absence
of international agreement, the fact was that there had ceased to
be a Czechoslovakia to guarantee. The Slovak secession had
simply dissolved the republic: "The condition of affairs which
was always regarded by us as being only of a transitory nature
has now ceased to exist."* He saw, apparently, no reason to alter
his confidence in the coming Golden Age or to suppose that the
Munich Treaty could not still bring "peace for our time." "It is
natural," he said, "that I should bitterly regret what has now
occurred. But do not let us on that account be deflected from our
course. Let us remember that the desire of all the peoples of the
world still remains concentrated on the hopes of peace."

This tranquil acceptance of the situation was not his final
word. The change in tone that followed was sudden, and looks
tidal in scope and nature. In actuality, Chamberlain and the
appeasers were not deflected from their course; they merely
followed it in a different vessel, but the change of ship was in
itself startling. The impression of a revolution was so strong that
the appeasers were themselves affected by it. The declarations of

---

*Quoted in Martin Gilbert and Richard Gott, *The Appeasers* (London: Weidenfeld and
Nicolson, 1963), p. 230.

war on September 3, 1939, were signs that the appeasers had been trapped by their own methods, not indications that the goals had altered or their understanding deepened.

The change in policy after Prague was, then, much less basic, and in some ways less important, than it looked. It becomes, thereby, easier to understand the curiously infecund gestures that now began to be made toward building a new anti-Axis coalition.

One fact had concretely and publicly appeared. Hitler had repeatedly said that he wanted no foreigners in Germany, that all his actions were aimed at freeing racial kinsmen from the tyrannous governance of racially inferior foreigners,* uniting them into "One Race, One State, One Leader," his compelling slogan. With the Czechs under German dominion, this most basic, and often iterated, statement of Nazi aims was proved a lie, and there was every reason to apprehend an indefinite expansion of the German empire, in Poland, and through the rest of central Europe and the Balkans. And (the Italian deputies in the chamber had ominously prophesied it) quite possibly an expansion elsewhere. If Hitler's renunciation of all additional territory in Europe, made so explicitly at Munich-time, were not to be believed, there was certainly no reason to believe his earlier renunciation of the old German lands of Alsace and Lorraine. No one, in short, was safe. And safety was the principal purpose of appeasement. Even if the British Cabinet did not at once grasp these implications, the British public did. Political pressures mounted. By the summer of 1939, according to a Gallup poll, more than three quarters of the British public felt that it was worth going to war to stop Hitler.

This fact would probably in time have dictated a change of method. The particular occasion for the change was curious and, because it was based on misinformation, revealing. The Rumanians told London that they had definite information that Hitler was going to take over Hungary and immediately "disintegrate" Rumania. This was not true; the Rumanians, understandably nervous, had accepted a false rumor. But it was lent plausibility

---

*The Czechs belonged in this category, of course, but their kinsmen, the Slovaks, being on the German side, were now approvingly described as a "small culture-bearing people."

by the fact that Rumania had oil, which Germany urgently needed, and that Rumania was almost as unstable a compound of national minorities as Czechoslovakia. In France, the ministry was receiving warnings from its ambassador at Berlin, Robert Coulondre. The French government and public were thoroughly alarmed. Representations—not so vigorous as to suggest any great decision—were made in London the next day. And representations were also being made within the bosom of the appeasement family. Lord Halifax had been disillusioned and discouraged by Munich. It is interesting, for he was in many ways the paradigm of the appeasers. Like many of them he was a man of patent good will and virtue with religious enthusiasms. Like most of them he had believed in Hitler's "sincerity." Like all of them he was very respectable as the world viewed respectability. He had the appeasers' common characteristic of being consistent to the point of obstinacy. In the end he was more determined than any of the others (although he was not alone) in persisting in his belief that Hitler must and could be negotiated with for a general settlement, long after war was declared. Up until the spring of 1940 he was trying to make contact with the Germans in the hope that the war would be called off if Germany were conceded all the territory that it had so far conquered.* But it was Halifax who seems to have converted Chamberlain to the view that the occupation of Prague could not be benevolently regarded as a regrettable but meaningless event. He was evidently much shaken by the Rumanians' report of an imminent attack.

There was also a personal element in the conversion. Hitler had said to Chamberlain at Munich, "I shall not be interested in the Czech state any more, and I can guarantee it. We don't want any more Czechs." The facts recalled, the whole edifice of faith in Hitler's sincerity crumbled. His guarantees must all be seen as persiflage. Chamberlain's ego was touched; he was, as Churchill noted in *The Gathering Storm*, a man who did not like to be tricked.

On March 17, in Birmingham, Chamberlain gave a scheduled speech (which was originally to have dealt with the social ser-

*Gilbert and Gott, *op. cit.* pp. 334–5.

vices) and denounced Hitler as a liar and a public menace. He described Hitler's action as wanton, and the Czechs (people "of whom," in September, "we know nothing") became a "proud, brave people." The disorders which were claimed to have disrupted the rump state had been fomented from outside. "Is this, in fact, a step in the direction of an attempt to dominate the world by force?"

It sounded, then, like a revolution. In fact it was half of half a revolution. The purpose, to lead the world to peace, had not changed. The belief in Germany's crushing power had not changed. What had changed was the mistaken view of Hitler's character.

The quarter-revolution in conception led in short order to a full revolution in the techniques of policy. There was strong public demand that something be done. *The Times* found that there was no "moral case" for Hitler's action, and it is possible that purely political considerations had played a role in Halifax's persuasions. But there was debate and caution about what to do to protect Rumania, which was believed to be the next victim. The Soviet government, still persisting in its ostentatious efforts to galvanize an anti-Hitler coalition, proposed, on March 18, a conference of governments of all states that seemed to be threatened, and might be expected to be co-operative, to discuss it. This was rejected by the British cabinet. Instead, Chamberlain hoped to invoke Poland as the protector of Rumania. This would contain Hitler, it was hoped, without directly involving Britain. But Poland had to be promised something in exchange. Chamberlain proposed a joint guarantee by Britain, France, and the Soviet Union, of Poland's integrity.

This was rejected by Poland. The Poles were overly confident of their ability to manage Germany, and they had no wish to become Red Riding Hood to a grandmotherly gesture from the Russian wolf. The cynical Polish Foreign Minister, Beck, was calm in the face of the news that his neighbor, Rumania, was likely to be devoured next. Chamberlain and Halifax shared his extreme distrust of the Soviet Union. Still, they felt that something had to be done to bring Poland into line as guarantor of frontiers in eastern Europe.

This dilatory debate about the complexities of doing something helpful was simplified by a new German initiative. On March 23, the German Fleet, with Hitler himself aboard (although incapacitated by seasickness) appeared in the roadstead of Memel. Memel was an old East Prussian port, mainly German-speaking, which the Lithuanians had occupied since 1923. The Lithuanians had been given an ultimatum demanding its immediate restitution, and had agreed. Memel made it clear that Hitler meant business in the Baltic. Only two days before, the Poles had been presented anew with German demands for the reincorporation of Danzig in Germany and for special, extraterritorial privileges for transporting German goods and passengers across the Polish Corridor. The German demand was again accompanied by the customary promises of permanent peace and respect for Poland's frontiers, but nobody now took these sweet addenda very seriously. The pace of German advance seemed to be quickening ominously. On March 31, Chamberlain announced that the British government would be prepared to give all necessary support to Poland.

The guarantee, although it was not intended to preclude concessions about Danzig and the Corridor, included unlimited British backing "in the event of any action which clearly threatened Polish independence, and which the Polish government considered it vital to resist." The phrasing was important; it transferred to the Poles Britain's right of decision about when, where, and whether to fight. (It also, incidentally, pledged Britain to go to war against the Soviet Union if the Poles felt it desirable to do so, although this was no doubt an unintentional consequence of an effort to avoid flagrantly labeling Germany as an aggressor and possible enemy.) The Poles were cautious about accepting the present, and they were even more cautious about giving a guarantee to Rumania. Beck eventually agreed to a mutual assistance pact with Britain, but he made no promise to help defend Rumania. A week after the incautious gesture of March 31, a preliminary pact was signed.

The odor of rashness persisted. A few days later joint French and British guarantees were given to Rumania and Greece.

The inclusion of Greece in this wholesale offering of precisely the kind of guarantee that Chamberlain had fought so hard against in the weeks before Munich was due to another act of Axis aggression whose complicated nature indicates both the sense of quickly approaching doom which was so strong a factor in the world in those days, and its singularly fortuitous and misleading nature. On Good Friday, April 7, 1939, the Italians occupied the kingdom of Albania (not without serious difficulty, although their landing was unopposed), expelled its king, and then proclaimed it annexed to Italy. The whole structure of the European state system seemed to be collapsing.

Albania was a small, mountainous, and very obscure kingdom, largely Muslim and tribal, that lay less than fifty miles across the mouth of the Adriatic from the heel of Italy. It had for generations been an object of intense interest to Italian expansionists, who endlessly reiterated a phrase, evocative if elusive, "The Adriatic Sea should be an Italian lake." The utility of Albania to the achievement of this aim, which harkened back to the sixteenth century, when Venice had controlled some of the eastern Adriatic coast and its ports, was that the Italians might hope to close the sea to others if Albania were in their hands. It was basically meaningless, since it depended on the supremacy of the Italian Navy in the Mediterranean which, if achieved, would have made Albania unnecessary. But in the late twenties one of Mussolini's more destructive whimsies had led to the establishment in Tirana, the Albanian capital, of a faithful client, King Zog I. The Yugoslavs were outraged and permanently alienated; they were exceedingly sensitive to Italian ambitions, which threatened the existence of their country—and, indeed, which did destroy it, from 1941 to 1945. Albania, although it did Italy no good at all, remained firmly under Italian domination thereafter. The invasion changed nothing except the name of the king, from Zog I to Victor Emmanuel III.

The sudden exploit looked like another example of the inexorable march of the Axis toward European domination, of the carefully plotted and perfectly co-ordinated schedule by the united dictators, on the shores of both the Baltic and the Mediterranean. Albania had a frontier with Greece. The Greeks were seriously alarmed. (So indeed were the Turks, and Britain gave *them* a guarantee on April 12.) In point of fact it was one of Mussolini's more abrupt and gratuitous adventures; it was received by Hitler (who had little warning) with irritation, which indeed it had been intended to provoke. Mussolini had become restive in his role of junior member. Hitler was getting all the publicity and all the spoils, and he resented it. "Every time Hitler takes another state," he said, "he sends me another message."* He had quite suddenly decided to get some for himself by occupying Albania. Mussolini preened himself; Hitler felt that he was being committed to unseemly adventures by an irresponsible ally.

Like the Ethiopian War, the Albanian coup had unexpected effects. The mutual irritation of the Axis partners did not adversely affect their relations. As always, Mussolini was alarmed by his own boldness. In May, in a renewed spirit of enthusiasm for Hitler and in the face of grave Italian naval and military inadequacy, he agreed to a military alliance, which he called the Pact of Steel. It provided, for the first time, a formal alliance, and bound the parties to support one another by all means should either become involved in war. The Italians warned that they would not be prepared to fight a major opponent for several years. The Germans affably reassured them by saying that they wouldn't either, although very detailed plans for a possible war with France and Britain, to begin in September, were then being drawn up. Mussolini had accepted another liabiity, and received another false promise. Hitler was finding that a weaker ally was a nuisance and danger, in much the same way that the Germans had found out the same thing about Austria-Hungary in 1914. But, as in those days, the need for an appearance of unshakable unity was deemed necessary, and it was achieved. It completely nullified, of course, the Italo-British agreements of the year before, by which Chamberlain set such store. It also frightened and estranged the more rational people in Italy, including the king.

The British were still working out their policy of guarantees. It was awkward. There was—Lloyd-George pointed out the fact

*Quoted in Elizabeth Wiskemann, *Rome-Berlin Axis* (New York: Hillary House, 1966), p. 137.

in the House of Commons—no possible way to help the Poles directly if they were attacked, much less the Rumanians or Greeks. Strategically, the guarantees were not only ill-considered but ridiculous; they could be defended only as deterrents, a new stage in the program of substituting words for a willingness to consider action. While official support of Poland was publicly reiterated, the diplomats made efforts to induce the Poles to negotiate with Germany about the demands for the incorporation of the Free City of Danzig into the Reich. (The British consul-general in Danzig was summarily recalled for expressing to the Foreign Office his view that giving Danzig to the Germans would be the first step in the destruction of Poland.) Beck, still believing in Poland's ability to cope with Germany by footwork and the threat of his cavalry, promised to do so. (As a matter of fact he lied to the British about it. He refused to consider concessions.) As late as July, when Hitler's propaganda campaign against the Poles had become even more violent than that against the Czechs the year before, Lord Halifax still thought that Hitler would be willing to leave Poland alone if he got Danzig, and at the end of August he was still trying to negotiate its cession and promising Germany to put pressure on the Poles. Despite his role in the March turnabout, Halifax thought a new Munich was both possible and desirable.*

It is true that the British and French had been rearming. The extent of their rearmament was exaggerated by the German military, who overrated the Royal Air Force and the French Armored Forces, and in particular overrated their willingness to use them offensively. Even Hitler, who was usually confident that boldness would prevail against stolidity, was anxious about the vulnerability of the German industrial heart in the Ruhr, which (he was told) could be attacked by air and perhaps even brought under French artillery fire in a few days. As early as November 1938, he had called the Ruhr his "Achilles' heel."†

There is reasonably reliable evidence on the air forces. The Germans in September 1939 had about 4,200 planes. (Not the

*Gilbert and Gott, *op. cit.*, pp. 264ff. Their startling revelations on the point are solidly based on British and German official documents.

†Quoted in Jon Kimche, *The Unfought Battle* (London: Weidenfeld and Nicolson, 1968), p. 56.

8,000 Lindbergh said they had a year earlier.) Of these, more than 500 were transports or trainers. Of the combat planes, both fighters and bombers, a high percentage were obsolete, and a small percentage were fighters, which were essential both as the defensive arm and as protection for the bombers on offensive missions. The rate of production was high and increasing by 1939. But—and this was the decisive weakness of the German Air Force—neither pilots nor bombs were being produced in sufficient numbers for sustained air battles. As the result of Marshal Göring's incompetence, the German flying officers were neither well-trained nor well-organized. There was, moreover, a serious shortage of petroleum reserves.

British and French strength in first-line aircraft was smaller in the summer of 1939; it amounted to something like 2,700 planes. But the British planes were better; and in both aircraft production and pilot training, as well as in munitions and gasoline supplies, the pace of increase was faster than Germany's; coming from behind, Britain's aircraft production equalled Germany's in September of 1939. The British air command was now in the hands of able and determined men. Plans for a considerable expansion of the Royal Air Force had been decided on in the summer before Munich, and for the first time an intensive and intelligent effort was made to strengthen the air defenses. This was most notably true, and useful, in regard to industrial capacity. In the year before war was declared, airplane production had increased from a monthly 240 to 660. It was to prove sufficient to the needs of Britain's defense in the appallingly close Battle of Britain a year later.

The comparative figures, which were actually somewhat more accurately known in London than in Berlin, were on the face of it enough to cause some apprehension if the supply insufficiencies in Germany were not understood. But they certainly showed no disparity great enough to justify imaginings about the total destruction of London and Paris. In fact, considering the exigencies of a campaign in Poland, the war which Hitler contemplated for September 1939 was going to be an extremely risky business, and his extreme sensitivity to the threat of damaging RAF raids on the Ruhr was justified. Or would have been had it not been for one decisive fact.

It is true that the balance of air power was changing in favor of the western powers in the year between Munich and the declarations of war. One of the frequent justifications offered for Munich was that France and Britain needed time to prepare themselves—this indeed was something that had been said for three years. As Churchill pointed out, the breathing space they got by Munich was a breathing space for Germany as well, and the German Army undoubtedly was growing faster than the French. But the controlling point is that the problem of defense was precisely that; the whole strategic picture was seen in London and Paris from the standpoint of providing security against German assault. The Germans may have been technically correct when they worried about a quick French advance to the Ruhr, but in France no plans were made, and no intention existed, to undertake offensive action. This decisively shaped both diplomatic and strategic policy up until after the French defenses had failed, in June of 1940. The defensive conception meant that no effective force could be brought to the support of Poland, any more than it could have been to prevent the Rhineland episode in 1936 or the evisceration of Czechoslovakia. The French and British had been thinking since 1933 of how to ward off attacks from Germany, not of how to prevent them. And this they continued to do, before and after the war started, until 1941.

This state of mind was the basic feature of the situation. It was supported by certain blind spots, areas of ignorance. The democracies were hypnotized by the idea of a monolithic, highly efficient German economy geared for war. Despite the high percentage of national income devoted to arms, this was a most inaccurate picture. The German economy was very incompletely mobilized, and there were serious deficiencies in it. In October 1938, Göring, the commander in chief of the Air Force who was also in charge of German economic development, had addressed his economic planning staff in gloomy terms. The reserves of foreign exchange, replenished in Austria, were now again at the vanishing point. This meant a curtailment of imports which meant, inevitably, a curtailment of armament. German industry, already operating at capacity, was behind schedule in filling orders. Rail and road transportation were in an unsatisfactory state. The picture, confirmed by the records, was one of very limited achievement greatly aggravated by the administrative disorder and jurisdictional jealousies that characterized all aspects of the Nazi state. The military potential of the German economy was—as events showed—vast, but it was so far organized for short, decisive actions. For a long war it was quite insufficient until it was supplemented by the resources of eastern Europe. In 1939, there were real shortages, of which oil, high-grade iron ore, and foreign exchange were the most serious and the most difficult to remedy. It was estimated that in a war of any length 23 million tons of petroleum would be required annually, and only 3½ million were readily available. Supplies of iron, steel, magnesium, and rubber were available for only a few months. Taken all in all, the figures seem to show what a good many German authorities at the time nervously believed and what recent careful appraisals of them have confirmed, that Germany in 1939 could not face even a short war on two fronts and could not face a long one on any terms without substantial improvements in its supply and production. All of the economic planning had been based on the assumption of a *Blitzkrieg*, a very brief and stunning blow that would bring decisive success before any strain was put on Germany's resources. A short war against Poland followed by a period of undisturbed build-up was the only military prospect that Germany could face with confidence, and the generals—and many other responsible people in Berlin—were certain that the British and French would not permit them such a breathing spell. It was Hitler's most stupefying success that they were wrong and he was right.

The French and British were unable to understand or exploit the situation. In June 1939 they were specifically invited to do so by a nervous German staff officer who quietly visited England and urged the British government (through the unfortunate medium of Tom Jones, permanently beguiled by the vision of instant and total destruction of London should war break out) to inform the German government in precise terms of the extent of allied strength and of their determination to use it immediately and to the fullest extent should Hitler make another aggressive move. The proposal was not taken seriously. There was by then a very lively expectation of war in London, but the authorities, still with an appeasement tropism, were thinking of waging it through a naval blockade, and an effort to "gain time" for an expansion of defensive forces (which meant, under the circumstances, giving time to Hitler). After the guarantees to Poland, in short, the British government was prepared, if necessary, to declare war; it was not prepared to fight. And the French were prepared to fight only if invaded.

The other aspect was the reverse of the first. Hitler was prepared to run risks and was trying to minimize them by publicly exaggerating his own power. He brooded a good deal that summer, and ranted restlessly against the turn events had taken, against British policy, but he did not falter in his intention to settle matters with Poland that autumn, at whatever risk of war in the west. Audacity and resolution were his most powerful weapons.

Planning went ahead. Plan White was being thoroughly prepared for action aganst Poland, since it now looked as if Poland probably would resist his proposed annexation of Danzig and his demands for a German corridor-within-the-Polish-Corridor. Hitler's motives were, as they had been when the decision for expansion had first been taken in November 1937, compounded of his own remarkable personality and its needs and obstinacies, and of cold economic necessity. The very condition which made further German expansion dangerous also made it necessary. On May 3 he had given the commanders in chief a briefing to this effect. His knowledge of economics was impressionistic and disdainful, but recent research has shown that it was tolerably accurate. The economic problem could be solved only by living space —that meant opening up the resources of eastern and southeastern Europe to German control. Given the pressure on gold and foreign exchange, given the necessity of a "power-state" to which other states would refuse to supply resources voluntarily, territorial expansion was indispensable to German economic expansion, and it could be got only by conquest. Poland was, very definitely, seen as a first step. "Danzig," he said, "is not the subject of the dispute at all. It is a question of expanding our living space in the East, of securing our food supplies. . . . There is no other possibility." On May 23 he added, "We cannot expect a repetition of the Czech affair. This time there will be war."

The strategic conception now evolving called for a *Blitzkrieg* against Poland—the Germans were in no doubt about its feasibility—and purely defensive operations in the west. By the middle of July, planning was largely complete. Some of the German officers had grave reservations. Admiral Canaris, chief of counterintelligence, tried as late as August 23 to warn Hitler of Germany's extreme vulnerability to economic warfare. But Hitler, his own doubts abating, was now calm. He said that the moment was ripe, politically and strategically, that Poland's enmity made it essential to defeat it promptly, that from now on time would work against Germany. There were provisions for calling off the invasion should Poland prove amenable to argument. This much —but no more—the stiffening of French and British policy had achieved.

It was known, of course, that Chamberlain was still radically averse to war, and efforts to modify British policy continued. It is possible that Hitler realized that while the British and French might declare war, they would not immediately fight. One of the many German analysts of Britain that summer had sent him a carefully prepared memorandum stating that "great gaps in British armament remain, especially in the army in the field, but that is not so very important (to the British) because their tactical plans, particularly at the beginning of the war, do not assign any sizable tasks to the British army in the field."[*] In any case, it appears that by midsummer Hitler had decided that unless a complete surrender by the Poles could be achieved without fighting, he would fight.

The crucial fact therefore emerges: the great powers were all, including Germany, unprepared to engage in an all-out war effort. The plan of the west was to stand on the defensive. The plan of Germany was to win European dominion by a series of short, sharp, cheap thrusts.

*Quoted in Kimche, *op. cit.*, p. 63.

THE NEGOTIATIONS IN MOSCOW

If Britain and France were to maintain their defensive posture and still contain Hitler in the east, it was urgently necessary to invoke some additional power to assist Poland. The imperative need was for Soviet aid. But there were serious obstacles. Nobody, least of all the Poles, wanted to bring the Soviets into European affairs and territory. Nobody had any real confidence in the mangled Red Army. (Events were to justify the most serious doubts when the Soviets tried to invade Finland that fall.) On the other side, it was perfectly clear in Moscow that the west wanted the Soviets to do their dirty work for them. Still, the imperative remained, and it was acted on. An effort was made to reach an agreement with the U.S.S.R. to re-form an anti-Nazi bloc.

The course of negotiations illuminated the whole dilemma of European politics. The difficulties immediately encountered arose from the serious misgivings London and Paris felt about the project, and from a remarkable lack of confidence that it was necessary. Once again the governments were affected by the reports of the Service chiefs who told them that "Poland was a more valuable ally than the Soviet Union." In fact, as events showed, neither had any military value in 1939 as part of British-French strategy which required a purely defensive war in the west.

Ironically, the Germans were now hoping to achieve the former British purpose of keeping the Soviet Union isolated. Since it was much simpler to find satisfactory terms for keeping outsiders out than for getting them in, they succeeded. In April, the President of the United States had made another effort to assert American leadership in world affairs. He had challenged Mussolini and Hitler to give pledges to twenty-nine nations, from Finland to Persia, that they would not be attacked for twenty-five years. The German and Italian press replied, not unnaturally, with oceans of vituperation and abuse. One superpower was thus disposed of. Disposing of the other was not much more difficult. On May 30, the Germans had made their first soundings at the Soviet Embassy in Berlin on the terms on which the Soviet

Union would agree to isolate itself from the west by promising to stay out of any German conflict with Poland or the democracies. The head of the German Foreign Office wired to the German ambassador at Moscow, "We have now decided to undertake definite negotiations with the Soviet Union."

The British and French negotiations with the Soviets had gone unpromisingly from the first. There were two inherent obstacles, both of them arising from the conservative nature of western aims: they wanted to preserve a situation, not to change it. This meant that they were asking of the Soviet Union the promise of an enormous effort, quite probably involving a war against Germany, in return for nothing. The second obstacle was more subtle and even more revealing. The Europe which they were trying to save, with its moral principles, was the Europe of independent states, large and small, which should all be free to work out their destinies without direct interference from foreign powers. This was the Europe of the late nineteenth century—the embodiment of the liberal dream of free men in free societies, of international security based on good will and the good law of sovereign states, of political organization based on nationality. The dream had never been exactly fulfilled; but it was the basis of the only arrangements that had ever promised stability, and it was very, very deep in the souls of liberal democrats and old-fashioned conservatives. It was not a dream shared by Josef Stalin. And his antipathy to it rose not from ideological imperialism which, with suitable guarantees and concessions, might have been evaded, but from hard strategic facts.

The Polish government was quite as hostile to the Soviet Union as to Germany. The Poles did not want Soviet forces crossing their territory. They did not even want Soviet promises of aid. The Soviets, moreover, insisted that guarantees against *indirect* aggression (which would have seriously impaired the freedom of action of the beneficiaries) must be given whether Poland wanted them or not, and must be given willy-nilly to seven other nations. This looked like an entering wedge for Soviet domination. Moreover, the Russians said that the military dangers of a campaign against Germany could not be faced unless they were in a position to defend their exposed Baltic flank. This would involve, they thought, control of the three small Baltic republics which had been provinces of the Russian empire before 1917—Estonia, Latvia, and Lithuania. For purely military reasons if for no others, there was a good deal to be said for the Russian argument. They were being asked to collaborate with powers that had spurned their earlier offers of aid, to assist people who were terrified of assistance, and in ways that were both insulting and terribly dangerous. The British, on their side, could hardly begin their defense of freedom and independence of small powers by sacrificing three or four of them to Soviet occupation; but nonetheless, piecemeal concessions to Soviet demands were regularly made. Foreign Minister Molotov replied to them with new demands. He added Switzerland and Luxembourg to the countries that must be guaranteed as well.

These facts gave to the negotiations between the Soviets and the western powers an atmosphere of nagging, endless argument which was really a thin veil for almost farcical unreality. It is probable that there was never any chance of even limited success; certainly by July the Soviets didn't want it, and it is even possible that there had never been any wish in Paris and London (as enemies of appeasement and friends of communism loudly complained at the time), or in Moscow (as the enemies of communism, with some justice, insisted), that they should succeed. The fact that they were conducted by British and French personages of inferior rank was taken, perhaps correctly, as evidence of their extreme dubiety. Halifax and Chamberlain both refused invitations to go to Moscow.

The negotiations had begun on April 14, and by July they were deadlocked. The Russians then asked for a military agreement, stating exactly what was expected of them and how it was to be achieved, before they would talk further about a political agreement. The westerners boggled, but they eventually agreed, and the military missions arrived on August 11. On August 21, after a total failure to make any progress, the military discussions were adjourned.

By then a great deal had happened. The westerners were distressed and frightened by the insistent and apparently limitless Soviet demands. Even before they had begun to converse seriously, they had been alarmed by the dismissal of Litvinoff, who had long been the symbol of the Soviet policy of co-operation with the west, and his replacement as Foreign Minister by the dour and hostile Molotov. They began to be aware of the deep and sullen resentment which the Soviet exclusion from Munich had bred, and of the Soviet fear that any agreement with the west would now bring a German attack upon them instead of preventing it. The Russians suspected, and the British suspected they suspected, that the negotiations might in fact be designed to produce this result. And the British also suspected that the Soviets were in some kinds of conversation with Germany. In fact the agreement to undertake formal German-Soviet negotiations was reached, after long but amicable preliminaries, three days after the western military missions reached Moscow.

The two transactions then proceeded simultaneously, but those with Germany were cloaked with effective secrecy. It seemed to most people unthinkable that interest could be strong enough to overcome doctrine—although in the case of Mussolini it had been thought impossible that doctrine could be strong enough to overcome interest. For years the Nazis had stridently presented themselves as the saviors of Germany, and indeed Europe, from the abominable menace of communism. They had contrived an improbable Anti-Comintern Pact, uniting the vigorous opponents of communism—Italy, Germany, and Japan. They had preached, denounced, vituperated, and shrieked for fifteen years. And for five the Soviets had given the impression of bending every effort to organize a force to destroy fascism in all its forms. Fascism and nazism were excoriated as the most vile forms of capitalist imperialism. The horrors and atrocities of the German regime were flamboyantly publicized as evils too hideous to tolerate, conspiracies by capitalists to murder the German workers.

The interests were, however, very strong. The Soviet Union, its military strength low, was perfectly glad to consider a nonaggression pact and the prospect of safety from German attack. Nobody in Moscow had any real interest in the Popular Front enthusiasm for democracy and freedom, which was no longer useful. They asked, of course, a price, and were paid one gratifyingly high. They were to get back the eastern parts of Poland, partly occupied by Russian-speaking people, which they had lost after the Russian-Polish war of 1920. They were to have an eminent influence (actual annexation was not mentioned) in the Baltic republics. Their "interest" in Rumania, and their claim on the Rumanian province of Bessarabia, which had been taken from Russia in 1918, were recognized. There was to be no direct German intervention in the eastern Balkans.

These terms, which even today look both skillful and sordid, were agreed to in a very short time, although they were not made public, and were not known in detail until the German archives fell into American hands in 1945. What was made public, on August 23, while the French and British were still in Moscow, was a mutual nonaggression pact to run for ten years. Ribbentrop went to Moscow to sign it, and German-Soviet friendship was toasted by Josef Stalin.

It was in many ways the most startling of Hitler's achievements, and the shock it caused was enormous. It had far-reaching effects, even beyond the essential consequences to Poland, effects that illuminated the obsolescence of the system of national states. For one thing—and this was to prove, in the end, important and perhaps decisive in determining the fate that awaited France—it turned the French Communist Party against the anti-Hitler policy. Until now the French Communists had been the most vigorous, in some ways the only really vigorous, supporters in France of a determined opposition to Germany. Now they became ardent saboteurs of that policy, and continued, after war was declared, to be ardent saboteurs of the war effort. They were numerous enough, and skillful enough, to make a difference.

But the effect of the Nazi-Soviet pact was not to weaken the French and British governments' resolve to make good their guarantee to Poland. In some ways, and in some circles, that resolve may even have been strengthened. The extreme distaste for the Soviet Union that most conservative people in France and Britain felt for a Soviet ally, the confusion of employing a thief to catch a thief, were now removed. A certain relief was felt that the two great totalitarian ideologies were now united against freedom and democracy. The war which was to be declared would be, ideologically, a clean war.

DANZIG

The story of the last weeks of the Danzig crisis, which ended in the invasion of Poland, has been told repeatedly, with almost morbid attention to detail. It scarcely deserves it. No essential German plan was changed, no wavering of German determination took place. Sometime during the spring, when Polish obstinacy, concealed by Beck's slithering, became clear, Hitler decided definitely to "smash" Poland. The decision was probably made before the Pact of Steel with Italy was signed on May 7. The opening of negotiations with Moscow was merely a means of implementing it. Early in August Ribbentrop told Ciano, the Italian foreign minister (who heard it with horror) that Germany was no longer interested in Danzig, but in destroying the Polish state. "We want war," he said, and Ciano noted this in his diary. "The decision to fight is implacable." The attention attracted by the details of the endless negotiations may be interpreted as a product partly of contemporary ignorance of Hitler's intentions, and partly of the analogy with 1914, when fate really did hang on the outcome of diplomatic interchanges.

But at this time this element of fantasy could not be known by anybody except the German, Italian, and Soviet authorities. The world waited with horror to see whether at last the European war would come. In all countries concerned preparations for it proceeded. Home defense was activated in Britain on August 24, and an emergency powers bill passed by Parliament. That day Chamberlain wrote to Hitler, warning him to make no mistake about Britain's intentions. He was determined that there could be no misunderstanding, as there had been in 1914, that Britain would not go to war. If certainty could prevent it, as he hoped it might, he was prepared to state it in categorical terms, and did. Chamberlain's letter also expressed assurance that the question of Danzig, and of the German demands on the Polish Corridor, could be settled without war. It ascribed the tension to the unbridled German press campaign (of a sort made familiar the summer before) which had been raging since spring, accusing the Poles of being monsters who had since 1918 delighted in committing unspeakable atrocities on the "Race Germans" who lived in Poland.

Hitler had thought Britain might back down after the Nazi-Soviet Pact and was furious that it had not done so. He had gotten encouraging reports from the emissaries who, through the summer, had been conversing with leading appeasers. Sir Horace Wilson had told one of them that Chamberlain hoped he could schedule a General Election for the autumn, and campaign on the basis of having saved the peace. But now there was Chamberlain's letter and, on August 25, an Anglo-Polish Treaty of alliance, signed in London. Hitler, in reply to Chamberlain, sent Nevile Henderson off to London with an "offer." He was determined to settle the question of Danzig and the Corridor; if Britain agreed to restrain the Poles from resisting a peaceful settlement, he would be glad to "guarantee" the British Empire. The British were led to hope there might be something in it. They urged the Poles, who were now more obstinate than ever, to negotiate, while telling them (in contrast to the treatment of the Czechs) that they "would come to their aid" if the negotiations failed. They told Hitler that they had done so, and still hoped for peace. Hitler replied, on August 29, that he would receive a Polish emissary, if he arrived, with full powers to make decisions, the next day. Beck, in Warsaw, authorized Lipski, his ambassador at Berlin, to negotiate, but not within the time limit and not with full powers. On August 31 Henderson was given the list of German demands and urged Lipski to consider them. But by then the German order to invade had already been given and could not, according to the way things had been planned, be withdrawn. On September 1, before dawn, the German army crossed the border and the bombardment of Warsaw began.

The effort to avoid war was not quite over in Britain, however. It was believed that Hitler might be induced by an ultimatum to call back his armies. Even after the Cabinet had unitedly decided on war, Halifax was trying to induce Mussolini to re-enact his role of *deus ex machina* and propose another conference—an initiative that the most forthright of appeasement's chroniclers term "betrayal."* That night, Chamberlain told the House of Commons of this proposal, and that he was sending to hear whether Hitler might agree to withdraw. Arthur Greenwood of the Labour Party rose to denounce this equivocating statement, made while the Poles, whom Britain had promised to defend, were already being slaughtered, and their capital was being heavily bombed. He said he spoke for Labour. From the Conservative benches Leopold Amery, an ally of Churchill now reduced to horror at the possibility of another surrender, shouted to him across the House of Commons, *"Speak for England!"*

THE LAST EUROPEAN WAR

On September 3, 1939, Chamberlain broadcast to the nation. "No reply having been received from Berlin to our message," he announced, "I have the duty to tell you that Germany and Great Britain are at war." The air raid sirens interrupted his speech and were taken as a symbolic coda to the years of peace. But the sirens were a false alarm. The exchange of declarations of war meant nothing. No major military operations were begun by Britain and France after them. In London, private hopes persisted that a general settlement could still be negotiated with Hitler, and Lord Halifax sedulously performed what actions he could (they were not very numerous) to pursue them. The western governments believed that a staunch defensive posture on the French frontier, combined with a naval blockade of Germany, would bring peace through attrition of the German economy and will-power without the dreadful need for battles. There was no consideration of any offensive action (which was certainly feasible in theory, and might well have succeeded had any plans been made for it) while Germany was occupied with the destruction of Poland.

The technique that the Germans had chosen for battering down the partitions of Europe was brilliantly successful. The war against Poland, undisturbed by any action on the western front, brought total victory within a month. The German and Soviet armies met as the strains of Chopin's *Polonaise*, the signature

* Gilbert and Gott, *op. cit.*, p. 305.

tune of Warsaw Radio, died on the air-waves of Europe, and planning for a campaign in the west began at once. It was prefaced by a preliminary action against Norway and Denmark, which were successfully occupied in the spring of 1940. On May 10, the attack on Luxembourg, Belgium, the Netherlands, and France was launched. It lasted a week longer than the war in Poland. By the middle of June the French armies had been defeated and the French government, remodeled to make it acceptable to the Nazis, signed an armistice which left the Germans in occupation of half of the country and in virtual control of the rest of it. In the spring of 1941, the whole of central and southeastern Europe was occupied. The Hungarians, Rumanians, and Bulgarians simply agreed to allow the Germans to move into their territories. The Yugoslavs and Greeks fought and were defeated. The Balkan campaign was won in six weeks.

Not all essays at *Blitzkrieg* were successful. The Soviet Union attacked Finland in November 1939, and the Red Army bogged down. The Finns, their total population an infinitesimal percentage of the Soviets', proved remarkably successful in holding their own through most of the winter, although they were inevitably beaten and obliged to sign an armistice. Mussolini, who had prudently remained at peace in 1939, entered the war at the moment when France appeared to be defeated. Then, in October of 1940, acting on another of his quixotic whims, he attacked Greece. The Greeks, like the Finns, fought effectively against a vast but ill-prepared enemy, and it was not until Hitler's advance into the Balkans six months later that the Greek defense crumbled. The Germans themselves were unable to devise a strategy for the quick reduction of the British Isles. They had hoped that the British would make peace after the defeat of France, but by then Churchill had replaced Chamberlain and invoked the flaming determination of his countrymen to save themselves. An invasion across water was something the Germans had not attempted before. They were weak in the necessary naval strength, and Hitler was psychologically ill-equipped for overseas operations. The counsels of the German leaders were as usual divided, and this time Hitler could produce no bold and simple plan for action. He vacillated among various schemes. It was decided, at

Göring's suggestion, to reduce the defenses of the British Isles by air attack; when the British had been decisively softened, the hazardous invasion would be undertaken. The point was never reached. "Softening" was an imprecise objective, and they were not agreed on what they wished to achieve, whether to paralyze Britain's national will by attacks on civilian centers, to neutralize its industrial capacity, to weaken its Navy, or to destroy its Air Force and so open the way for further strategic operations. By mid-September of 1940, the *Blitzkrieg* against Britain failed, because it was unfocused and because the British means of resistance were enough—barely enough—to balance German air power.

The technique of the sharp, decisive blow required supreme focus and a wide margin of superiority. It is conceivable that had the Germans organized their attack better in the summer of 1940 they could have occupied Great Britain. It is certainly conceivable that if they had set themselves the task again, having learned the lessons of the Battle of Britain, they might have won. But they set themselves quite a different task instead.

It was immediately after the fizzling out of the air attack on Britain that Hitler decided to turn to the Soviet Union. This was the decisive and fatal moment in his career, but there were reasonable grounds for his action. The conquest of Russia had always been his ultimate objective, and now the moment appeared to be ripe. The Soviet Union had displayed its military incompetence in the Finnish campaign, while Germany had been spectacularly successful in every land operation they had attempted. The Soviets, too, presented a serious potential threat to any eventual strategy for reducing Great Britain; if the necessary all-out effort were made in the west, a prudent Stalin might well decide that the time had come to invade Germany from the east. No complementary threat existed in reverse; it was quite impossible for the British to contemplate an invasion of the continent while the Germans were disposing of Russia. The resources of Russia would provide the necessary economic backing for the ultimate attack on Britain and for the construction of a German-dominated Europe. Accordingly, the attack on the Soviet Union appeared both feasible and necessary, and the successful, although costly, Balkan campaign was undertaken as preparation for it. With Germany in control of all of central and southeastern Europe, as it was by June of 1941, the whole of the Soviet frontier was exposed and the danger of a flanking attack from the south was removed.

The mistake made was a double one, and in both its aspects it reflected the narrowness of Hitler's horizon. He had won, up until that time, for precisely the same reason that the French and British had lost, because he was operating within the geographical boundaries of the old European system. He had understood quite clearly how to destroy the many-chambered mansion of the old Europe; he had understood its flimsiness, and he had exploited the impossibility of shoring it up, which the British and French had attempted, by old methods of diplomacy and defense. Most of all, he had learned a lesson from 1914–18, that a general, protracted war would prove too costly and place on the economy of Europe a burden too heavy to be borne. The shaky edifice could be easily pushed down, without danger or damage to Germany, by a series of blows.

His vision, however, stopped at the boundaries of the world he had known during his formative years, before 1919, just as Chamberlain's had, and it was this that destroyed him. He thought of the Soviet Union as if it were the old Russia, a Europeanized Great Power. He disastrously underrated the resources and the determination of the Russian peoples and the Soviet government. In particular, like Napoleon, he underrated the resource of distance, which enabled the Russians to defeat the tactics of the *Blitzkrieg* through retreat. The essential quality of Europe was compactness, and the confusion of the Germans when faced with space was quite as great as their confusion when faced with the water that protected Great Britain. They had planned, and even attempted, to build an invasion fleet of canal barges in 1940 and were surprised at what happened to them in surf. They were as much surprised by what happened to their tactic of the breakthrough in the thousands of empty miles that separated Leningrad, Moscow, and Kiev.

The second and more important of the Germans' failures, however, was their misunderstanding of the United States. Hitler barely took it into consideration when making his world strategy, except rather vaguely to imagine that Japan could distract it. It is illuminating that of all the lessons of 1914–18, this was the one he most notably failed to learn, that the dimensions of American power were of a sort entirely different from those of the tight, professional, military forces of Europe.

The decision to attack Russia while Great Britain was still in existence as an independent power meant that there was time for American resources, and American minds, to be brought to bear on the struggle. The Neutrality Act, which forebade the export of arms to Europe, was repealed, and in the interim between the defeat of France and the attack on the Soviet Union, the Roosevelt administration succeeded in passing the "Lend-Lease" Act, which not only made supplies available to Great Britain but obviated the accumulation of indebtedness that had stultified international financial relations after 1918. The Americans, too, had learned a lesson from World War I.

By the autumn of 1941 the German offensive in Russia had stalled, and American power was being brought to bear upon the defense of Britain. American opinion, always volatile, was now reversing its unreasoning dedication to isolation. The European war became a world war, and the defeat of Germany was certain. It was, as Churchill called it, the end of the beginning; it was also the end of the European world.

The French and British declarations of war had no effect on the process. Hitler continued his course of *coups d'état*, both political and military, exactly as he would have done had the western powers remained at peace. He attacked Poland, Scandinavia, Belgium, Luxembourg, the Netherlands, and France at the times, and in the order, when he would have attacked them anyway. The British and French continued to occupy their defensive positions as long as they were allowed, while Hitler accumulated the resources that were necessary to assault them. In particulars, the British defense was strengthened by events: the German naval losses in the Norwegian campaign; the very suddenness of the French collapse, which left Germany for the first time without a formed plan for the next operation; the escape of the British Army from a trap the Germans had prepared for it in France by its evacuation from Dunkirk; the skill and fortitude of the Royal Air Force; perhaps most of all, the magnetism of Churchill.

For the west had at last found leaders who were prepared to attack. Churchill galvanized British patriotism, as Charles de Gaulle, who had escaped to London, galvanized French. It is logical that they were always at odds in Allied councils, for they represented the disparate aims of their two countries, the quest for national greatness. They were the leaders of an old crusade, the last knights of Europe. They called forth the national will to glory.

But in the end Britain and France were rescued by the English Channel and the power of Russia and America. Britain and France and Germany would not again make the great decisions. Churchill had bravely said, "I did not become the King's first minister to preside over the liquidation of the British empire," but the days of kings and empires that he so splendidly embodied were over.

Hitler's imperial design was a vision as ancient as the crusades, the achievement of dominion over Europe by one of its parts. It was, as much as the formalism of Daladier and Chamberlain or the chivalry of Churchill and de Gaulle, an epilogue to a long millennium. The Europe of the fatherlands—equal, diverse, and fruitfully competitive—the Europe that had won the world, the Europe of the knights, was gone.

A Note on the Bibliography

The literature on international relations between the wars is now quite as great in quantity as that on the years before 1914, but most of it, especially that on the 1930s, is of a different sort, reflecting changes in the historical profession as well as in the character of events. There have been— so far anyway— no general studies of the sort like the classic works of Sidney Bradshaw Fay, Bernadotte Schmitt, and, most imposing of all, Luigi Albertini, which aimed to be exhaustive and definitive, almost epic, in scope. Historians are less given to epics these days, and the notion of "diplomatic history" has become, in some measure, anachronistic. Younger historians would, most of them, find it not only inadequate but misleading to study the conduct of affairs by cabinets and ambassadors in isolation from social and economic and political contexts. And this is more than a change of fashion; if there ever *was* any warrant for diplomatic history, it disappeared with the First World War. Foreign affairs in the twenties and thirties *were* conducted in much less isolation. The class of cultivated gentlemen manipulating other cultivated gentlemen who staffed missions and foreign offices had become obsolete, although it had not disappeared. Diplomacy, no less than elections, was a matter for ordinary politicians.

The twenty years between the wars was the age of the politician, but it was also the age of the specialist whose advice was often disregarded but was even more often solicited. The profession of history has shared in the general tendency to greater specialization. Historians, rarely writers of epics, are today almost always technicians. Their emphasis is more and more upon detail, and particularly upon administrative detail. In this respect history is catching up with historians; the politicians listen more often today to the advice they solicit from the specialists, more often, certainly, than in the days of Adolf Hitler or Neville Chamberlain. The first move of the intelligent revolutionary in the sixties is to seize not the royal palace, as in the nineteenth century, or the radio station, as in the 1930s, but the filing cabinets.

There is a fairly distinct chronological break in the history-writing of the interwar years. For the period before about 1930, the literature is, logically, more often of the old-fashioned sort. Produced largely in the thirties, forties, and early fifties, writing about the twenties tends to be narrative and political history. With the coming of the Great Depression and the Nazi regime, the literature changes. It is for the most part more voluminous and more sophisticated.

In 1939 as in 1914, belligerent governments rushed into print with collections of official documents purporting to demonstrate the culpability of the enemy. There was, once again, a British Blue Book and a French Yellow Book, and many others. They were taken less seriously than in the First World War, partly, perhaps, because the distortions of the earlier harvest of "colored books" were so well known, and they were in fact all misleading as well as fragmentary. Later, as had happened in the twenties, much larger collections began to be published in many-volumed series. The most important are the *Documents on British Foreign Policy 1919–1939; The Foreign Relations of the United States; I Documenti Italiani* (of which only the volumes covering 1939 are yet available); and *Documents on German Foreign Policy 1918–1945*. The last consists of the German Foreign Office archives, captured largely intact in 1945 by the British and Americans. Since the originals are available to scholars, the hazards of misleading editing are in this case unimportant.

But there are other insufficiencies about the documentary collections. It was true in the earlier twentieth century, but was much truer in the twenties and thirties, that private conversations and correspondence, telephone calls, and the reports of private contacts supplemented official dispatches in essential ways. The archives, while indispensable, nonetheless form only the part of the iceberg visible above the surface. In every country, and especially in Germany, regular diplomatic channels were increasingly bypassed before 1939. In Germany, indeed, they were often used as façades behind which the real business was conducted by private or party agents. The German ambassadors were frequently kept in deliberate ignorance of the policies they were supposed to be conducting.

The subsurface portion of the iceberg is partly accessible to study through the forty-two volumes entitled *The Trial of the Major War Criminals Before the International Military Tribunal, Proceedings and Documents*, published at Nuremberg 1947–49. They are cumbersome to use, and much of the material is in German. The testimony of the defendants is, of course, not at all reliable, since they were trying to save their lives, not to reveal the truth. Still, the volumes supply an almost inexhaustible amount of both misinformation and information, and almost all studies of European history in the Nazi era draw on them.

For the scholar, the most important supplements to published collections are usually the archives themselves and the files of contemporary periodicals. For both the scholar and the student, as well as the general reader, published diaries and memoirs are necessary and illuminating pieces in the picture-puzzle that is historical reconstruction. Many of the policy-makers kept journals. The most sensational is *The Ciano Diaries 1939–1943*. The Italian Foreign Minister, Mussolini's son-in-law, recorded his day-to-day activities and reactions with what appears to be startling candor. His diaries were smuggled into Switzerland by the Countess Ciano when German forces occupied Italy, and they give not only an enormous amount of inside information but an unnerving insight into the triviality and caprice of the Fascist leaders. Neville Chamberlain's diary was the foundation for Keith Feiling's imposing and important biography, *The Life of Neville Chamberlain* (London, 1946). Anthony Eden's memoirs are built largely on documents, including his diary, private and official, and the relevant volume, *Facing The Dictators* (Boston, 1962) is probably the most illuminating single book on the interwar period.

The flood of autobiographies and reminiscences has been oceanic. (Two decades ago Sir Lewis Namier collected three volumes of essays on those that had appeared theretofore: *Diplomatic Prelude, 1938–39* [London, 1948]; *Europe in Decay* [London, 1950]; and *In the Nazi Era* [London, 1952]. They are still important for the student.) Among those available in English, a number of the more readable and useful are noted below.

The German memoirs are very numerous, but relatively few have been translated, and even fewer are important for the general reader, since self-justification is naturally the most common purpose and, in the case of Nazi officials, the most difficult to achieve without distortion. The *Memoirs* (Chicago, 1951) of Ernst von Weizsäker, the wily chief of the Foreign Office, are important although unreliable. The bypassing of the German diplomats by the Nazis, and the restiveness of the old-line officials, are well illustrated in the memoirs of three German ambassadors who were, or claimed to be, anti-Nazi: Herbert von Dirksen, *Moscow, Tokyo, London* (Norman, Oklahoma, 1952); Ulrich von Hassell, *The Von Hassell Diaries* (London, 1948); and Franz von Papen's *Mem-*

oirs (London, 1952). The memoirs of the Austrian Chancellor Kurt von Schuschnigg give a moving and persuasive account of the crisis years in Austria and the Chancellor's incredible maltreatment by the Nazis. (*Austrian Requiem*, New York, 1946). Of rather special interest, but fascinating and revealing reading, is George Kennan's collection of papers from the time of his service in the American Legation at Prague, *From Prague After Munich* (Princeton, 1968).

Few of the important French memoirs have been translated, and those that exist reflect, in many cases, self-justificatory distortion almost as marked as in the case of the Germans—this is particularly true of Georges Bonnet's. An interesting exception is *The Fateful Years* (New York, 1949) by André François-Poncet, French ambassador at Berlin from 1931 to 1938.

Of the memoir material available in English, that of British statesmen is of course the largest and most interesting part. The most famous is Winston Churchill's *The Gathering Storm* (Boston, 1948).

Churchill's splendid prose and the fact that he was right on many points tend to obscure the fact that he was wrong on many others and that his resolute stand seems to have arisen less from a profound under-standing of affairs in his own days than from well-preserved, nineteenth-century nationalist reflexes. His book is vague or incorrect in many details, and the passing years, though they cannot diminish his gran-deur, certainly diminish the air of infallibility that earlier cloaked his dicta. Two other men who shared his general position (in addition to Eden) have also written memoirs: Sir Robert Vansittart, the bellicose permanent undersecretary for the Foreign Office, whose more impor-tant work is *The Mist Procession* (London, 1958); and Alfred Duff Cooper, *Old Men Forget* (London, 1953). Both are rich in detail for the indictment of appeasement.

The appeasers have indicted themselves almost as effectively as have their enemies. Tom Jones's *Diary with Letters* (London, 1954) is almost incredibly revealing. Sir Samuel Hoare's *Nine Troubled Years* (London, 1954) is a rather pathetic record of mistaken judgments, and Lord Si-mon's *Retrospect* (London, 1952) is more interesting for what it leaves out than for what it includes. Harold Nicolson's *Diaries* give a remarka-ble picture of the times and the clubby, sometimes silly, atmosphere in which public affairs were transacted in Britain.

There have, as noted above, been few major general histories of the developments leading to World War II. One of the best is by the distin-guished French diplomatic historian Pierre Renouvin. *World War II and Its Origins: International Relations 1929–1945* (translated by Rémy Inglis Hall, New York, 1969; published in the original in Paris, 1958) is an intelligent although poorly organized study, considerably less nar-rowly Eurocentric than much of the writing on the period. It begins with the Depression, which is logical enough, but the omission of the history of the twenties beclouds understanding of the reasons for the myopia of many western statesmen and for the opportunism of the dictators. For a routine account of the facts in interwar history as a whole, G. M. Gathorne-Hardy, *A Short History of International Affairs* (fifth edition, London, 1950) is still useful, being detailed and detached, but it was originally written before the war and still deals mainly with the outward, public, appearance of events. The best-known general work in English is A. J. P. Taylor, *The Origins of the Second World War* (London, 1951), which is cast in the same form as the classic works on the first war's origins. As noted in the text, it is highly controversial and now outdated, since some of its major themes have been effectively undercut by more specialized research. But it is brilliantly written, like all its author's works, and full of his characteristic erudition and insight.

Relatively few recent works, either general or specialized, have dealt with the twenties. Since the events were less dramatic and the scope for revelation much smaller, historians of the past decade have been less interested in the period between the treaties of 1919 and the coming of the Depression. A few works of particular interest may be mentioned. Gordon Craig and Felix Gilbert have edited *The Diplomats 1919–1939* (Princeton, 1953), containing admirable studies that not only illuminate the men who made policy but convey a good picture of diplomatic history in general. Arnold Wolfers' *Britain and France Between Two Wars* (New York, 1940) has become a classic and remains perceptive and stimulating although in important respects outdated. Hans W. Gatzke, *Stresemann and the Rearmament of Germany* (Baltimore, 1954) was a milestone in the interpretation of German policy in the twenties. Of the very extensive literature on Soviet policy and German-Soviet relations, Gerald Freund's *Unholy Alliance* (London, 1957), dealing with the peculiar German-Soviet connection in the early twenties, is exceptionally good.

For the thirties, there is an abundance of recent secondary works, many of which attain very impressive standards of quality. For example, George W. Baer, *The Coming of the Italo-Ethiopian War* (Cambridge, Mass., 1967) is not only a definitive study of its subject and one that throws much light on the entire European scene in 1935; it is also an example of historical scholarship and writing as nearly as possible at its best. Alan Milward's *The German Economy at War* (London, 1965) was of revolutionary importance, and while it deals mainly with the period after 1939, its information and arguments apply to the prewar years as well. Jon Kimche, a British journalist, has made a similarly important reappraisal of British policy, especially defense policy, in *The Unfought Battle* (London, 1968), demonstrating the single-minded determination of the British government to avoid taking the initiative or preparing for offensive action. Martin Gilbert and Richard Gott developed a similar thesis in *The Appeasers* (London, 1963) and presented it with dramatic impact.

There are two first-rate studies of Munich available (replacing the earlier excellent but now outdated *Munich: Prologue to Tragedy* by John Wheeler-Bennett, New York, 1948). They are: Keith Eubank, *Munich,* (Norman, Oklahoma, 1965), solid, thorough and admirably balanced, and Laurence Thompson, *The Greatest Treason* (New York, 1968). Thompson is a journalist, and his book is written in the rather intimate and flowing manner of British newspapermen. It is less professional than Eubank's, but it is good reading and contains much material, including personal interviews, to be found nowhere else.

Some other works remain to be noted. Alan Bullock, *Hitler* (New York, 1953) is the standard biography and a book of major stature, although later findings suggest modifications of some of his interpretations. Two fine studies of the German Army, both older, are Telford Taylor, *Sword and Swastika* (New York, 1952), beautifully written for the general reader, and John Wheeler-Bennett, *The Nemesis of Power* (New York, 1954). Derek Wood and Derek Dempster, *The Narrow Margin* (New York, 1961), is an absolutely fascinating study of Britain's air defenses. Gordon Brook-Shepherd, *The Anschluss* (Philadelphia and New York, 1963) is a very good account of the extinction of the Austrian Republic. John Connell, *The 'Office'* (London, 1958) is an informal history of the Foreign Office that strikingly reveals the curious jurisdictional struggle over foreign policy in the appeasement years. Ian Colvin, *Vansittart in Office* (London, 1965) is interesting in its parts although full of holes. Christopher Thorne, *The Approach of War 1938-39* (New York, 1968) is up-to-date in its scholarship and brilliant in its presentation.

Index

ment talks and, 109–12; non-aggression pact with Poland, 118-19, 128, 132; Communist Party in, 125–26; introduction of military conscription in, 139; appeasement of, 160, 190–97, 211, 219, 230–37, 240–42; repudiation of treaty obligations, 161; economy (1937), 183–85; annexation of Austria, 187, 200–207; Army placed under Nazi control, 187, 199, 215; economy (1938), 249–50; negotiations with Russia, 254, 256–57; non-aggression pact with Russia, 257; invasion of Poland, 258–60; World War II and, 260–65. *See also* Hitler, Adolf; Nazis and Nazism

Good Neighbor policy, 94
Göring, Hermann, 182, 193, 201, 249, 262
Great Britain: attitude toward continental affairs after World War I, 51–52; economy after World War I, 52–53, 85; isolationism, 53, 85; Great Depression and, 86–90; Peace Ballot, 147–48, 151; General Election (Nov., 1935), 151–52; reaction to Hitler's Rhineland invasion, 159–60; intelligence services, 166–67; rearmament, 167, 176–78, 218, 247–48; Spanish civil war and, 174–75; foreign policy (1937-38), 188–97; agreement with Italy (1938), 197–98; reaction to Germany's annexation of Austria, 206–7; Czech crisis and,

211–28, 233–34; Poland guaranteed support of, 244; negotiations with Soviet Union, 235-56; World War II and, 261–62
Great Depression, 79–95, 98–99
Greece, 67, 83, 84, 244, 245; World War II and, 261
Greenwood, Arthur, 260
Grey, Sir Edward, 159
Grynszpan, Herschell, 234

Hacha, Emil, 236, 237–38
Haile Selassie I, 138, 153
Halévy, Elie, 34
Halifax, Lord, 191, 192–93, 215, 218, 222, 234, 242, 243, 247, 255, 259, 260; distrust of Soviet Union, 243
Hawley-Smoot tariff, 91
Henderson, Sir Nevile, 192, 206, 211, 236, 240, 259
Henlein, Konrad, 210, 212–13
Herriot, Edouard, 24
Hindenburg, Paul von, 83, 100
Hitler, Adolf, 6–7, 8, 12–16, 19, 78, 83; attitude of German Army leaders toward, 7; emergence of, 58; diplomacy and, 71; rise of, 96–108; aims of, 104–6; early actions of, 108; passive attitude toward, 121; Mussolini and, 133–34, 153, 172, 204–6, 232, 246; attitude toward Franco-Soviet alliance, 156; Rhineland and, 156–68; attitude toward Versailles Treaty, 158; murder of Storm Troop leaders, 134; Spanish civil war and, 171–72, 174, 175; plans of, 179–87, 200,